OKANAGAN UNIV/COLLEGE LIBRARY

D0454163

CRITICAL MORAL LIBERALISM

Studies in Social, Political, and Legal Philosophy
General Editor: James P. Sterba, University of Notre Dame

This series analyzes and evaluates critically the major political, social, and legal ideals, institutions, and practices of our time. The analysis may be historical or problem-centered; the evaluation may focus on theoretical underpinnings or practical implications. Among the recent titles in the series are:

OKANAGAN UNIVERSITY COLLEGE
LIBRARY
BRITISH COLUMBIA

CRITICAL MORAL LIBERALISM

Theory and Practice

Jeffrey Reiman

ROWMAN & LITTLEFIELD PUBLISHERS, INC.
Lanham • Boulder • New York • London

ROWMAN & LITTLEFIELD PUBLISHERS, INC.

Published in the United States of America
by Rowman & Littlefield Publishers, Inc.
4720 Boston Way, Lanham, Maryland 20706

3 Henrietta Street
London WC2E 8LU, England

Copyright © 1997 by Rowman & Littlefield Publishers, Inc.

All rights reserved. No part of this publication may
be reproduced, stored in a retrieval system, or transmitted
in any form or by any means, electronic, mechanical,
photocopying, recording, or otherwise, without the prior
permission of the publisher.

British Cataloging in Publication Information Available

Library of Congress Cataloging-in-Publication Data
Reiman, Jeffrey H.
    Critical moral liberalism : theory and practice / Jeffrey
Reiman.
    p.   cm. —(Studies in social, political, and legal
philosophy)
    Includes bibliographical references and index.
    ISBN 0-8476-8313-3 (alk. paper). — ISBN 0-8476-8314-1 (pbk. :
alk. paper)
    1. Liberalism.   2. Social ethics.   I. Title.   II. Series.
HM276.R45 1997
303.3'72—dc20   96-9480
                                                   CIP

ISBN 0-8476-8313-3 (cloth : alk. paper)
ISBN 0-8476-8314-1 (pbk. : alk. paper)

Printed in the United States of America

♾ ™ The paper used in this publication meets the minimum requirements of
American National Standard for Information Sciences—Permanence of Paper
for Printed Library Materials, ANSI Z39.48-1984.

for Sue

Contents

Preface

When I told a friend that I was working on a book defending liberalism, she replied, "Oh, I didn't think there were any liberals left." To this a philosopher is inclined to reply, "It depends on what you mean by 'liberalism.' " If you mean the political liberalism that occupied center stage in America for most of the postwar period—the liberalism that advocates government programs to help the needy and disadvantaged— that liberalism has taken some hard knocks in recent years, though no one seems quite ready to give it up entirely. If you mean the economic liberalism that flourished in America until the Great Depression and the New Deal—the liberalism that calls for minimal government involvement in the economy—that liberalism has many current defenders, though few who are willing to call themselves liberals, for fear, I suppose, of being identified with the political liberalism that seems to be the complete opposite of their doctrine. But if you mean either of these liberalisms, you don't mean by 'liberalism' what I mean.

The liberalism that I have in mind is the moral liberalism that was defended by John Locke in the seventeenth century, by Immanuel Kant in the eighteenth century, by John Stuart Mill in the nineteenth and John Rawls in the twentieth—the liberalism that champions the moral right of individuals to live as they choose so long as they respect that right in others. I think of the political and economic liberalisms mentioned above as competing theories of how best to achieve the objective championed by moral liberalism.

Moral liberalism has suffered an ambiguous fate in recent years. On the one hand, its defenders appear to be in retreat, with some now lauding liberalism's supposed neutrality toward different visions of the moral good rather than liberalism's own vision of the moral goodness of freedom and rational self-governance. Rawls himself now promotes

ix

a pared-down "political" liberalism that is scarcely more than a recipe for peaceful coexistence among people who can never be expected to agree about the moral good. On the other hand, moral liberalism seems to have abandoned the field only to have found its way into the hearts and minds of its opponents, who almost always have a place in their doctrines for the freedom of individuals to live as they see fit. This last fact suggests to me that moral liberalism is a hardier specimen than its recent defenders appear to believe, and that it can and should be given a more robust defense as the core of a vision of the good life and the good society. It is to this aim that this book is devoted.

I call the doctrine advocated in this book *critical moral liberalism.* It is moral because it is neither neutral about the moral good, nor merely a set of rules for peaceful coexistence. Critical moral liberalism contends that living one's life according to one's own rational judgments is a condition of living a good life; that promotion of the ability of individuals to so live is a moral ideal that all societies should foster; and that the right of individuals to so live (as far as this is compatible with all individuals being able to do so) is a right that all human beings have a moral duty to respect. It is critical because it recognizes—in the wake of Marxian and, more recently, feminist analyses—that our knowledge of what threatens freedom and of what is needed to protect it change in history, and therefore that any particular interpretation of what liberalism requires may, in effect, function ideologically to legitimate a situation characterized by unjust coercion. Critical moral liberalism takes this danger very seriously and therefore remains open to the idea that as-yet-unrecognized forms of coercion may be discovered and that new rights may be needed to defend freedom against them.

Moreover, critical moral liberalism aims to be not just a theory but a practical doctrine as well. As the chapters that follow testify, the theory itself emerged in the attempt to grapple with practical questions ranging from drug addiction to police discretion, from economic justice to just punishment. I hope that the theory sheds light on these practical issues, just as dealing with the practical issues has lit the way to the theory. The book is divided under the rubrics of "theory" and "practice," but the division is only one of emphasis. All of the chapters deal with issues of theory and practice.

Indeed, though the chapters of this book were written over a period of more than twenty years, they share a certain "style." That style combines the already noted interest in practical questions with a continued attempt to find resources in the history of philosophy to respond to those questions. So the reader will see that examination of drug addiction leads me to consideration of Aristotle's doctrine of virtue; that the attempt to clarify the problem of police discretion leads back to Plato's *Republic* and Hobbes's *Leviathan*; that my liberalism itself arises from reflection on the thought of Descartes, Locke, and Kant; and that similar excursions into the history of philosophy guide the other chapters as well. Here I see more clearly than ever the debt that I owe to my philosophy teachers. My undergraduate philosophy teachers at Queens College in New York City taught me the relevance of philosophy to the business of life, and vice versa. My graduate philosophy teachers at Pennsylvania State University taught me a deep reverence for the history of philosophy as an unending source of fresh insight. I thank my teachers at both institutions from the bottom of my heart for these lessons, and I hope that they may find in the chapters that follow evidence that their work was not in vain.

Nine of the chapters in the book have been published elsewhere; two chapters plus the introductory essay appear here for the first time. With respect to the chapters previously published, I thank numerous editors and referees for their helpful comments. These chapters are presented here largely as they originally appeared, although all have been revised in small ways either to show more clearly their contribution to critical moral liberalism or to achieve stylistic unity. I have taken the opportunity to correct what seem to me now to have been errors.

I credit American University in Washington, D.C., where I have taught for more than twenty-five years, for continually providing a lively and supportive atmosphere for my work, as well as the time and wherewithal to do it. I thank Rachel Levine for starting, and Sylvia Rolloff for doing the lion's share of, the scanning of previously published articles so that they could be revised for inclusion in this book.

I express my gratitude to Jim Sterba, professor of philosophy at the University of Notre Dame and general editor of the Studies in Social, Political, and Legal Philosophy series, for inviting me to include this book in that excellent series. I thank my editors at Rowman & Littlefield, Jennifer Ruark and Julie Kirsch, for their good counsel and hard work in shepherding the book from idea to reality, and Judith Copeland, for a sharp-eyed and intelligent job of copyediting that has contributed in no small measure to giving these chapters, written at different times, the feel of a book.

The book is dedicated to my wife, Sue Headlee, my partner in life for more than twenty years, my colleague, inspiration, and ray of sunshine.

Acknowledgments

The author and publisher gratefully acknowledge permission to reprint the following material.

Chapter 2, "Postmodern Argumentation and Post-postmodern Liberalism, with Comments on Levinas, Habermas, and Rawls," originally appeared in *Canadian Journal of Philosophy* supplementary volume 21, *On the Relevance of Metaethics: New Essays on Metaethics,* ed. J. Couture and K. Nielsen (1996), pp. 251–72.

Chapter 3, "Drug Addiction, Liberal Virtue, and Moral Responsibility," originally appeared in *Drugs, Morality, and the Law,* ed. S. Luper-Foy and C. Brown (New York: Garland, 1994), pp. 25–47.

Chapter 4, "The Labor Theory of the Difference Principle," originally appeared in *Philosophy and Public Affairs* 12, no. 2 (Spring 1983): 133–59. Copyright 1983 by Princeton University Press.

Chapter 5, "The Constitution, Rights, and the Conditions of Legitimacy," originally appeared in *Constitutionalism: The Philosophical Dimension,* ed. A. Rosenbaum (Westport, Conn.: Greenwood, 1988), pp. 127–49.

Chapter 6, "Privacy, Intimacy, and Personhood," originally appeared in *Philosophy and Public Affairs* 6, no. 1 (Fall 1976): 26–44. Copyright 1976 by Princeton University Press.

Chapter 7, "Driving to the Panopticon: A Philosophical Exploration of the Risks to Privacy Posed by the Information Technology of the Future," originally appeared with a slightly different title in *Santa Clara Computer and High Technology Law Journal* 11, no. 1 (March 1995): 27–44.

Chapter 8, "Abortion, Infanticide, and the Asymmetric Value of Human Life," originally appeared in *Journal of Social Philosophy* 27, no. 3 (Winter 1996).

Chapter 10, "Is Police Discretion Justified in a Free Society?" originally appeared in *Handled with Discretion: Ethical Issues in Police Decision Making,* ed. John Kleinig (Lanham, Md.: Rowman & Littlefield, 1996), pp. 71–83.

Chapter 11, "Justice, Civilization, and the Death Penalty," originally appeared under a slightly different title in *Philosophy and Public Affairs* 14, no. 2 (Spring 1985): 115–48. Copyright 1985 by Princeton University Press.

Introduction

Critical Moral Liberalism, an Overview

Liberalism: Moral, Critical, Rational, and Universal

I call the ethical theory that will be defended in these pages *critical moral liberalism*. At its heart is a moral principle, which I call the *ideal of individual sovereignty*. It holds that all human beings are entitled to the maximum ability to live their lives according to their own judgments, subject to the conditions necessary to realize this for everyone.

Critical moral liberalism is *liberal* in that it insists on the right of all human beings to freedom to live as they see fit, as far as this is compatible with the same freedom for all. But freedom is not the ultimate value here. Freedom is valued because it is necessary if people are to live their lives according to their own judgments. It is this, the living of self-governed lives, that critical moral liberalism takes as its chief value, holding that self-governance is a necessary condition of a good life for human beings and that all human beings have a right to the exercise of their capacity for self-governance because they are rational. Thus, critical moral liberalism is *moral* because it claims to identify a universal good and a universal moral right. And critical moral liberalism is *critical* because it recognizes—in light of Marxian and feminist analyses—that our understanding of what threatens freedom and of what rights are needed to protect it change in history, and therefore that a doctrine of moral liberalism must be self-critical. It must remain open to the possibility that as-yet-unrecognized forms of unjustified coercion may be discovered and that new rights may be needed to defend freedom against them. (In general, I use the term "moral liberalism" to refer specifically to the moral content of the theory defended here, and the phrase "critical moral liberalism" to refer to the whole theory including both its moral content and its critical dimensions.)

1

Critical moral liberalism aims to retrieve and rehabilitate the Enlightenment project of a universal moral liberalism. Later in this introduction, I set forth what I take to be the Enlightenment argument for the right of all human beings to freedom to direct their lives based on their possession of reason. In subsequent chapters, I try to show that such an argument can withstand the criticisms of feminists and multiculturalists who think Enlightenment universalism is biased in favor of a male or a Western view of the world, as well the criticisms of postmodernists who deny generally the possibility of a universal moral ideal. But critical moral liberalism is not simply a return to the Enlightenment. It is critical as a result of the encounter between Enlightenment moral liberalism and Marxian and feminist critiques of liberalism as ideological. Because any given interpretation of what is needed to protect freedom may overlook as-yet-unrecognized forms of coercion, any such interpretation may function ideologically by giving its moral approval to a situation marked by unjust coercion. No theory can be foolproof against such ideological functioning, but critical moral liberalism recognizes the danger and includes a way of testing whether newly recognized forms of coercion are unjust according to the ideal of individual sovereignty.

Critical moral liberalism insists on people's right to live the way they judge best, but this is not because critical moral liberalism is neutral regarding conceptions of the good life.[1] Quite the contrary, critical moral liberalism insists on people's right to live as they see fit because it squarely contends that living according to one's own judgments is a necessary condition of the good life. On these grounds, it includes a doctrine of *moral virtue*, a standard of personal moral excellence. Thus, critical moral liberalism is not "merely" political.[2] It applies to all facets of life, not only to political institutions. Nor is it justified merely politically, as a recipe for peaceful coexistence among people with differing moral views.[3] Rather it seeks to establish a universal moral ideal on a universal foundation, namely, the rationality of all human beings.

Notice that the ideal of individual sovereignty is a rather high-altitude principle. It doesn't tell us what to do in each case; it specifies neither particular actions nor general policies. Rather it gives us the standard to use in choosing actions and policies. We are to select those actions and policies that best maximize people's ability to live according to their judgments. For the most part, we achieve this by leaving people alone, not blocking them in the pursuit of their goals as long as they do not block others. This is so, among other reasons, because the goodness of self-governed lives lies in part in people being able to view them as their own creations. Consequently, freedom from interference—what is sometimes called "negative freedom"—is a central value, and critical moral liberalism shares traditional liberalism's opposition to paternalism. But critical moral liberalism is liberal, not libertarian. Insofar as self-governance rather than freedom itself is its ultimate value, critical moral liberalism accepts that more active intervention will sometimes be needed, say to provide people with education, health, or security, without which they cannot effectively govern their lives by their own judgments. Since such interventions may themselves interfere with some people's freedom (by forcing them to pay taxes to support public education or universal health care, for example), they will be justified only where needed to substantially enhance everyone's ability to govern their lives by their own judgments overall. But no formula can tell us in advance when the benefit is worth the cost. This will have to be argued out, in light of the best knowledge available. A moral principle is not meant to replace such arguments, only to guide them. And such guidance, particularly in these skeptical times, is plenty. It means that we at least know what it is that has to be proven in order to show that some course of action is right or wrong.

Critical moral liberalism shares both the Enlightenment's emphasis on *reason* as our distinctive capacity, and the Enlightenment's aspiration to moral *universality*. The Enlightenment's focus on reason puts some people off because they think that it slights our emotional or non-rational sides, or because they identify rationality (I use "reason" and "rationality" interchangeably) with some abstract system, like logic or mathematics, that seems too distinctively Western to be the basis of a universal moral principle. As to the first concern, there is no doubt that some Enlightenment thinkers overstated the degree to which we are rational.[4] However, nothing in the argument for liberalism presupposes this exaggeration. What is required is not that we be perfectly rational and nothing else, but that we be significantly rational whatever else we are. Learning that we are often irrational and even always influenced by emotions doesn't mean we are not rational; it means only that we are not perfectly so. Nothing that I shall say implies that we are more than imperfectly and episodically rational. Nor, by the way, does anything I say here require us to believe in a sharp distinction between reason and the emotions. It is enough that there is a reasoning process ready and generally able to distinguish more from less belief-worthy judgments, however mixed or imperfect the process is. When I talk of rational self-governance, then, I mean self-governance by individuals who arrive at their judgments in the imperfectly rational ways characteristic of normal, imperfectly rational human beings.

As to the second concern, if rationality is taken as mathematical cal-culation, as science, or, for that matter, as ideal consumer behavior, then it may seem to be a Western thing or a male thing—in any event, not universal to human beings. But what I mean by rationality is some-thing much more basic and, I think, therefore universal. I understand it as the general capacity to make and review judgments about what things are and how we ought to respond to them. "Review" is important here. Animals, no doubt, make some simple judgments. What distin-guishes us from them is the length and variability of the chain of con-nected reasons we can entertain and our ability at will to bring to bear representations of things or events not currently present, but, more even than these, the fact that we can deliberately review our belief-formation process and try to correct it.

Rationality is a universal capacity of human beings because, among other things, it is presupposed by the use of language. Language sounds to us like the direct transmission of sense or information, as if compre-hending it were merely a matter of direct perception, like seeing. But simple reflection shows that language must be more complicated. What reaches our ears is not sense but sound. Thus the comprehension of language must involve rational processing of sounds to infer what their producer meant by them. We hear a series of sounds and we rationally judge what someone who would utter those sounds must be trying to get across. We do it so well and so quickly that we don't notice it, except, of course, when communication breaks down and our capacity for deliberate review kicks in. We then check our beliefs about what the other is trying to say against other things she has said, or against our shared beliefs about the world, or, of course, by asking her what she meant.

Inspired by Bentham, the American philosopher Charles Sanders Peirce once characterized philosophy as *coenoscopy*: the study of those aspects of human experience that are so common that we don't notice them.[5] This is true, in the first instance, of reasoning itself. In any event, since even the most extreme postmodernist writers treat human beings as language users, text interpreters, culture bearers, and so on, they all think of human beings as rational in the sense in which I mean it here. Using this universal conception of reason, I shall, in the next section, "Four Arguments for Moral Liberalism," develop the Enlightenment argument for moral liberalism and follow it with three contemporary arguments: the respect argument, the universal interest argument, and the antisubjugation argument. Then, in the section entitled "The Liberal Good," I shall lay out moral liberalism's vision of the good life and what makes it good. It goes without saying that this amounts to a fifth argument for moral liberalism. Following that, in the section on "Making Liberalism Critical," I explain how particular versions of liberalism may function ideologically to legitimate as-yet-unrecognized forms of unjust coercion, and I describe the mechanism available to critical moral liberalism to test for the justice of coercive social practices. I conclude, in the final section, "From Liberal Theory to Practice," with an overview of the rest of this book.

Four Arguments for Moral Liberalism

The Enlightenment argument

Before plunging into the Enlightenment argument itself, one preliminary point needs to be made, namely, that I don't think any of the great Enlightenment thinkers actually succeeded in making the argument. My view is that an incomplete, but oddly persuasive, argument lies just below the surface of, and, indeed, is the driving force behind, the two great Enlightenment formulations of liberalism, that of Locke and that of Kant. The argument aims to prove that moral liberalism is a true moral doctrine because it corresponds to the only way to treat human beings that is appropriate to their nature as rational beings. To make this argument requires showing what it is about rational beings that makes moral liberalism the only appropriate response to them. And though both Locke and Kant wrote as if this argument could be made—indeed, as if it had been made—neither of them actually succeeded in making it or even in stating the problem very clearly. I contend that we can complete this argument by filling in the blanks in Locke and Kant with an argument that is implicit in the writings of Descartes. But, first, consider the blanks.

Locke, arguing for our natural rights to liberty and property in his *Second Treatise of Government*, claimed that it is possession of reason that fits us to run our own lives. But, when it comes to why anyone else is obligated to stand aside and allow us to do so, his explicit answer is that, as creatures of God, we belong to God and therefore no one has the right to harm us or use us as a resource.

> The *state of nature*, has a law of nature [that is, a natural moral law] to govern it, which obliges everyone: and reason, which is that law, teaches all mankind, who will but consult it, that being all *equal and independent*, no one ought to harm another in his life, health, liberty, or possessions:

for men being all the workmanship of one omnipotent, and infinitely wise maker . . . ; they are his property whose workmanship they are, made to last during his, not one another's pleasure.[6]

While this may say why it is wrong for others to aggress against us, it doesn't say why we have a right to live as we see fit. (That we are owned by God gives us as little right over ourselves as it gives everyone else.) Moreover, the argument quoted above makes hash out of Locke's argument for our natural right to property. We have that right, Locke thought, because we own our labor and therefore come to own whatever we mix our labor with.[7] But we only own our labor if we own ourselves, and Locke had already claimed the reverse, that we are owned by God. This is really quite strange. Locke's whole defense of liberalism presupposed that we own ourselves; Locke spoke (at least whenever he was not directly addressing the issue) as if we obviously do own ourselves, and yet Locke stated no argument for this conclusion whatsoever. Worse, what he did state is that we belong to God.

Kant did not get much further. About a century after Locke, in his *Groundwork of the Metaphysics of Morals*, Kant contended, in effect, that we have a natural right to liberty (not to property, by the way, since Kant understood the right to property as socially created) because our rational nature marks us out as "ends-in-ourselves": entities that are valuable because of what they are rather than what they can be used for. This, in turn, rules out treating us as mere means to other people's ends. We are always to be treated at least also as ends.[8] And what is it to be treated as ends-in-ourselves? Kant said that it is to be treated always according to ends—goals, purposes, values—that we ourselves could rationally embrace.[9] This makes a lot of sense. What is wrong with the robber, murderer, or rapist is precisely that he uses his victim as nothing but a means to his own ends, without regard to his victim's ends. Anyone who has ever felt objectified or manipulated, treated like a thing or a tool, will resonate with Kant's dictum that we are to treat humanity, in ourselves and others, never merely as a means and always as an end.

But how do we acquire the status of ends-in-ourselves? In response to this question, Kant offered precious little in the way of argument. It is not clear why we are ends-in-ourselves. Nor is it clear why that status implies the wrongness of treating us as means. As to the former, Kant declared, "Now I say that man, and in general every rational being, exists as an end in himself and not merely as a means to be arbitrarily used by this or that will."[10] "Now I say that . . . " might work for an old-style German philosophy professor, but it surely isn't an argument. (I will not go into those aspects of Kant's thought that might seem to support his view by reference to his distinction between a phenomenal and a noumenal realm. This distinction is now generally regarded as indefensible, and its main force is to rule out any knowledge of the noumenal anyway, so the claims that Kant made about the noumenal would be ruled out by his own theory if the theory weren't otherwise implausible.) As to the latter, suppose we are ends-in-ourselves. What follows from this? To me, it seems to imply only that we *needn't* be used by others to have value, not that we *may not* be used by others because we have value. I suppose that great works of art are ends-in-themselves; they have value independent of what use they may be put to. But this means only that they needn't be put to use to have value; it doesn't prohibit our so using them, say, by trading them for medicine or for other great works of art.

Both Locke and Kant wrote as if they had made the argument that our rational nature entails our right to be free (from aggression, for Locke; from being used by others contrary to our own ends, for Kant)— but, in fact, neither quite made the argument. As to how to make it, we get a clue from an argument that was advanced quite frequently during the Enlightenment, though normally in the narrower context of an argument for freedom of conscience.

Arguing for religious tolerance, numerous writers, Locke among them, pointed to the interesting fact that religious faith cannot be coerced. Belief happens as a free response to evidence and arguments, or else it isn't belief. Forced faith is no more faithful than forced laughter is mirthful. While this argument was not put forth as the basis of moral liberalism as such, it was raised in defense of two crucial liberal principles, tolerance and the limitation of state control to external conduct, rather than thought. So, in *A Letter Concerning Toleration*, Locke asserted that

> the care of Souls cannot belong to the Civil Magistrate, because his Power consists only in outward force; but true and saving Religion consists in the inward perswasion [sic] of the Mind, without which nothing can be acceptable to God. *And such is the nature of Understanding, that it cannot be compell'd to the belief of any thing by outward force.*[11]

Voltaire wrote,

> The sovereign . . . has no right to use coercion to lead men to religion, which in its nature presupposes choice and liberty. My thought is subject to authority no more than is sickness and health. . . .

> Our soul acts internally. Internal acts are thought, volition, inclinations, acquiescence in certain truths. All these acts are above coercion.[12]

And Jefferson said, "Almighty God hath created the mind free, and manifested his Supreme will that free it shall remain by making it altogether insusceptible of restraint."[13]

Here is seen, at least, the natural antipathy between belief formation and coercion, the natural alliance of reason and freedom. But gaps remain. Most importantly, this alliance of freedom and reason is simply a fact, the fact of the impossibility of commanding people to believe this or that. To arrive at the idea that our rational nature is the basis for our right to make our own decisions and to live by them, we need an argument that is implicit in the writings of Descartes.

Descartes wanted to place scientific knowledge on a foundation of certitude. His method was to doubt all his beliefs until he found one that he could not doubt. What he found was that he could not doubt that he was doubting. In order for him to doubt, he had to exist. But this is hardly enough to found the sciences. So, Descartes set out to prove that God existed and, being perfect, would not deceive him at least with respect to those of his beliefs that were clear and distinct. Descartes thought that mathematics gave us the only clear and distinct ideas that we have of the material world. It followed, then, that God would not allow us to be deceived about the mathematical aspect of the material world. Which is to say, God is the warrant for the certainty of modern science in the form of quantitative physics.

Descartes appeared, then, to prove that God is the authority that justifies our trust in our beliefs. I think, however, that what he actually proved was virtually the opposite of this! Note, at the outset, the obviously circular nature of the argument: Descartes had to trust the beliefs used in his proof of God in order to prove that he didn't have to doubt all his beliefs. But, this presupposition of trust is actually fundamental to Descartes's entire project. The crucial point is that when Descartes doubted, he always doubted for a reason: that he might be dreaming, or that there might be an evil demon bent on deceiving him. That is, he always assumed that he could trust his belief that a certain fact was sufficient to justify doubt. Rather than undermining our confidence in our beliefs, then, Descartes's doubt presupposed it.

Indeed, whatever his intent, Descartes taught the modern world a different lesson from the one that God is the authority for the validity of our beliefs. What he taught was that we, and we alone, can be, must be, and are the only authority for our beliefs.

A rational being cannot but trust her beliefs. Even when she distrusts them, it is only by trusting some other belief to the effect that this one is worthy of doubt. But this means that a rational being implicitly asserts her authority to believe in her beliefs, including the authority to believe which of her beliefs are not to be trusted.

That a rational self claims authority for his beliefs doesn't necessarily mean that his claim should be granted. However, there are good grounds for thinking that this claim should be. As Descartes's argument shows more clearly than it says, a reasoning being cannot take one step without presupposing his authority to believe in the validity of that step. The working of reason itself presupposes our authority to believe in our beliefs. And thus such authority must be valid, since it is the necessary condition of our having any knowledge at all.

In short, Descartes has proven the natural right of the rational subject to authority over her beliefs. I believe that this unformed argument, implicit in the failure of Descartes's explicit strategy, is the real historical impact that Descartes's teaching had on his successors. It is the "light" in the Enlightenment. Now let us see how Locke's argument for natural rights looks in this light.

In the *Second Treatise,* Locke argued against treating monarchical authority as Adam's paternal authority over his offspring passed down to latter-day kings. Locke contended that parental authority is a temporary trust existing only for the purpose of guiding children to maturity, at which point they come to have over themselves just that same authority that their parents had over them. What, then, must a person achieve in order to come out from under parental tutelage and earn the right to freedom? "I answer," wrote Locke,

> a state of maturity wherein he might be supposed capable to know that [natural] law, that so he might keep his actions within the bounds of it. When he has acquired that state, he is presumed to know . . . how far he may make use of his *freedom*, and so comes to have it.[14]

Why is understanding of the law enough to earn its possessor a right to run his or her life? After all, we belong to God. But, said Locke, still in the context of his discussion of the limits of parental power,

> God having given man an understanding to direct his actions, has allowed him a freedom of the will, and liberty of acting, *as properly belonging thereunto*, within the bounds of that law he is under.[15]

Here is at least the core idea: liberty of action properly belongs to a creature with a rational understanding to direct her actions. Somehow it is appropriate to beings whose nature includes the capacity to arrive at rational judgments about how to act that they be allowed to exercise that capacity and thus live their lives according to their own judgments.

This idea of what is proper or appropriate to a rational being takes on even more weight when Hume enters the debate. His contribution is to make things even more difficult by insisting on the logical gap between *is* and *ought*. From one fact or many, no moral conclusion can be deduced. That rational beings assert authority, even exercise it as a necessary condition of reason itself, entails nothing about how such beings should or ought to be treated. But deductive entailment is the strictest possible logical relationship—and not the only possible rationally discernible relationship—between facts and values, between *is* and *ought*. Another relationship, less strict but not therefore feeble, is that of *appropriateness*.

The relationship of appropriateness is not one of logical entailment, but it is the object of a rational judgment. In fact, the capacity to judge appropriateness is presupposed by judgments of logical entailment, since, to make judgments of logical entailment, one must first judge the premises appropriate to the task of supporting the conclusion, and so on. And though it would be wrong to ask for a set of rules for the proper application of "appropriateness," I think we can say that, if there is reason to believe that some X is good, then, in the absence of competing rational considerations, what is appropriate to X is what allows X to be what it is and to follow out its natural tendency. There is reason to believe that the claim of reasoning beings to authority is good because that authority is a necessary condition of knowledge. And there is an absence of competing rational considerations because nothing else in the natural world besides reasoning beings naturally and necessarily asserts authority. Thus, we can say that there is a treatment appropriate to rational beings. Kant named this treatment *respect*.

Kant thought that human beings are worthy of respect because their rational nature stamps them as ends-in-themselves. Of ends-in-themselves, we saw that Kant said little more than that treating people as ends-in-themselves is treating them only according to ends—goals, purposes, values—that they themselves can rationally embrace. Though Kant did not prove that human beings are ends-in-themselves, or show why such treatment is due them, I think that viewing Kant's argument against the background of the implicit Cartesian argument can supply what is lacking. Specifically, we can say that human beings are ends-in-themselves because their rational nature endows them with a natural right to authority over their beliefs, and treating human beings only according to ends they can embrace is appropriate because it acknowledges their authority over the beliefs—about what is valuable—that govern their lives. Allowing this natural exercise of authority corresponds to Kant's understanding of the duty of respect: "When I observe the duty of respect, I . . . keep myself within my own bounds in order not to deprive another of any of the value which he as a human being is entitled to put upon himself."[16]

Respect for an individual's authority over her beliefs about values leads naturally to respect for her authority to act on those values. This is natural because a reasoner uses her reason, not simply to reach value-beliefs *period*, but to reach value-beliefs to determine the kind of actions that she thinks worth doing, the kind of life she thinks worth living. In short, the natural tendency of a being who claims authority over her beliefs is to claim authority over the beliefs that govern her life, and the appropriate response to such a being is to let her live according to those beliefs—to give her, in a word, respect.

With this, we have a way of saying how moral liberalism is true: The appropriate way to treat beings who naturally and necessarily claim authority over their beliefs is to allow them to exercise that authority, which means allowing them to subject their lives to that authority. The ideal of individual sovereignty, then, is true as well: all human beings are entitled to the maximum ability to live their lives according to their own judgments, subject to the conditions necessary to realize this for everyone. Consequently, all societies should promote this ability and all individuals should respect every other individual's right to exercise it.

The respect argument

The argument from respect is essentially the Enlightenment argument run backwards. Instead of starting with the authority of the rational subject and arguing to his or her respect-worthiness, we start with the idea of a moral society as one in which human beings are treated with special respect and, further, as one that aims to protect or, where possible, enhance the respect-worthiness of human beings. Then we look for what could be the plausible condition of such special respect as human beings deserve. It seems to me that there is no way to accord special respect to human beings without according special value to their reaching their own judgments about how to behave. Any alternative would have to hold either (*a*) that what earns human beings respect is something they share with other animals (inasmuch as rational judgment—

including the competencies that presuppose it, such as language—is the only important capacity of ours that animals lack); or (*b*) that what earns human beings respect is their behaving in some particular way, whether or not they have figured out for themselves that this is the best way to behave. Now, from (*a*), it would follow that human beings are no more worthy of respect than other animals and thus not worthy of special respect at all. With (*b*), likewise, there could be no special respect for human beings, since humans who have been drugged or hypnotized, animals that have been trained or conditioned, and robots that have been programmed to act in the desired way would have the same value.

It follows that human beings will be worthy of special respect to the extent that their actions are the outcomes of their own judgments. That, in turn, implies that a social arrangement designed to maximize the respect-worthiness of human beings will maximize the range in which individuals govern their own lives by their own judgments, compatible with a similar range for all. Therefore, insofar as a society realizes the ideal of individual sovereignty, it maximizes the degree to which human beings are worthy of special respect.[17]

The universal interest argument

Kant realized that for a person to have a duty, she must be able to recognize it as her duty. Recognizing something as a duty is more than feeling that it is one's duty. It is, as the word "recognize" suggests, a cognitive act. To recognize something as one's duty requires that one have a reason for acting on the duty that holds even when one feels or judges that one should act to the contrary. Moreover, since moral duties are generally held to apply to all rational human beings, if there are any moral duties, then recognizing them will require that all rational human beings have a reason for acting on them. It follows that if there are moral duties at all, they must be such that everyone at all times has a reason for acting on them.

What could such a reason be? Kant thought he had found it in the categorical imperative. But the commonest version of that imperative, namely, the requirement of universalizability ("Act only according to that maxim whereby you can at the same time will that it should become a universal law"),[18] doesn't give us what we need. All that universalizability requires is sincere willingness to have others act toward me for the same reasons as those upon which I act toward them. If I am a masochist, then I can universalize a principle that allows me to hurt others. This, by the way, shows the general flaw in the universalizability approach. Universalizability works only if we can assume that people have the same standard desires. Hence, it is not really universalizability as such—that is, consistency with *my* desires—that makes an action morally acceptable. Rather, because my desires are expected to be the standard ones shared by others, consistency with my own in fact amounts to accommodation to the desires of others. It is this latter that is absent when the masochist universalizes his desire for pain and thus "justifies" his infliction of it on another who is not a masochist. It is the accommodation to the desires of others that morally justifies my action, and universalizability simply mimics this accommodation as long as my own desires are not too exotic.[19]

The universal reason for moral action must be a universal interest, one that all rational human beings have at all times. This interest cannot be equivalent to every individual human being's overall self-interest, since moral requirements are precisely requirements to limit one's pursuit of one's self-interest. Moral requirements wouldn't have to be requirements if all they asked was fully self-interested behavior. Likewise, we cannot suppose that the universal interest is an interest in happiness, since this is equivalent to self-interest.

Is there, then, an interest that every rational human being has at all times that can support moral requirements? I think there is. A rational being has a continuing interest in living according to how he judges that he should. We may differ in what we judge happiness to consist in, and we may differ in the value that we judge suffering to have. What we share is the interest in being able to live according to our judgments, whatever they are. Even the person who wants another to run his life wants to be able to live according to his own judgment that that other knows best. Any rational human being has an interest in being able to live according to his judgments about how to live. This is an interest that, so to speak, comes with being rational. And this is just the interest that the ideal of individual sovereignty serves.

Note that I am not saying that the ideal of individual sovereignty serves everyone's full self-interest—that would be too much to ask of a moral ideal. What I am saying is that the ideal serves a real and important interest that rational human beings always have. Since people's ability to act according to their own judgments is vulnerable to the ability of others to block them from so acting, everyone has an interest in principles that maximize each one's ability to act according to her own judgments as far as this is compatible with a like ability for everyone else. Thus everyone has an interest in the ideal of individual sovereignty.

This shows that the ideal of individual sovereignty is uniquely suited to spell out moral requirements. Any other moral ideal may appeal to an interest that some or all people contingently have—for example, an interest in pleasure or in being charitable. But some people may not have this interest. They would have no reason to act according to the ideal that corresponds to it. There would be no grounds for holding them to have a duty to so act, since that, as we saw, requires showing that they have a reason to so act. If the existence of such a reason is a necessary (though not a sufficient) condition for holding something to be a duty, then we can say that only the ideal of individual sovereignty satisfies the necessary condition for being a universal human duty. This isn't as good as satisfying the sufficient condition, but since no other moral ideal can satisfy the necessary one, it follows that if there are moral duties at all, they are indicated by the ideal of individual sovereignty.

The antisubjugation argument

The ideal of individual sovereignty indicates a set of duties or moral requirements. Moral requirements spell out ways that people must act even if they are not inclined to, even if they do not endorse the requirement. If duties depended on people wanting to, or judging that they should, act on them, they wouldn't be duties. To show the validity of a moral requirement, then, we must show that it is binding on people who disagree with it. We must demonstrate that the requirement overrides the contrary judgments of dissenters. To understand what is at stake in satisfying this condition, imagine a situation in which one person asserts that another is morally required to act in some way other than the way he judges he should act. Unless and until we can demonstrate that the asserted requirement really should override the recipient's judgment, any case in which it does in fact override may be no more than a case of one person simply imposing her will on another—a matter of might, not right.

When a person is gotten to act according to the judgment of another (about what he morally should do) at the expense of his own judgment (about what he should do, morally or otherwise), one of two things has happened: Either the requirer's judgment has prevailed because it should prevail, or it has prevailed because (somehow) it could prevail. If it prevailed because it could prevail, not because it should, I call this *subjugation*. "Subjugation" here refers, not to the motives of the people involved, but to the relationship between two wills, one of which has prevailed over another without justification. Anytime one person gets another to comply with an asserted moral requirement against his will, the possibility of subjugation is present.

In light of this, a person confronted with a requirement to act contrary to the way she judges that she should act is always entitled to suspect that the requirer is attempting to subjugate her, that is, trying—consciously or otherwise—to get her to act according to the judgment of the requirer, without justification. As long as that is a possibility, the recipient of the asserted requirement is entitled to think that she is not really morally required to comply. It follows that to show that she is morally required to comply, it is necessary to refute the suspicion of subjugation. How can this be done?

It seems to me that there are only two possibilities. One would be to prove beyond a reasonable doubt that the asserted requirement is a true moral requirement. Then, the recipient is being asked to override her own judgment because she should—her own judgment is wrong. Now, on the possibility of proving some moral requirements true beyond a reasonable doubt, the prevailing view among moral philosophers is negative. I shall, then, for the present, treat this option as, for all intents and purposes, impossible. This does not, by the way, commit me to moral agnosticism or moral skepticism. It amounts, rather, to recognizing that in real interactions between individuals with differing moral beliefs, we are not, in fact, able to prove the truth of one of those beliefs in such a way as to show that the one who differs is wrong beyond a reasonable doubt. There may be, nonetheless, true moral ideals, and we may even know the truth of some or all of them, even if we cannot prove their truth beyond a reasonable doubt.

The second alternative is to show that the requirement asserted is needed in order to defend people against subjugation itself. If subjugation is a danger, then those requirements on behavior that are needed to prevent it can hardly be called subjugating. Since subjugation amounts to unjustified overriding of people's own judgments about how they should behave, requirements justified as necessary to maximize each person's ability to act according to his own judgments are not subjugating. These requirements are equivalent to those entailed by the ideal of individual sovereignty.

The point here is simple but, I think, quite far reaching in its implications. Any moral requirement must be a matter of right, not might. To establish this, we must prove—not just believe firmly—either that the requirement is truly right beyond a reasonable doubt or that it is needed to restrict to a minimum the role of might in human affairs. This shows that the liberal ideal has an advantage over all others. Unless and until one of those others can be proven truly right beyond a reasonable doubt, only the liberal ideal can satisfactorily rebut the suspicion of subjugation. It is the only one that can withstand the charge of being might, not right.[20]

The Liberal Good

In *The View from Nowhere*, Thomas Nagel makes constructive use of the distinction between the third-person, objective viewpoint characteristic of science and the first-person, subjective viewpoint that we have because we are individual subjects.[21] This distinction between third-person observation and the sort of first-person awareness one has of oneself by virtue of being oneself, while new to Anglo-American philosophers, has been a staple of European philosophy at least since the beginning of the century when it figured in the work of Henri Bergson and Edmund Husserl. Crucial to this distinction is the notion that the knowledge one has of oneself from the subjective viewpoint is different in kind from, and not translatable into, the knowledge available to objective observation. In *Being and Time*, Martin Heidegger, following upon Husserl, launched a full-scale exploration of human being from the standpoint of the special awareness available to the human subject by virtue of being it. Heidegger maintained that as I live my life in the first person, I find that my being is *at stake*.[22] Contrary to the appearance from the third-person point of view, I am not a thing whose being is, so to speak, complete, and that traverses a life in which the last event is death. Rather, from the first-person point of view, my mortality is part of my present, rendering my being itself fragile, not a completed thing, but a task that I must take up and yet at which I can fail. And my life is not a path I traverse; it is the action of the task of being me.

In the first person, I grasp my mortal being as a one-time *chance to be*. By putting an edge on my being, mortality transforms living into living *a life*. As that life is the sum of my being, bounded on the far side by endless darkness and silence, mortality makes my life into a special kind of challenge. Aware of the fact that I have one finite chance to be in all eternity, I am confronted by the need to live a life whose worth to me somehow satisfies me that I have used my chance well. This is what I take Heidegger to mean in calling the being of human beings, *care*. Indeed, I think that we find here the natural factual basis of human moral equality: However different we are, we all confront our lives as our once-in-eternity chance to live a life whose nature we care about.[23]

Readers who are familiar with the writings of Heidegger will know that his philosophy is marked by a deep antirationalism, and that, in response to mortality's challenge, he counsels "resolve," an act of sheer will by which one undertakes to live one's own life "authentically" rather than give in to the temptation of letting the world script one's life for one. Such antirationalism has, of course, no counterpart in critical moral liberalism and, I think, it betrays the existentialist project as well. It seems obvious to me that an act of sheer nonrational will is more like an unexpected accident than like a resolve to live one's own life, and that a true resolve to live one's own life would have to be marked by the sort of evaluation of one's nature and possibilities that can only be called rational. Be that as it may, my approach is to appropriate Heidegger's valuable insights about the human condition for critical moral liberalism, and leave behind his antirationalism. This has the added benefit of leaving behind just that feature of Heidegger's thought that led him to sympathy with Nazism.

What I take from Heidegger, then, is the idea that the challenge of mortality, brought home to us in an ultimate way in the first person, puts a distinctive shape on the human good. That we live our lives in response to the challenge of mortality means that it is, above all, important in each person's life, not just that she lives some particular way or another, but that she *intentionally* lives a life that somehow *satisfies her* that it is worthwhile in the face of the inevitable nonbeing on the other side. No life can answer the challenge of mortality unless it is judged to do so by the one whose life it is.

That my life is my once-in-eternity opportunity to meet this challenge means that I cannot simply leave to chance whether I live a life that I can judge worthwhile. Indeed, it is just here that the warnings of Heidegger and other existentialists about "inauthenticity"—the temptation to go along with the crowd, to shrink from facing one's mortality and slip easily into a role handed one by the society in which one finds oneself—have their point. To give into such temptations is, in effect, to let my life be shaped by the society's judgments about how to live, not by my own, and thus not to live a life that truly satisfies me that it is worthwhile in the face of my ultimate nonbeing. To resist such temptations, to live such a life, I cannot just follow the course of least resistance. I must aim intentionally at living a life that satisfies my standards for a worthwhile life. This, in turn, implies that I must live my life as the outcome of my own judgments about how to live.

In short, the existentialist account implies that at least a necessary condition of any human life's being good is that the person whose life it is intentionally live it in a way that he or she can recognize as good. But, then, it is a condition of living a good life that one's life be the outcome of one's rational judgments about how best to live. Thus rational self-governance—critical moral liberalism's rational version of authenticity—is the sine qua non of the good life.

However, since lives can be governed well or poorly, self-governance is a necessary, but not a sufficient condition, of a life's being good. A rationally self-governed life, we might say, meets the formal condition of goodness but still might be substantially bad. There are, however, ways in which rational self-governance contributes toward making lives substantially good. First of all, a rationally self-governed life is one lived intentionally according to reflectively endorsed beliefs about what makes a life good. To so live is to be willing, in the face of evidence, to revise those beliefs. This means that a rationally self-governed life is lived in an intentionally self-correcting fashion. Just as the steady use of scientific method must generally improve the quality of our hypotheses (even if in particular cases errors are made), so the steady disposition to review rationally the beliefs according to which one lives must generally improve the quality of those beliefs. And this "generally" means both "on the average for large groups of rationally self-governing individuals" and "on the average over the course of the lifetime of any single rationally self-governing individual." It follows that a rationally self-governed life has the best chance of being a substantially good life.

Moreover, I contend that a life lived according to our rational judgments is a free life. Freedom is not whimsy, chance, accident or indeterminacy, any or all of which would turn our actions into unpredictable eruptions. Freedom is being able to act on one's considered judgment about how one should act. Then, a rationally self-governed life is a life whose nature expresses the will of a free person. This opens the possibility of seeing our fates as earned and our lives as accomplishments or failures, as objects of pride or disappointment. This means that, in addition to a life's feeling pleasant or painful, a new possibility enters: *personal significance*. Life becomes a drama whose unfolding means something to the one whose life it is because it is that individual's self-creation.[24] And this, by enhancing what is at stake in the living of a life, increases the chances of that life's being good substantially.

Making Liberalism Critical

I said at the outset that critical moral liberalism's ideal of individual sovereignty is a high-altitude principle that specifies neither particular actions nor general policies. Consequently, anyone or any society that aims to realize this ideal will do so subject to some interpretation of what is needed to maximize people's abilities to live according to their own judgments—normally, some set of basic rights. Such interpretations will be no better than the best available understanding of what threatens freedom and what is needed to promote it. That we can be mistaken about this, that unjustified coercion can occur without being noticed as such, means that we may be satisfied that the liberal ideal is being realized when, in fact, it is not. And then our interpretation of what the ideal requires will function ideologically because we will bestow liberalism's moral approval upon a situation marked by unrecognized and unjustified coercion. For this reason, any honest moral liberalism must be critical, that is, self-critical. It must remain open to the idea that knowledge of what threatens freedom changes in history, and therefore it must be ready to revise the set of basic rights it currently recommends, in light of newly recognized forms of unjust coercion. Recognition of this need is stimulated by, but not tied to the specifics of, Marx's challenge to capitalism.

Marx held that private ownership of the means of production is unjust and coercive: Where a small number of people in a society own the machines and resources, the others will have no choice but to work for those owners on those owners' terms in order to make a living, that is, in order to live at all. Of equal importance, however, is the idea that workers in such a society may not notice that they are being coerced insofar as they view property arrangements as obviously justified or in no need of justification. If people don't notice the unjust and coercive nature of property arrangements, then they will agree to work for owners without feeling that any power has been exercised over them.

Marx has really made two discoveries here that profoundly affect our moral situation. Moreover, these discoveries are not tied to Marx's specific views about capitalism. Thus they can be useful even to those who doubt or deny that ownership of the means of production is coercive.

First, Marx has discovered the potentially unjust and coercive nature of social practices, such as, but not limited to, forms of property ownership. This discovery applies as well to the social maintenance of gender roles. The system of gender roles is also a putatively unjust coercive social practice, effectively narrowing women's and men's alternatives and thus limiting their choices.

Marx's second discovery is of the tendency for the coerciveness of social practices not to be recognized as such. Since social practices are all around us, they fade into the background like the smell of the air or the feel of your chair. This means that their coercion works effectively and doesn't feel unjustly coercive. Said Marx of capitalism, it is a system of "forced labour—no matter how much it may seem to result from free contractual agreement."[25] With this, we get not only the way ideology works in capitalism, but the general form of the critique of liberalism as ideology.

An ideology is a belief system that is false in a way that allows unjust coercion to function unrecognized as such, and thus unchallenged. The general form of the criticism of liberalism as ideology is that (*a*) liberalism effectively defends freedom by establishing rights against recognized forms of unjust coercion; (*b*) there exist putatively unjust social practices (for example, property arrangements, sexism, racism, poverty) that limit people's choices coercively, but which are not recognized as doing so; and (*c*), because of (*a*) and (*b*), liberalism ignores (leaves unrecognized and thus unchallenged) these forms of coercion, which, then, simply work through the existing system of liberal rights. Indeed, liberalism does worse than ignore them, since the effect of (*c*) is that liberals will pronounce the situation—with its unrecognized and presumably unjust coercion—free and thereby bestow upon it liberalism's own moral approbation.

But, notice that this is not an objection to liberalism as such. Quite the contrary, it appeals to liberalism's own core value, freedom. The critique of liberalism as ideology is always a critique of an existing version of liberalism as not doing enough to protect individual freedom, in light of unrecognized unjust coercion. Consequently, the critique of liberalism as ideological is a call, not for the abandonment of liberalism, but for its revision to include protections against newly discovered forms of unjust coercion.

For Marxism, the unrecognized unjust coercion is that which is built into private ownership of the means of production by a few and which is hidden by, and thus allowed to function by, "equal" liberal rights to sell one's property without being subject to overt coercion by the buyer. For feminism, the unrecognized unjust coercion is the existence of gender roles characterized by male dominance, enacted by social practices (patterns of behavior and attitudes), and hidden by, and thus allowed to function by, "equal" liberal rights to marry, to take "women's jobs," and so on, without being subject to overt coercion.

Consider the feminist form of the critique of liberalism as ideology in the work of Catharine MacKinnon. Here she speaks of the U.S. Constitution as typical of the liberal state:

> The Constitution—the constituting document of this state society—with its interpretations assumes that society, absent government intervention, is free and equal. . . . Speaking descriptively . . . , the strategy is first to constitute society unequally prior to law; then to design the constitution, including the law of equality, so that all its guarantees apply only to those values taken away by law. . . . Then, so long as male dominance is . . . effective in society . . . , not even a legal guarantee of sex equality will produce social equality.[26]

All the elements of the critique of liberalism as ideology are here. Inequality, in the form of presumably unjust and coercive male dominance over women, is built into existing social practices; it "constitute[s] society . . . prior to law." The existing liberal legal system is blind to the coerced inequality; it "assumes that society . . . is free and equal." Then, only overt deviations from the status quo, such as legally enforced inequality—"values taken away by law" itself—or (we can add) violations of the law by citizens, will appear as transgressions against freedom and equality. Consequently, the preexisting coercive system of male domination is allowed to flourish even though there is "a legal guarantee of sex equality."

Though MacKinnon goes to great lengths to distinguish her views from those of Marx and Engels, her picture of the way liberalism functions ideologically is essentially the same as the Marxian model. Engels, also discussing the liberal legal systems of his day, applied the Marxian model to both the oppression of women by men and the oppression of workers by capitalists, thereby making the similarity of structure clear:

> Modern civilized systems of law increasingly acknowledge first, that for a marriage to be legal it must be a contract freely entered into by both partners and secondly, that also in the married state both partners must stand on a common footing of equal rights and duties. If both these demands are consistently carried out, say the jurists, women have all they can ask.
>
> This typically legalist method of argument is exactly the same as that which the . . . bourgeois uses to put the proletarian in his place. The labor contract is to be freely entered into by both partners. . . . The power con-

ferred on the one party by the difference of class position, the pressure thereby brought to bear on the other party—the real economic position of both—that is not the law's business. . . .

In regard to marriage, the law, even the most advanced, is fully satisfied as soon as the partners have formally recorded that they are entering into marriage of their own free consent. What goes on in real life behind the juridical scenes, how this free consent came about—that is not the business of the law and the jurist.[27]

Here, too, all the elements of the critique of liberalism as ideology are present. Liberal legal rights protect against recognized forms of coercion. Unrecognized, and presumably unjust, coercion is built into existing social practices—as "the real economic position of both," "what goes on in real life behind the juridical scenes"—and is allowed to function through the freedoms kept clear by existing liberal legal rights.

Notice that the criticism of liberalism as ideology contains a factual claim and a moral claim. The factual claim is that unrecognized coercion exists. The moral claim is that the coercion is unjust. A social theory, such as Marxism or feminism, can tell us that unrecognized coercion exists, by pointing out the way in which social practices effectively close off (or make costly or dangerous) certain otherwise attractive options. But, that a social practice coerces people is not enough to condemn that social practice morally. Established social practices are necessary for the smooth functioning of any society; and the way they narrow choices may be necessary for social life to be predictable and relatively conflict-free. Indeed, without some such narrowing, people might be overwhelmed, even paralyzed, by the seemingly limitless range of alternatives from which to choose. The issue is whether the coercion works justly, that is, to everyone's benefit alike, or unjustly, that is, to force a disadvantage on some for the benefit of others. To determine whether any existing interpretation of liberalism is functioning ideologically, we need a way of testing the justice of coercive social practices.

Since the coercion in social practices is normally unrecognized, we cannot test its justice by asking members of the society whether they find the coercion acceptable. Even if they are made aware of the coercion, say, by being introduced to a social theory like Marxism or feminism, asking them won't do since their answers may simply reveal how they individually are affected by the system, or how well they have been indoctrinated into it, and not whether it is really in everyone's interest. Consequently, we need a theoretical test to determine the justice of the social practice.

For critical moral liberalism, the justice of a coercive social practice lies in whether it is limiting people's freedom as, and only as, is needed to maximize everyone's ability alike to live according to their own judgments. Asking whether a given social practice does this is, in effect, asking the theoretical question embodied in the doctrine of the social contract: namely, whether it would be reasonable for (imaginary rational) people (interested in maximizing their ability to govern their lives by their own judgments, and supplied with the best available knowledge, but ignorant of how they in particular will fare under any particular social arrangement) to agree unanimously to live under that social arrangement given the possible alternatives. Since the contractors do not know where they in particular will end up in any arrangement to which they agree, they must test each potential arrangement by whether it is in the interest of everyone. Since the interest of everyone is in living as far as possible according to their own judgments, applying the social contract test amounts to determining whether the ideal of individual sovereignty is being satisfied to the maximum degree possible—or, equivalently, that no individual's ability to live according to his judgments is being limited except as necessary to maximize this possibility for all individuals alike. This is how the social contract tests for the justice of coercion in light of the ideal of individual sovereignty.

It is by this special use of the social contract doctrine that *moral liberalism* becomes *critical*. That is, it becomes open to the need to revise its current version of what must be done to protect all individuals' rights to govern their lives by their own judgments. Some, of course, think that the social contract doctrine itself is ideological. But I think they confuse the doctrine with particular ways it has been formulated and with particular uses to which it has been put. The core idea, in my view, is the very opposite of ideological.

If the capitalist relations of production that Marx identifies as coercive are thought to be unjust, this surely means that it would be irrational for freedom-loving people (who are imagined as not knowing whether they will be capitalists or workers) to adopt them voluntarily and unanimously where, say, socialist relations of production were possible. If the social relations of male dominance that MacKinnon identifies as coercive are thought to be unjust, that surely means that it would be irrational for freedom-loving people (who are imagined as not knowing whether they are of the dominant gender or the dominated) to adopt them unanimously where relations of gender equality were possible.

What will be crucial in applying the social contract doctrine to determine whether some version of liberalism is functioning as ideology is what knowledge our imaginary freedom-loving contractors are thought to have. The imaginary contractors will only come out agreeing with Marx and Engels about capitalism if they are taken as knowing (that is, accepting as true) Marxian theory. They will only come out agreeing with MacKinnon if they are taken as knowing feminist theory. The same will hold true for other versions of the critique of liberalism as ideology. This is just what should be expected, since those who claim that liberalism is ideological do so on the basis of assuming that Marxian or feminist (or some other) theory about the coercive nature of social practices is true, that is, should be part of the knowledge had by the imaginary parties to the social contract. Criticisms of liberalism as ideological will only be as strong as the arguments for the social theories (Marxist, feminist, or other) on which they are based.

That determination of when liberalism is functioning ideologically requires such arguments shows that a theory can only go so far in protecting itself against being used ideologically. After that, it will need a little help from its friends. If those friends succeed in identifying as-yet-unrecognized forms of coercion, and if those forms of coercion cannot pass the test of the social contract, then critical moral liberalism will have to revise its currently recommended set of rights to include new ones to protect against the newly discovered threats to people's ability to live according to their own judgments.

From Liberal Theory to Practice

Though this introduction comes first, it was written last. It is not rightly seen as stating the doctrine from which the rest of the book flowed. The introduction is, rather, an afterthought, a reconstruction of the liberal view that was aborning and abuilding in the chapters that follow. These chapters show how critical moral liberalism deals with specific policy problems, as well as how that doctrine emerged in the course of trying to shed philosophical light on those problems. Below, I shall suggest briefly how each chapter relates to critical moral liberalism.

Chapter 1, "Liberalism, Feminism, and Multiculturalism: The Ironic Destiny of Western Philosophy," places critical moral liberalism in the context of the history of Western philosophy from the ancient Greeks to the present day. I contend that Western philosophy's self-conscious rationalism makes it inherently self-critical and, ultimately, liberal. I argue that current feminist and multiculturalist critiques of the Western intellectual tradition presuppose that tradition's own commitment to liberal ideals and rational self-criticism. Rather than steps beyond the Western tradition, these recent critiques are steps within that tradition. Since both feminists and multiculturalists attack liberalism's supposed individualism in the name of more communitarian values, I defend liberalism's focus on individuals, pointing out that it is only by protecting the rights of individuals that we can prevent the subjugation of some by many. Further, I argue that community is a value only if a community's members freely embrace their shared life, and thus community itself presupposes the "individualistic" liberal ideal. I also take up the problems of cultural relativism and the supposed opposition between the justice approach and the care approach in ethics.

In chapter 2, "Postmodern Argumentation and Post-postmodern Liberalism, with Comments on Levinas, Habermas, and Rawls," I contend that the common postmodernist charge—that universal moral principles (such as those of the Enlightenment) have been used to exclude some individuals or groups from full moral standing—is paradoxical: it amounts to criticizing moral universalism for not being universal enough! It follows that postmodernists presuppose a universal moral standard in their very critique of moral universalism. I try to supply this standard by developing in greater detail the Cartesian argument for the subject's authority over her beliefs, and showing that it yields a universal liberal moral principle—the ideal of individual sovereignty—that can be defended subject to the postmodern requirements of argumentation. Since these postmodern requirements are, in fact, widely endorsed in the contemporary intellectual situation, the argument reaches beyond those who call themselves "postmodernist" to everyone on the contemporary scene who has doubts about the possibility of universal moral principles. I conclude by showing that this universal liberal principle provides just what is missing in the moral theories of Emmanuel Levinas, Jürgen Habermas, and John Rawls.

In chapter 3, "Drug Addiction, Liberal Virtue, and Moral Responsibility," I develop a liberal theory of the moral virtues as those dispositions that promote the sovereignty of practical reason. I show what this theory shares with, and how it departs from, the Aristotelian account of the virtues.

In chapter 4, "The Labor Theory of the Difference Principle," I defend a version of John Rawls's "difference principle" as a standard of economic justice. I interpret economic distributions as, in the first instance, distributions of the labor that goes into the products that are traded on the market. This is appropriate for a critical liberal theory that recognizes the possibility of unrecognized coercion in social practices such as those that support a given set of property arrangements. If such coercion functions in the economy, then what appear as freely contracted exchanges of labor for money may be socially coerced labor of some for others. The only way to determine if this is so is to view the economic distribution in light of how much each is laboring for others. Moreover, viewing economic distributions this way shows, much more clearly than Rawls has been able to, that the difference principle is a principle of mutual benefit. And, it shows the conditions under which capitalist, socialist, and communist principles of distribution are just.

In chapter 5, "The Constitution, Rights, and the Conditions of Legitimacy," I show how the social contract doctrine functions as a critical tool for testing whether oppression exists even in social institutions that we have come to take for granted. Though argued in the context of a defense of a liberal theory of constitutional interpretation, this chapter suggests how the social contract idea can make good on the critical nature of critical moral liberalism, by keeping it open to the need to revise any existing interpretation of what rights are needed to realize the ideal of individual sovereignty.

In chapter 6, "Privacy, Intimacy, and Personhood," I contend that privacy has value beyond such practical effects as protecting our reputations. It is a way of enacting a society's belief that each individual is the owner of his or her own body. It is also a crucial element of the cultural training by which we shape selves who believe in their authority over their destinies and thus who are ready for life in a liberal society.

In chapter 7, "Driving to the Panopticon: A Philosophical Exploration of the Risks to Privacy Posed by the Information Technology of the Future," I develop further the ideas discussed in chapter 6 into a general analysis of the value of privacy, and I explore the moral risks posed by the threats to privacy from the new information technology.

In chapter 8, "Abortion, Infanticide, and the Asymmetric Value of Human Life," I argue that, in view of the way we value human life, nothing about fetuses can justify protecting their lives in the way we normally protect the lives of children or adults. I argue that the value we place on childrens' and adults' lives is a form of respect for them as persons, and that the value we place on infants' lives is a matter of love rather than respect. What results is a liberal defense of a pregnant woman's right to an abortion at any stage of gestation.

In chapter 9, "On Euthanasia and Health Care," I contend that biographical life—the conscious life of a being who understands him or herself as the same individual continuing over time—is more important to human beings than biological life, the latter being important only as a condition for the former. On this basis, I argue for a liberal right of individuals to passive and active euthanasia. I take up the "slippery slope" problem and some issues related to the fair allocation of health care.

In chapter 10, "Is Police Discretion Justified in a Free Society?" I look at the political philosophies of Plato, Hobbes, Locke, Montesquieu, and Rawls and develop a liberal view of the nature of both law and the public force that backs it up. I conclude that discretionary police enforcement of serious laws is not justified in a free society. Freedom is threatened both by the overreach of the law and by arbitrariness in its enforcement.

In chapter 11, "Justice, Civilization, and the Death Penalty," I develop a liberal conception of crime (as the disruption of equal relations of sovereignty among citizens) and of punishment (as the restoration of equal sovereignty). Included are explanations of just desert, of the proper status of the *lex talionis*, of the varieties of retributivism, and of the roles of social injustice and deterrence in the justification of punishment. I conclude that, though the death penalty is just punishment for some murders, abolition of the death penalty is part of the civilizing mission of modern states.

Notes

This introduction is based on my University Senate Distinguished Faculty Lecture, delivered at American University in Washington, D.C., on 27 March 1996.

1. See Ronald Dworkin, "Liberalism," in *Public and Private Morality,* ed. S. Hampshire (Cambridge: Cambridge University Press, 1978), pp. 113–43; and Bruce Ackerman, *Social Justice in the Liberal State* (New Haven, Conn.: Yale University Press, 1980).

2. See John Rawls, *Political Liberalism* (New York: Columbia University Press, 1993).

3. Ibid., pp. 12–13.

4. Interestingly, Locke maintained that the irrational association of ideas is a form of madness, and that virtually no one is free of it in some degree. See John Locke, *An Essay Concerning Human Understanding*, abridged and ed. John Yolton (London: Everyman, 1994; originally published 1690), pp. 218–24.

5. Charles Sanders Peirce, *The Philosophical Writings of Peirce*, ed. J. Buchler (New York: Dover, 1955), p. 66.

6. John Locke, *Second Treatise of Government* (Indianapolis, Ind.: Hackett, 1980; originally published 1690), p. 9.

7. "Though the earth, and all inferior creatures, be common to all men, yet every man has a *property* in his own *person:* this no body has any right to but himself. The *labour* of his body, and the *work* of his hands, we may say, are properly his. Whatsoever then he removes out of the state that nature hath provided, and left it in, he hath mixed his *labour* with, and joined to it something that is his own, and thereby makes it his *property.*" Locke, *Second Treatise*, p. 19 (emphasis in original).

8. "The practical imperative will therefore be the following: Act in such a way that you treat humanity, whether in your own person or in the person of another, always at the same time as an end and never simply as a means." Immanuel Kant, *Grounding of the Metaphysics of Morals*, trans. J. W. Ellington (Indianapolis, Ind: Hackett, 1981; originally published 1785), p. 36. (Note that in the text, and henceforth in the notes, I use the more common translation of the title of this work of Kant's: *Groundwork of the Metaphysics of Morals*.)

9. "[T]he man who intends to make a false promise will immediately see that he intends to make use of another man merely as a means to an end which the latter does not likewise hold. For the man whom I want to use for my own purposes by such a promise cannot possibly concur with my way of acting toward him and hence *cannot himself hold the end of this action.*" Kant, *Groundwork*, p. 37 (emphasis in original).

10. Ibid., p. 35.

11. John Locke, *A Letter Concerning Toleration* (Indianapolis, Ind.: Hackett, 1983; originally published 1689), p. 27 (emphasis mine).

12. François-Marie Arouet de Voltaire, "The Ecclesiastical Ministry," quoted in *The Portable Enlightenment Reader*, ed. I. Kramnick (New York: Penguin Books, 1995), p. 116.

13. Thomas Jefferson, "A Bill for Establishing Religious Freedom," in *Papers of Thomas Jefferson,* ed. Julian Boyd (Princeton, N.J.: Princeton University Press, 1950), vol. 2, p. 545.

14. Locke, *Second Treatise*, p. 33.

15. Ibid., pp. 32–33 (emphasis mine).

16. Immanuel Kant, "The Metaphysical Principles of Virtue," pt. 2 of *The Metaphysics of Morals*, in *Ethical Philosophy*, trans. James W. Ellington (Indianapolis, Ind.: Hackett, 1983; originally published 1797), p. 114; see also Kant, *Groundwork,* pp. 35–37.

17. In my *Justice and Modern Moral Philosophy* (New Haven, Conn.: Yale University Press, 1990), especially pp. 112–28, I take a different approach and argue that respect is a cognitive attitude that is required for gaining knowledge of human subjects. This cognitive attitude, however, brings with it liberal normative commitments.

18. Kant, *Groundwork*, p. 30.

19. For an extended critique of the universalizability strategy, in both Alan Gewirth's and R. M. Hare's versions, see my *Justice and Modern Moral Philosophy*, pp. 108–12, 314.

20. In my *Justice and Modern Moral Philosophy*, I attempt to show that the true principles of justice (which turn out to be liberal principles of the sort defended here) can be found by determining the terms under which rational human beings ought to agree that they are not being subjugated. I also contend that this is the implicit logic of the social contract approach to moral theorizing and thus accounts for the perennial appeal of that approach.

21. Thomas Nagel, *The View from Nowhere* (New York: Oxford University Press, 1986), p. 18, inter alia.

22. Martin Heidegger, *Being and Time* (New York: Harper & Row, 1962), pp. 236–38.

23. I develop this argument in my *Justice and Modern Moral Philosophy*, especially, p. 49.

24. In a seminal essay, Herbert Morris spells out what we would lose if we thought of our actions as symptoms of underlying conditions rather than as expressions of free choice. Among the things he lists are our belief in our capacity for "creating, among other things, ourselves"; our "range of peculiarly human satisfactions that derive from a sense of achievement"; and our belief that important features of our fates are "earned." Herbert Morris, "Persons and Punishment," in *Punishment and the Death Penalty: The Current Debate*, ed. R. Baird and S. Rosenbaum (Amherst, N.Y.: Prometheus Books, 1995), p. 69. Morris's essay was originally published in *Monist* 52 (October 1968): 475–94.

25. Karl Marx, *Capital*, vol. 3 (New York: International Publishers, 1967; originally published 1894), p. 819.

26. Catharine MacKinnon, *Toward a Feminist Theory of the State* (Cambridge, Mass.: Harvard University Press, 1989), pp. 163–64.

27. Frederick Engels, *The Origins of the Family, Private Property, and the State* (New York: International Publishers, 1973), pp. 135–36.

Part I

Theory

1

Liberalism, Feminism, and Multiculturalism: The Ironic Destiny of Western Philosophy

Intellectual life in the present era is marked by a widespread and radical skepticism, a thoroughgoing agnosticism that rejects claims to objective knowledge, by which I mean knowledge that is true and valid for all human beings. This skepticism began with doubts about knowledge that erupted in Europe in the nineteenth century in response to Hegel's attempt at a grand synthesis. It has been hemorrhaging ever since. However, its nature changed profoundly in the wake of Nietzsche's charge that Western notions of reason, truth, and goodness are tools of domination. With this, skepticism took a moral turn. Claims to objective universal knowledge made on behalf of the Western tradition now appear to be not only false but evil.

Western ideas about reality and morality, we are told, are biased by Western cultural attitudes in ways that justify Western subjugation of non-Western peoples, and, being dominated by white males, the Western tradition represents as universal the experiences of only part of the population, thereby legitimating their domination over the rest. Nineteenth-century Europeans "knew" that civilizing the dark-skinned peoples of the southern hemisphere was the white man's burden, as nineteenth-century Americans "knew" that their manifest destiny required conquering the Indians who stood between them and the Pacific. In the twentieth century, Stalin "knew" that history was on his side, and Hitler "knew" that Aryans were the superior race. When to this list is added all the so-called knowledge about the inferiority of blacks, the irrationality of women, the sickness of homosexuals, the defectiveness of the poor, the criminality of foreigners, the primitiveness of Africans, and the inscrutability of Asians, the threat posed by knowledge becomes palpable—and skepticism, which started life as a theoretical headache, comes to look like a moral cure.

But skepticism is no ally against evil, because the condemnation of evil presupposes knowledge—historical knowledge and moral knowledge. For us to condemn morally the oppression of women, blacks, or non-European peoples, we must be confident that such oppression has actually occurred (and thus confident that we have knowledge of the historical record), and we must be confident that this oppression is truly wrong (and thus confident that we have knowledge of what is morally right and wrong). But the skepticism of which I am speaking is the belief that we cannot have such knowledge. Thus it undermines moral condemnation.

A case in point is the very popular skepticism that takes all thinkers to be biased by their culture or personal predilections. Biased thinkers produce biased theories, and biased theories are false in that they distort reality either by outright misrepresentation or by putting forth part of the truth as the whole thing. If all thinkers are biased, then all theories are false (or, if true, only by accident and in no way that we can distinguish from false), and this includes the theories upon which our moral condemnations are based. Consider the following example, which is typical of current attitudes: The editor of a recent anthology of writings on feminism and postmodernism tells us that some feminist scholars have challenged the notion of scholarly neutrality, holding that what has generally been presented as objective is not. So far, so good. The editor goes on to say, however, that these scholars "claimed that such biases were inevitable; all scholarship reflected the perspectives and ideals of its creators. Avoiding narrowness in the academy could only be possible through ensuring the inclusion of a multitude of points of view."[1] Now I ask you: Why avoid narrowness in the academy? Is the desirability of avoiding narrowness just a bias reflecting some scholars' ideals and perspectives? If so, then it is no more worthy of support than the opposite bias. If it is not a bias, then bias cannot be inevitable. You can't have it both ways. Bear in mind that I agree that much supposedly neutral scholarship is biased, that postmodernists and feminists have done much to expose this, and that we should, for moral and intellectual reasons, avoid narrowness in the academy. My point is that, once you say that bias is inevitable, you cut the ground out from under these very claims.

We cannot have both thoroughgoing skepticism and moral condemnation of oppression. My hunch is that, forced to choose between these, we will give up skepticism first. It is here, by the way, that the late Allan Bloom went wrong in his diagnosis of the American mind.[2] He rightly saw that the prevailing skepticism (or "relativism," which for all intents and purposes amounts to the same thing) wreaks havoc on our intellectual and moral life, but he failed to understand the deep moral longing that undergirds it. Our skepticism is only skin-deep. Beneath it lies its opposite: An unskeptical belief that human beings truly are equal in worth and truly are entitled to live their lives according to their own ideals and choices. Because of this belief, we condemn oppression as morally wrong.

This belief is the core of the moral doctrine of liberalism, about which I shall soon say more. For the moment, suffice it to say that those who would condemn oppression morally must assume that this liberal belief is true. And at least Westerners who condemn oppression got this belief from the Western tradition. These Western foes of oppression need a way of thinking about the effect of cultural traditions that allows the possibility that such a belief is true and that we can know it to be true. I want to propose such a way, namely, that we think of cultural traditions, not as biasing us, but as positioning us. Cultural traditions constitute the place and angle from which we see the world. At first, thinking of them as positioning us may seem to be no real change from thinking of them as biasing us. Positioned here rather than there, we may be able to see some things, and we may be blocked from seeing others. The resultant view may then be as partial—in both senses of that term, selective and partisan—as it seems to those who think that traditions bias us.

But, while all biases distort, some positions give a better and wider view than others. And this implies an enormous shift in how we understand the influence of traditions. If we think of traditions as *biasing* their members, it follows that, since all thinkers work out of some tradition, all thinkers are biased. Therefore, we can conclude in advance, a priori, and automatically, that all theories are distortions. Enter general skepticism, sowing destruction indiscriminately to the beliefs of friend and foe alike. If, however, we think that traditions *position* us and that positions may be better and worse, then, while it is an ever present possibility that theories are distorted, it is not an automatic, inevitable conclusion. We must see, on the basis of case-by-case analysis rather than a priori argument, which theories are distorted and which are not. Exit general skepticism and enter, instead, what I would call "healthy suspicion." By this, I mean a general inquiring stance that stays on the lookout for bias but remains open to finding knowledge instead. Healthy suspicion is the only authentic skepticism because, unlike our contemporary skepticism, it is even skeptical about skepticism.

To draw together the strands of my argument so far, I contend, first, that the notion that all human beings are of equal worth and that all are equally entitled to live according to their beliefs is presupposed by the moral condemnation of oppression. This notion, then, is one that the defenders of the oppressed must believe to be true. Believing it to be true, they cannot reject all claims to knowledge, nor can they hold the general view that all traditions bias their members. Somehow their own tradition has enabled them to see at least the truth about the equal worth of all human beings (as well as the truth of the factual claims that make up the record of oppression). They must think of traditions as positioning their members for better or for worse, rather than irretrievably biasing and blinding them. Further, a tradition that has positioned its members to see the equal worth of human beings must be providing its members with a very good and wide view indeed. At least the defenders of the oppressed must believe this. And the Westerners among them must face the fact that it is their Western cultural tradition— ethnocentric and male-dominated as it undoubtedly has been—that has positioned them in this way. Then, staying ever alert to bias, they must ask: What is it about this tradition that accounts for this positioning?

When I address this question, I do so from the standpoint of that particular thread of the Western cultural tradition that is called Western philosophy. I do not think that this is the only thread, and I recognize that it itself is woven of strands from many sources, including foreign imports. I contend only that—as cause or effect or, more likely, as both—Western philosophy has embodied certain themes that are distinctive of Western culture.

Of these themes, the one that is central for my purposes here is Western philosophy's self-conscious rationalism. In the remainder of this chapter, I shall show how this self-conscious rationalism leads to moral liberalism. I shall take up the feminist and multicultural critiques of the Western tradition and show that feminism and multiculturalism rely on central values of that tradition, namely, rationalism and liberalism. Note here that I am not saying that these values occur only in the Western tradition, though I think they appear there with an uncommon salience. What I am saying is that, even if Western critics of Western values could have gotten their values from other traditions, for the most part they did not. They got them, in fact, from the Western tradition in which they were raised and educated. Indeed, I suspect that rationalism and liberalism are so much a part of us that we often don't notice them at work. We find ourselves critiquing Western culture, without realizing that our critiques are based on Western rationalism and liberalism. This is what strikes me as ironic. Since rationalism and liberalism are inherently critical, I take it as Western philosophy's ironic destiny that it gives rise to critiques of itself based on its own deepest values.

If I am right here, it means that the feminist and multiculturalist critiques represent, not the death of the Western tradition, but its continued life. They are cause, not to reject the tradition, but to celebrate its continuing power for self-reflection and to wonder at and wonder about the source of that continuing power. None of this is to deny the negative features of the Western tradition. It is, rather, to say that, in addition to these, or in spite of these, the tradition has a progressive self-correcting center, a core that always pushes it to reflect on, and thus to surpass, its limitations. Though the tradition has its sexism, ethnocentrism and other evils, it also has an inner dynamic that leads beyond these.

Self-conscious rationalism is this inner dynamic. Earlier I said that moral condemnation requires knowledge. Now, knowledge is more than mere belief or faith. If all we have are mere beliefs, then we have no ground for holding our beliefs to be more correct than the opposite beliefs. To claim that a belief is more than mere belief, but knowledge, requires pointing beyond the belief to something independent of it that supports it. This pointing is called arguing or reasoning, and it is the only thing that has a chance of distinguishing the true from the false among any two competing beliefs. Strength of conviction is no substitute for force of argument. This is why it is wrong to think that appeal to reason is itself appeal to a kind of faith. Faith takes strength of conviction as evidence for the truth of its beliefs, while reason begins with recognition that the most deeply held belief may be false and thus that the grounds for the truth of our beliefs must be found outside of the passion with which we hold them. The reasoner always looks for something beyond her belief itself that is evidence for the belief; she always looks to someone other than herself for confirmation or challenge. Thus reasoning is always inherently public, either directly as dialogue or indirectly as monologue presented to a critical audience.

It is in the recognition of the opposition between reason and faith that Western philosophy was born. We commonly tell our students that Thales was the first philosopher, a title he earned for saying that "everything is water." This announced the characteristic philosophical aim to understand everything and, because water's capacity to take different forms was easily perceived, represented as well the characteristic philo-

sophical notion that everything can be understood by our ordinary reasoning faculty. But Thales's doctrine was as much protoscience as philosophy. Philosophy only truly distinguished itself as such when
Socrates turned reason on itself. Then Thales's rationalism became self-
conscious and philosophy emerged as the attempt, not only to understand everything rationally, but to understand how that very understanding was possible. This self-conscious rationalism remains, in my view,
the defining characteristic of philosophy, even when, as of late, some
philosophers are led to conclude that rational understanding is ultimately impossible. Even they reason to that conclusion.

Socrates, as you know, went around Athens questioning people about
their beliefs and generally getting them to see that what they thought
was knowledge wasn't. For his troubles, Socrates was tried, convicted
of impiety, and sentenced to death. At his trial, Socrates explained that
he was questioning people in order to understand the Delphic oracle's
statement that Socrates was the wisest of all men. Socrates was puzzled
by this pronouncement because he believed himself ignorant. Consequently, he sought out those who were reputed wise and questioned
them. Discovering that these men thought they had knowledge but did
not, Socrates concluded that the oracle's statement was true in that,
while the reputed wise men thought they knew something but didn't,
Socrates was the wisest of all because he alone knew that he knew
nothing.

It is common to interpret this as meaning that a modest recognition
of one's inevitable ignorance is the highest wisdom. Undergraduates
are only too happy to believe that there is nothing to know, since this
promises easy sledding in their college careers. I, however, must regu-
larly deny them this comfort by pointing out that Socrates's statement
is too paradoxical to be interpreted in this way. It is paradoxical because
to know that one knows nothing is to know something. But what?

To know that one knows nothing is to know that there is a difference
between knowing and merely believing that one knows. This is "knowing nothing" in that it implies no knowledge of any particular doctrine.
Nonetheless, the recognition of the difference between knowing and
just believing is a momentous piece of wisdom, announcing the imperative to subject all beliefs, even those most deeply and widely held, to
tests—in the context of open-ended dialogue. Thus Socrates represents
the call to carry on self-consciously and radically the work of reasoning
itself, and philosophy enters Western history, not just as protoscience,
but as radical questioning before which no belief is sacrosanct. This, of
course, is a threat to every dogmatism—of state, religion, culture, or

tradition—and Socrates paid for it with his life. He was for philosophy what Jesus was for Christianity.

The reasoning that Socrates brought to self-consciousness should not be identified with any set of specific procedures. Reasoning is and must be open ended. Whatever procedures of reasoning are identified, we remain capable of reasoning about them. To capture this open-endedness and self-reflexivity, I shall say that reasoning is anything we do to improve the success rate of our beliefs. By this, I mean primarily the testing of beliefs with the aim that the beliefs we hold and act upon be the ones with the greatest chance of being true. Reasoning also includes such related activities as inventorying our beliefs, seeing which ones lead to or conflict with others, and adjusting our actions to our beliefs about what we want, what is possible, and so on.

This general and active conception of reasoning is enough to debunk the myth that reasoning is applying some pre-given set of rules. This myth leads to the idea that reason is a kind of doctrine and thus that appeal to reason, far from being neutral, is a partisan appeal to some theory about the world. This conception of reason has led many thinkers to give up on reason. But, on my view, such thinkers are doing nothing but reasoning. Those, for example, who turn away from scientific method because it strikes them as imposing a distorting objectivity on reality, those who turn away from logic because it seems to rigidify thought or freeze concepts into oppositions that do not correspond to the fluidity of reality, and even those who question rationality itself because it seems based on privileging what is present or enduring, are all reasoning. They are questioning strategies of reasoning because those strategies are suspected of distorting reality, and that amounts to trying to improve the likelihood that our beliefs about reality are true, which is to say, it amounts to reasoning. Because people are almost always reasoning—sifting beliefs, making inferences and judgments, and so on—it is so familiar that, as with breathing, people don't notice that they are doing it. It is the naturalness of reasoning to us, its very inescapability, that makes people think that they can give up on it.

The myth that reasoning is applying some pre-given set of rules also leads people to think that reasoning is some kind of Western or male thing. This seems to me to be not only false but little more than an updated version of the idea that non-Western peoples are primitive and that women are irrational. In any event, the open-ended capacity to inventory and check beliefs is surely possessed by all human beings, no matter how differently they may exercise the capacity. Nor is the West the only area with a rationalist tradition. There are rationalist traditions in India, China, and elsewhere. What is distinctive about the West is to have made such a fuss over reason, to have made rationality so central, to have devoted so much time and effort to its study, improvement, and celebration.

A related myth is the notion that reason is the enemy of emotion. A rationalist need not deny that emotion, passion, feeling, or intuition can be the source of true beliefs. On the contrary, reason remains open to the possibility that true beliefs can come from anywhere. What reason denies is that emotion or feeling can show that beliefs are true. That requires testing, which is to say, reasoning.

Socrates saw that the capacity for reason qualified those who had it for sovereign rule, but he, like Plato and Aristotle after him, interpreted this conservatively. Socrates, Plato, and Aristotle saw that people differed in their rational abilities and that it was common to seek counsel in any field from those who seemed to have special abilities in that field. Thus, they easily supposed that some people were meant to rule others, as men were to rule women, masters to rule slaves, parents to rule children, and humans to rule animals. The discovery of reason led them to a preference for aristocracy, understood literally as government by the best.

It was Descartes who democratized reason. And, since liberalism is little more than reason democratized, it was he who brought philosophy to the threshold of its liberal destiny. Descartes wrote after the rise and fall of the Christian Middle Ages in Europe. He aimed to establish a foundation for scientific knowledge; to do this he set out to doubt everything he had hitherto believed, in the hope of finding some truth that could not be doubted and that would thus serve as an Archimedean point upon which scientific knowledge could be built. And so he doubted that he was really perceiving a world, since he just might be dreaming; he doubted that he even knew the truths of mathematics and logic, since he just might be being deceived by some evil demon. He found one truth that he could not doubt, namely, that he existed: "I think, therefore I am." This, however, is rather a thin reed upon which to build science. Thus, Descartes went on to argue that a benevolent God existed who would not deceive him in those of his scientific judgments that were most clear and certain.

But this argument was never very convincing. If an evil demon might be deceiving him about the truths of math and logic, Descartes could never be sure that the demon wasn't deceiving him as he argued for the existence and veracity of God. In short, no argument could prove that Descartes wasn't being deceived, since the possibility of deception would cut down any argument before it could reach its conclusion. Thus the ultimate message of Descartes's project—not the message he expressly stated, but the one that actually got read by his successors—is that God cannot guarantee the truth for us. Indeed, nothing can guarantee the truth for rational beings except themselves. Rational beings have no alternative but to trust their own reason. Descartes himself always presents reasons for his doubt, thereby admitting that confidence in reason is presupposed by suspicion about it. Nothing can be either doubted or believed by a rational being unless she judges that it is reasonable to doubt or believe it. Consequently, nothing can stand as an authority for a rational being unless she judges that authority worthy of belief. But this means that human beings replace God as the ultimate authority for the certainty of their beliefs, since even God's authority must be proven to human beings' satisfaction before they will believe it. It is, then, no coincidence that in proclaiming, "I think, therefore I am," Descartes took for the thinking subject the biblical name of God: *I am.*

And he took it for every single rational subject. Descartes understood reason as a "method" that could be taught to, and mastered by, anyone.[3] He wrote in French (or had his works translated into French) in order to break beyond the circle of the educated whose language was Latin. In particular, Descartes sought to reach women who were deprived of Latin because they were excluded from formal education.[4] Descartes gave us nothing less than a secular version of the Judeo-Christian notion of the imago Dei, the idea that all human beings are created in the image of God and worthy of special respect and treatment because of that fact. But the secular version, rather than being based on human beings' soul or spirit, is based on their capacity to reason. As the Greeks saw this capacity as the grounds for sovereignty over others, so it became in the post-Cartesian world the ground for each rational being to be sovereign over himself or herself. Democratizing reason, Descartes opened the way to liberalism.

Since what is true is true for all, Descartes's democratization of reason brought in its wake a new practical definition of truth. The truth is what can earn the assent of all rational beings. In science, this underwrote the move toward public methods of verification. For morality, it means that what is truly right is what all rational beings can agree to. To see how liberalism emerges from this democratization of reason, imagine a world of rational individuals who strive to test their beliefs about the world and, most importantly in this case, their beliefs about how to live. What will it be rational for them all to agree to? Each will insist on his own right to live according to beliefs that he finds worthy of assent. None will willingly allow himself to be subjected to beliefs of others that he does not find worthy of assent. What all can rationally agree to, then, is the egalitarian principle that everyone should be able to live according to his or her own beliefs as much as possible without imposing those beliefs on others.

This liberal egalitarian principle, which I have earlier termed the ideal of individual sovereignty, is not the same as the political liberalism that says don't tamper with the existing distribution of power, just give everyone equality before the law, let them vote, and so forth. Nor is it the same as the economic liberalism that says don't tamper with the existing distribution of wealth, just give everyone equal opportunity, and so forth. If inequalities in power and wealth work to reduce the capacity of those with little of either to live according to their beliefs, then those inequalities are in violation of the principle of individual sovereignty. Liberalism (unlike libertarianism) is not simply a principle of noninterference. Consequently, liberals are willing to countenance interference that seems needed to promote individual sovereignty over-all, such as prohibiting racial discrimination or taxing people to pay for public education.

To better understand how we reached this liberal egalitarian principle, consider again the difference between Socrates and Descartes. Socrates gave us dialogues, and Descartes gave us meditations—that is, mono-logues. Socrates saw the reason of others from the outside, Descartes looked at his own reason from the inside. For Socrates, reason was an expertise; for Descartes, it was an experience. Since people differ in their expertise at reasoning, Socrates's view led to aristocracy. Unlike expertise, however, the experience of reasoning is shared by all alike, and thus Descartes's view led to democracy and to liberalism. The experience of reason is that one cannot accept a belief without judging for oneself that it is worthy of belief. This means that anytime people have to act according to beliefs they do not themselves judge to be true, they experience this as going against their grain, as a violation, a trampling on their very selves. Thus human beings must be allowed the greatest possibility of living according to beliefs they judge true, or they will experience themselves as undermined, as denied their nature, reduced to things, treated as objects. This way lies liberalism and egalitarianism.

It is common in these postmodernist days to think that the argument I have just sketched has been refuted by recognition that we are crea-tures of culture and impulse, of ideology and desire, rather than impar-tial rational spectators. There is considerable truth in this recognition of our partial rationality, but its negative implications are overstated. No doubt we are not the little gods Descartes took us to be. The Cartesian rational subject was an exaggerated idealization. But this recognition does not, as some think, amount to the death of the Cartesian subject. That obituary is as much an exaggeration in the other direction as the Cartesian subject was in its. Recognition of the various forces that shape our subjectivity does not destroy subjectivity; it cuts it down to its real size. That we are imperfect at reasoning about our beliefs does not imply that we cannot do it at all. It still remains true that the way to improve the success rate of our beliefs is to test them to the best of our ability. That human beings differ in culture and so many other ways does not deny that they are alike in having this imperfect rational ability. And their similarity in this latter respect is all that is needed to keep alive the notion that because all human beings are rational, they must all be treated as sovereign over their lives or denied their nature. I contend that this ideal of individual sovereignty is a universal truth that underlies feminism and multiculturalism.

Following feminist philosopher Alison Jaggar, I understand by "feminism," the movement of "all those who seek, no matter on what grounds, to end women's subordination."[5] In the context of theoretical reflection, this amounts to "identifying various forms of male bias concealed within apparently gender-blind assumptions or conceptual frameworks," which tend to "rationalize women's subordination or devalue their moral experience."[6] And following Molefi Kete Asante, recent defender of Afrocentric education, I understand by "multiculturalism," both the rejection of "the dominance and hegemony of the Eurocentric view of reality [in] a multicultural society" and the "idea that the educational experience should reflect the diverse cultural heritage of our system of knowledge."[7]

The general point I want to make about feminism and multiculturalism is that, when you dig down into them, you find Western rationalism and liberalism. Feminism and multiculturalism embody the self-conscious rationalism of the West in insisting that hitherto accepted beliefs be subjected to tests, and they embody the egalitarian liberalism of the West in insisting on the equal rights of all human beings to live according to their own beliefs and judgments. Far from stepping outside of the Western tradition, feminism and multiculturalism are steps in that tradition, new ways in which that tradition comes to question the truth and universality of its own beliefs, new ways to challenge existing institutions to live up to the West's liberal and egalitarian values.

Insofar as feminism and multiculturalism call upon us to fill in the gaps in the historical record that result from the invisibility of the ac-

complishments of women and of nonwhite and non-Western peoples to
the Western white men who have written our history, these two approaches reflect the very same commitment to questioning prevailing
"certitudes" for which Socrates died. It is wrong to teach students that
Columbus discovered America as if human beings were not already
living here for centuries, that all great intellectuals were men, that all
the heroes of the American Revolution were men, and that all the heroes
of the civil rights movement were whites. It is wrong to teach Western
culture as if it were the only one (or the only one worth our attention)
or to fail to recognize that the accomplishments of ancient Greece and
Rome had roots reaching back into Africa and Asia, that the High Middle Ages and the Renaissance relied on the work of North African and
Spanish Muslims, and so on.[8] But these teachings are wrong according
to Western rationalist standards of truth. They are factually false. The
reason that schools and universities should correct these and kindred
falsehoods so as to reflect accurately the contributions of women and
nonwhite and non-Western peoples is not, as is sometimes suggested,
because we now have large numbers of women, nonwhites and non-
Westerners in our classes (as if education were a matter of tailoring the
truth to consumer demand). The reason is that schools and universities
are in the business of equipping students to find the truth, the *whole*
truth, and that these diverse contributions are part of the whole truth.

Beyond the call to make the historical record more accurate, feminism and multiculturalism rest on moral judgments whose core is captured by the liberal principle of individual sovereignty. This is easiest
to see in the case of feminism, since it arises from moral condemnation
of the subordination of women to men. What makes the subordination
of women morally wrong? It can be morally wrong only if everyone
has the equal right to live according to his or her own judgments, a right
violated by the subordination of women. This is not only recognized
by what is called "liberal feminism." Radical, Marxist, socialist, and
postmodernist variants of feminism all criticize the liberal variant for
not going deep enough in rooting out the causes of women's oppression
and for not going far enough in establishing women's control over their
bodies, work, and relationships. Which is to say, they criticize liberal
feminism for falling short of the principle of individual sovereignty.

Some feminists, however, have criticized liberalism precisely because
of its focus on individuals. Liberalism, it is objected, falsely assumes
that human beings are essentially nonsocial. Thus, Jaggar criticizes liberalism for its "assumption that human individuals are essentially solitary, with needs and interests that are separate from if not in opposition

to those of other individuals."[9] Note, first, that this assumption is by no means held unanimously in the Western philosophic tradition, since that tradition contains many who affirm that human beings are essentially social: Socrates, Plato, Aristotle, Aquinas, Rousseau, Hegel, Marx, and Dewey, to name a few. John Locke's social contract doctrine is often thought to presuppose that humans are naturally nonsocial, but what the contract creates is a political regime. It is the state, not society, that is artificial for Locke; nothing in his doctrine requires the assumption that people are naturally asocial.[10]

In any event, there certainly hasn't been an important liberal thinker in over a century who has held that human beings are nonsocial. That is because there is nothing in the liberal moral ideal that depends on viewing human beings as nonsocial. Whether individuals are essentially social or not is a matter of descriptive analysis, while liberalism is a normative standard. It holds that individuals' lives *should be* the outcome of their free choices. Beyond affirming that free and rational choice is possible, liberalism says nothing about how individuals or their choices are formed.

Second and more important, the reason why liberals believe that people's lives should reflect individual choice, rather than the will of the group, is this. Either the will of the group is unanimously shared, in which case it meets the liberal requirement of reflecting every individual's choice, or the will of the group represents the judgments of the majority or strongest part of the group, in which case it threatens to oppress the dissenters. Appeal to the will of the group, then, either is in line with liberal requirements or is a potential cover for oppression. This is why liberals countenance majority rule only when it is hedged with protections of the rights of the minority.

A related charge is the suspicion, recently voiced by Carol Gilligan and others, that liberalism reflects a male picture of the moral life. Gilligan's early studies purported to show that males and females have distinctive moral sensibilities, with males taking a *justice* approach (emphasizing impersonal rules, rights, and obligations) and females taking a *care* approach (characterized by sympathetic responsiveness to the actual needs of particular persons).[11] This led to the view that there are two distinct basic moral orientations and that Western philosophy's emphasis on the justice orientation at the expense of the care orientation is due to the fact that moral theory (until very recently) has been done by men and has reflected typically male experience.

Later studies by Gilligan and others soften this opposition somewhat. It turns out that both sexes use both the justice and the care approach, with men tending uniformly to give priority to justice, while women are more varied, some emphasizing justice, some care, some both.[12] All of this research has been challenged because its subjects almost exclusively have been educationally advantaged North Americans. Nonetheless, since liberalism—with its focus on rules and on rights of individuals—is part of the justice orientation, the research creates a strong suspicion that liberalism reflects a one-sided, male-biased conception of morality.

The first thing I want to say about this suspicion is that it is an excellent example of the West's self-conscious rationalism in seeking out new ways to challenge and test our beliefs. Second, though it is generally true that Western moral philosophers have tended to favor the justice approach with its impersonal rules over the care approach with its emphasis on sympathetic responsiveness to the needs of others, it is false to think that the care approach has lacked Western champions. Plato designed his republic with the aim of so unifying its citizens that each would experience the pains and pleasures of the others. Hume traced morality to our natural sentiment of benevolence, which he took to be an instinctive desire for the well-being of others. And the idea that care brings something that justice lacks is an updated version of the claim that early Christianity made about Judaism.

Third, it seems to me that the idea that liberalism is a male orientation and care a female one should also be suspect as a possible product of sexism. It is worth noting that training in liberalism may make one more willing to insist on one's own rights and desires and thus more resistant to oppression, while training in caring and conflict-avoidance may make one less willing to insist on one's own rights and desires and thus more vulnerable to oppression. It might be that liberalism is correct for all human beings and that, because of sexism, young girls have been introduced into a false or partial understanding of morality. This, by the way, was Mary Wollstonecraft's view.[13] And some feminists have seen in care the self-destructive tendency of women to subordinate themselves to others, a tendency whose natural corrective is liberalism's insistence on individual sovereignty.

The suspicion that the opposition between liberalism and care is an artifact of sexism is only strengthened when one sees feminist philosophers, such as Nel Noddings, characterize care as "nonrational."[14] Fortunately, when, in her book *Caring: A Feminine Approach to Ethics and Moral Education*, Noddings describes examples of care, what she portrays is a responsiveness to the needs of others that is so fine-tuned that it couldn't possibly be nonrational.[15] Unless carers are thought to be fitted out with some magical power of intuition (and you know where that leads), we must accept that sizing up the needs of another person, whether child or adult, and determining the appropriate response to those needs, involve just that sifting and checking of beliefs and evidence that characterize reason. Noddings has fallen prey to the mistake of failing, because of rationality's very familiarity, to see how deeply it pervades everything we do—an oversight that, in this case, leads to the more pernicious mistake of identifying the feminine with the nonrational.

On the other hand, Noddings's perceptive descriptions of care are testimony that the attempts of feminist moral philosophers to develop the care approach have led to many rich insights into the moral life. I don't, however, think that these insights show care and justice to be different moral orientations. Care and justice live within a single moral framework in which the beliefs underlying liberalism play a fundamental role. To see this, ask yourself what is morally good about caring. Caring cannot answer this question itself, since standing alone it is just a feeling or an attitude, and no feeling or attitude can, so to speak, present the credentials for its own moral goodness. If caring is good, it must be because of something about the objects of care. Caring for our fellow human beings is good because something about our fellow human beings makes it good to care about them. What could that be?

Caring is, as Noddings rightly says, sensitive responsiveness to the needs of others. Thus, the good of caring must lie in the good of meeting the needs of others. This much is true even of caring for animals or trees. What is special about caring for our fellow human beings lies in the special nature of human needs. Human needs, other than those that humans share with animals, are special in that they are the needs of beings who, not only want to avoid pain, but also want to live according to their beliefs about how they should live. They are the needs of rational beings. Insofar as the goodness of caring for human beings is different from that for animals or trees, it lies in the goodness of helping rational beings live according to their own beliefs about how they should live. That means that the goodness of caring rests on the principle of individual sovereignty. Interestingly, this is confirmed in Noddings's account. When she distinguishes genuine caring from its manipulative counterfeit, Noddings writes, "The one-caring is motivated in the direction of the cared-for and she must, therefore, respect his freedom. She meets him as subject—not as an object to be manipulated. . . . The [one] genuinely cared for is free to respond as himself, to create, to follow his interests without unnecessary fear or anxiety."[16]

Caring is the spontaneous desire to support the sovereignty of another. The goodness of caring, then, lies within, not outside, liberalism.

Moreover, when care is taken as nonrational, what is missed is that, like virtually all human emotions, care is riddled through with judgments of the sort that only rational beings can make. Humans do not experience anger or sadness as if they were blind feelings like a headache or a hot flash. Our anger includes the judgment that someone did us wrong, and our sadness includes the judgment that something important has been lost. Likewise, Noddings's account suggests that care is no blind feeling. Rather, care includes the judgment that the other's needs should be responded to because rational beings should be enabled to live as they judge they should. I think that care includes as well the judgment that responding to this person's needs violates no obligation to others. We would not think of someone as very caring who, out of affection for a dangerous maniac, allowed him to run free and imperil innocent strangers. Both the judgment that the other should be cared for because rational beings should be enabled to live as they judge they should and the judgment that caring for one violates no obligations to others are judgments of justice. This suggests that, rather than care and justice being alternative orientations, carers are already making judgments about the justice of what they do. It should not surprise us, then, that Gilligan's more recent research subjects can and do use both justice and care.

All this suggests that the feminist critique stands firmly within the Western tradition of liberalism. I want, now, to suggest that the same is true of multiculturalism. Multiculturalists may respond to this suggestion with yet another version of the charge that liberalism is excessively individualistic. Asante, for example, denies that individual liberty is a universal value, pointing out that African cultures exalt the ideal of "community."[17] But, if community is to have moral worth, it must be more than people living near one another. People must share interests and concerns and feel toward one another some measure of affection. None of this is compatible with force. There is no real community between master and slave or jailor and prisoner. Forced community is like forced laughter. It is to true community what forced religious observance is to true faith. Real community must be a free expression of shared commitment. But, to be free, it must arise in just the space that liberalism protects. Real community must be a shared involvement that free individuals freely undertake. Once again, digging into the multicultural critique, we find the liberal values that mark the Western tradition.

But I want to say more than that seemingly anti-individualist moral ideals such as community rest on liberal values. I contend that multiculturalism's condemnation of the subjugation of non-Western peoples and their cultures by Western peoples and their cultures also rests on liberal values. It is hard to see the implicit appeal to liberalism in the moral condemnation of cultural imperialism, since that condemnation seems to rely on a principle protecting the rights of groups or cultures, rather than of individuals. But groups of people matter morally because they are people, not because they are groups. People's cultures matter morally because they belong to people, not because they are cultures. And people must be protected as individuals because it is as individuals that they suffer. Even if all of us suffer together over some shared loss, there is no "group-suffer" that occurs over and above the suffering that goes on for each of us within the envelope of his or her skin.

Moreover, the way in which human individuals suffer is not the same as the way animals do. Though humans share with animals a vulnerability and aversion to physical pain, humans are also vulnerable to the special suffering that comes from being prevented from living according to their beliefs about how they should live. This is a kind of suffering to which only rational beings are vulnerable. Cultures are valuable precisely because they constitute beliefs about how people should live. And cultural imperialism is evil because imposing an alien culture on people against their wills forces them to live according to beliefs that are not their own. Thus the condemnation of cultural imperialism and of the suffering it produces rests on the affirmation of the right of individuals to live according to their own beliefs, which is to say, the principle of individual sovereignty.

If I am right that the moral condemnation of cultural imperialism rests ultimately on the principle of individual sovereignty, then whoever condemns cultural imperialism will have to accept the truth of this principle. This will have two consequences that may make multiculturalists uncomfortable. First, it implies that Western culture has hit upon a true moral principle that applies to all cultures. Second, how well any particular culture satisfies this principle will be an open question. Thus it will be possible to judge different cultures comparatively along a moral dimension, such that some may turn out to be morally superior to others, in one respect or several. For example, cultures that recognize the equal rights of women will be, in that important respect, morally superior to cultures that do not.

The multiculturalist may deny that there are any moral principles that apply to all cultures, arguing instead that each culture can be judged only by its own standards. However, according to this argument, if a culture doesn't have a standard condemning cultural imperialism, it will not be wrong for that culture to engage in it. In fact, it will not even be wrong for cultures that do have standards condemning cultural imperialism to engage in it, if they will simply change their standards. But, then, cultural imperialism stops being morally wrong at all. Cultural relativism is incompatible with the moral condemnation of cultural imperialism in just the same way that radical skepticism, or a belief in the inevitability of bias, is incompatible with the condemnation of women's oppression. Cultural relativism will not support multiculturalism, since any reason for respecting cultures will apply to all cultures and thus be a transcultural reason. And any reason for thinking that cultures are good will be a reason for thinking that some may be better than others.

Thus when Asante decries the teaching of Western culture as superior to all others, I agree with him if he means that we shouldn't slyly convey that Western culture is superior by ignoring all others and thus treating our own as the only one worth considering. Nor should we assume that Western culture is superior because it is ours. I disagree, however, if he means that no culture *can* be superior to others. If cultures are good at all, then some may be better than others, in one respect or many. Thus to hold that no culture can be superior to others denies the very values that make cultures worthy of respect in the first place, and it denies our students the capacity to make judgments about the value of the practices and products of different cultures because it teaches them that such judgments can never be true.

I hope I have said enough to show that the feminist and multicultural critiques stand on, rather than against, Western liberalism and rationalism and thus that they are steps in that tradition, rather than steps outside of it. I want to close this chapter with one final observation. I have argued that we generally fail to see the liberalism underlying the current skepticism and that this is part of a general tendency not to notice the pervasiveness of liberalism and rationalism due precisely to that pervasiveness. Liberalism and rationalism are so present and familiar that they go unnoticed, like the smell of the air or the feel of our clothes. The unnoticed presence of liberalism under our current skepticism makes that skepticism a much less dangerous doctrine than it would be alone.

Alone, as we saw at the outset of this chapter, skepticism implies that we can never know that anything, including intolerance and oppression, is wrong. It should not be forgotten that, though Nazism was far from a coherent philosophy, it had a strong component of antirationalism, which led to moral skepticism and, from there, to the idea that anything is permitted for those who are strong enough. That is what threatens when skepticism floats loose of a liberal mooring. I tend to think that the current notion of cultural diversity is subject to a similar danger. Tied to a liberal commitment to the value and rights of all human beings, cultural diversity is an opportunity to celebrate and profit from the rich and varied creations of human ingenuity. Set loose from that commitment, it threatens to become a kind of ethno-fascism in which the beliefs of any group are held to be beyond question, no matter what they may direct about the treatment of others. It is, I think, this danger above all that calls on us to find and to hold the liberal truth that our tradition has positioned us to see.

Notes

This chapter is a revised version of my inaugural lecture as William Fraser McDowell Professor of Philosophy, delivered at American University in Washington, D.C., on 11 April 1991.

1. Linda J. Nicholson, ed., *Feminism/Postmodernism* (New York: Routledge, 1990), p. 3.

2. Allan Bloom, *The Closing of the American Mind* (New York: Simon & Schuster, 1987).

3. Descartes gave instruction in mathematics to one of his servants, Jean Gillot, who eventually became the director of the school of engineering at Leiden. See Jack Vrooman, *René Descartes: A Biography* (New York: G. P. Putnam's Sons, 1970), p. 195.

4. Genevieve Lloyd, *The Man of Reason: "Male" and "Female" in Western Philosophy* (Minneapolis, Minn.: University of Minnesota Press, 1984), p. 44. See also Vrooman, *Descartes*, p. 93.

5. Alison M. Jaggar, *Feminist Politics and Human Nature* (Totowa, N.J.: Rowman & Littlefield, 1988), p. 5.

6. Alison M. Jaggar, "Feminist Ethics: Some Projects and Problems," *From the Center: A Newsletter* (Center for Values and Social Policy, University of Colorado at Boulder) 9, no. 2 (Fall 1990): 2.

7. Molefi Kete Asante, "Multiculturalism: An Exchange," *American Scholar* (Spring 1991): 267–72.

8. See, for example, James A. Banks, "A Curriculum for Empowerment, Action, and Change," in *Empowerment through Multicultural Education*, ed. Christine E. Sleeter (Albany, N.Y.: State University of New York Press, 1991), pp. 129–33, for concrete examples of the kind of changes that need to be made to fill in the historical gaps.

9. Jaggar, *Feminist Politics and Human Nature*, p. 40. Cf. Will Kymlicka, *Liberalism, Community, and Culture* (Oxford: Clarendon Press, 1989), p. 14.

10. Locke begins his discussion of language in *An Essay Concerning Human Understanding* with these words: "God, having designed man for a sociable creature, made him not only with an inclination and under a necessity to have fellowship with those of his kind, but furnished him also with language, which was to be the great instrument and common tie of society. *Man*, therefore, had by nature his organs so fashioned as to be *fit to frame articulate sounds*, which we call words." These hardly seem the views of someone who thinks of human beings as naturally asocial. See John Locke, *An Essay Concerning Human Understanding*, ed. and abridged John Yolton (London: Everyman, 1994; originally published 1690), bk. 3, ch. 1, p. 225 (emphasis in original).

11. Carol Gilligan, *In a Different Voice: Psychological Theory and Women's Development* (Cambridge, Mass.: Harvard University Press, 1982).

12. Carol Gilligan, "Moral Orientation and Moral Development," in *Women and Moral Theory*, ed. Eva F. Kittay and Diana T. Meyers (Totowa, N.J.: Rowman & Littlefield, 1987), p. 25.

13. Wollstonecraft wrote, for example, that "the most perfect education, in my opinion, is such an exercise of the understanding as is best calculated to . . . enable the individual to attain such habits of virtue as will render it independent. In fact, it is a farce to call any being virtuous whose virtues do not result from the exercise of its own reason. This was Rousseau's opinion respecting men: I extend it to women, and confidently assert that they have been drawn out of their sphere by false refinement." And further: "Love, in their bosoms, taking the place of every nobler passion, their sole ambition is to be fair, to raise emotion instead of inspiring respect; and this ignoble desire, like the servility in absolute monarchies, destroys all strength of character. Liberty is the mother of virtue, and if women be, by their very constitution, slaves, and not allowed to breathe the sharp invigorating air of freedom, they must ever languish like exotics, and be reckoned beautiful flaws in nature." Mary Wollstonecraft, *Vindication of the Rights of Woman* (New York: Penguin Books, 1982; originally published 1792), pp. 103, 121–22.

14. "While much of what goes on in caring is rational and carefully thought out, the basic relationship is not, and neither is the required awareness of relatedness. The essentially nonrational nature of caring. . . ." Nel Noddings, *Caring: A Feminine Approach to Ethics and Moral Education* (Berkeley: University of California Press, 1984), p. 61.

15. Ibid., pp. 53–59, inter alia.

16. Ibid., p. 72.

17. *Newsweek*, 24 December 1990, 54.

Postmodern Argumentation and Post-postmodern Liberalism, with Comments on Levinas, Habermas, and Rawls

The Paradox of Postmodernism

Modernism is, roughly speaking, the Enlightenment belief in a single unified rational perspective, founded on some indubitable evidence given in human experience—either innate concepts à la Descartes and the rationalists or sensations à la Locke and the empiricists—and elaborated according to reliable logical rules. This view was first attacked for its "foundationalism." Philosophers such as Nietzsche, Dewey, Heidegger, and the later Wittgenstein denied that there is any indubitable given upon which truth can be founded. There is no experience, no testimony of the senses or of reason, that blazons forth the undeniable truth. Rather, the "given" is, so to speak, constructed—which is to say, not given to us, but made by us. Some experience or other evidence is interpreted as this or that with this or that epistemological status, on the basis of beliefs that one already has about, say, space or mathematics or sense perception or the nature of what is ultimately real. Postmodernism is an intensification of this attack, with a distinctive political spin.

The intensification takes the following form. If there is no given, interpretation is "fundamental" (not, of course, in the sense of a new foundational given, rather quite the reverse, in the sense of something beneath or behind which we cannot get, something that stands eternally between us and any foundational given). Interpretation is fundamental in the sense that it is the furthest down we can ever get.[1] If interpretation is as far as we can ever get, then every experience is part of a tapestry (textile, text) of beliefs against which it gets its interpretation. And the beliefs themselves are only what they are for us as a result of interpretation of their meaning in light of other beliefs, and other interpretations, and so on.

Accordingly, there can never be just one interpretation of anything. This is sometimes exaggerated into the claim that there are unlimited valid interpretations of everything, a claim that would make it impossible to write a single sentence, since one would have no reason for choosing one string of words rather than another to express one's thoughts! The more modest claim is enough, however, to ground the distinctive postmodern strategy of *deconstruction.* Any supposedly canonical interpretation can be shown to have been purchased by the arbitrary exclusion of other possible ones. There can only be a canonical interpretation if some meaning in a text has been taken as if it were an unquestioned given from which the canonical interpretation then follows. The deconstructer finds the meaning that has been taken as if simply given and shows that it is in fact only one interpretation among other possible ones in view of the "textily" way in which it is woven together with other beliefs. Then, taking a different meaning than the supposedly given one as her starting point, the deconstructer shows that other interpretations of the whole text can be spun. Such alternative interpretations must still meet the normal standards for successful interpretation, namely, plausibility, fit with the text, and so on. This is not the "anything goes" that is sometimes associated with deconstructive technique. Rather, the canonical interpretation is deconstructed by means of showing its illicit appeal to sheer given meanings, and the way in which it has been promoted by excluding other possible plausible interpretations.

Related to this technique is the political dimension of postmodernism. Much as any canonical interpretation is necessarily based on excluding alternative possible interpretations, any universal vision is based on excluding what doesn't fit by defining it as "other," "lesser," "lower," "bad," "crazy," "primitive," and so forth. Consequently, Enlightenment universalism based on, say, the shared rationality of human beings reflects (in various versions of the critique) the definition of rationality by exclusion of deviants, or women, or third-world people. Or, at the very least, the establishment of the universal standard becomes a tool or weapon by means of which some can be defined as second rate because they are held not to share the prevailing trait, or not to embody it completely, or the like. Thus, for example, Zygmunt Bauman, in his *Postmodern Ethics,* describes the moral universalism of the modern era "as but a thinly disguised declaration of intent to embark on *Gleich-schaltung*, on an arduous campaign to smother the differences."[2] With this, deconstruction becomes a political weapon in defense of the people who have been oppressed because their natures or ways have been excluded from the universal standard—as the means to define that very standard.

Here enters the paradox: The critique of universal standards because they exclude certain individuals or groups of individuals is a critique of those standards for not being universal enough! Consequently, rather than abandoning or opposing universalism, the critique is itself based on an implicit universal valuation, albeit one that aims to be more inclusive than the ones critiqued.

In short, what postmodernism needs, what virtually every postmodern writer writes as if he or she had, but in fact does not have, is a universal standard for valuing human beings that is compatible with the postmodern critique of universals. I will argue that such a universal can be found and can be defended while keeping to postmodernism's own critical requirements of argumentation.

The Requirements of Postmodern Argumentation

If postmodernism understands itself as (*a*) a form of antifoundationalism and (*b*) a protest against the exclusion of certain human individuals and/or groups from the universal measure of full moral standing, then certain things follow about the way arguments must be made if they are to be acceptable to postmodernists. First of all, arguments must be explicitly based on assumptions actually held by those to whom they are addressed (rather than appealing to foundational givens). Second, arguments must be addressed to all human beings. Putting the two together, arguments must start from assumptions that are shared by all human beings. Arguments must be *universal* in their aim and *ad hominem* in their logical structure.

Actually, the second condition is already suggested by antifoundationalism. If there is no indubitable given, if all starting points are, so to speak, created by interpretation in light of other beliefs, then there is no Archimedean point from which all of a person's beliefs can be shown true or false. Consequently, all arguments must proceed from beliefs that people already hold, which is to say, they must be ad hominem.

Two examples from different contemporary philosophical directions will show the prevalence of ad hominem argumentation in present-day thought. Consider, for example, Rawls's political liberalism, which starts openly by appeal to beliefs held by participants in liberal democratic cultures, assumes explicitly that even within this framework there will be irreconcilable disagreements among reasonable people on fundamental metaphysical and moral beliefs, and proceeds to argue for its very modest liberalism from the hopefully actual overlapping consensus among those fundamental views that presumably permit allegiance to liberal ideals.[3] Consider, for a quite different example, the approach of Habermas's "discourse ethics," which starts from the presuppositions of rational argument aimed at justifying moral norms. Since the implicit aim of such argument is rational persuasion, and since rational persuasion is uncoerced assent in the face of open argumentation and full information, those who engage in justification can be taken as implicitly committed to seeking uncoerced and fully informed assent to their proposals.[4] Accordingly, one can justify only moral norms to which all can freely and informedly consent—the result being not very far from contractarianism of the Rawlsian sort.

There can be postmodern universals if there are ad hominem arguments that can appeal to assumptions necessarily made by all human beings. However, the demand that arguments must appeal to assumptions that all human beings can be taken to share surely seems impossible in the condition of postmodernism, with its objections to universalism and its emphasis on irreducible differences. But the situation is more hopeful than it appears at first, for postmodernists do assume that human beings are rational insofar as postmodernists speak of and to human beings as users of language, interpreters of texts, bearers of culture, and so on—all of which require rational operations. I shall argue that the assumption that human beings are rational leads to other beliefs, which form the basis for a universal moral principle.

Ironically, I shall find these beliefs in an unlikely place: Descartes's philosophy, which has been the target of considerable postmodernist criticism. What I am going to argue in the next section is that in Descartes's *Meditations* one finds a way of establishing a universal that does not violate the postmodern requirements for argumentation. That is to say, the very form of ad hominem I discussed above in connection with Rawls and Habermas is first hinted at in Descartes, and with more far-reaching implications. (Indeed, at the end of this chapter, I shall suggest how what we find in Descartes provides what is missing from Rawls's and Habermas's ethical theories.) In short, postmodernists, unable to resolve their paradox on their own grounds, can do so if they turn back to a discovery of the very Enlightenment they have criticized.

The Authority of Rational Beings: Descartes's Discovery

Descartes made a discovery whose nature is very much the opposite of that for which he is mainly credited—and yet, I contend, it is this very discovery that inspired his successors even when they were not able to put it into words.

Descartes subjected all his beliefs to radical doubt, deduced his existence from the fact of his doubting, and then proceeded to restore enough of his beliefs to ground physics by arguing that God exists and that it is contrary to God's nature to allow His creatures to be irremediably deceived. The apparently circular nature of this argument—that Descartes had to believe in his proof of God in order to prove that he didn't have to doubt all his beliefs—was not lost on Descartes's readers. The charge of circularity crops up numerous times in the seven sets of objections that Descartes published along with his *Meditations on First Philosophy*. And, in the replies to those objections, Descartes tried gallantly to show that there is no circle. I think it is fair to say that none of Descartes's important philosophical successors thought he succeeded.

Indeed, it seems to me that, willy-nilly, Descartes taught his successors a different lesson from the one that God is the authority for the validity of our beliefs. What he taught them, rather, was that we, and we alone, can be, must be, and are the only authority for our beliefs.

The important point is that when Descartes doubted, he always doubted for a reason: that he might be dreaming, or that there might be an evil demon bent on deceiving him. Thus, rather than undermining our confidence in our rational judgments, Descartes's doubt presupposes it. In a letter to Clerselier, Descartes gave his replies to Gassendi's replies to Descartes's original replies to Gassendi's objections, which were the fifth set of objections published along with the *Meditations*. In this letter, Descartes pointed out that "before we can decide to doubt, we need some reason for doubting: and that is why in my First Meditation I put forward the principal reasons for doubt." And then, a few pages later in the letter, Descartes added:

> Even with respect to the truths of faith, we should perceive some reason which convinces us that they have been revealed by God, before deciding to believe them. Although ignorant people would do well to follow the judgement of the more competent on matters which are difficult to know, it is still necessary that it be their own perception which tells them they are ignorant; they must also perceive that those whose judgement they want to follow are not as ignorant as they are, or else they would be wrong

to follow them and would be behaving more like automatons or beasts than men.[5]

What this means is that we must trust our own judgment in order to doubt, we must trust it in order to have religious faith, and we must trust it even to appeal to authority because of our own ignorance! *A rational being cannot but trust her judgments*. Even when she distrusts them, it is only by trusting some other judgment to the effect that this one is worthy of doubt. But this means that a rational being implicitly presupposes her authority to believe in her judgments, including the authority to believe her judgments about which of her judgments are not to be trusted.

And this is an "authority" precisely because judgments go beyond any general rules or any general competence. Even the generally competent judge may be wrong in any given case; his preceding correct judgments are never sufficient to assure correctness in the present case. But he must judge the present case, and he must trust that judgment, for reasoning to proceed at all. Precisely because he may be wrong in his current judgment and yet rightly trusts it, we are dealing, not with the rightness of his judgment, but with his right to make and trust it. Moreover, this must be the subject's right, since it is a condition of reasoning and thus of the very possibility of obtaining knowledge at all.

Note here the emphasis on judgments, acts of reason, actual conclusions actually reached by particular reasoning beings at particular moments. We are rational, not just in that we can entertain rational arguments, but here most importantly because we actually conclude arguments, actually judge this way or that. Focus on judging as the distinctive feature of rationality shifts attention away from rationality understood as capacity for the application of rules, logical or otherwise. Judging involves more than entertaining logical possibilities—it involves actually plumping for one possibility over another. Judgment brings to the fore that we are dealing, not with rationality as an abstract system, but with a rational being, a particular individual embodiment of rationality who doesn't just entertain possibilities but actually concludes, opts for particular thought products over other logically possible ones.

Indeed, judging implies a double individuation of rationality. First, rationality is individuated in the sense of being possessed by (instantiated by) a rational individual, traditionally a *person*. (Early Christian thinkers gave this word its modern meaning as they struggled to make sense of the doctrine of the trinity. In the sixth century, Boethius defined "person" as "an individual substance of rational nature.")[6] Second, it is individuated in the sense of describing, not a general capacity, but particular acts. Rational individuals engage in individual acts of reasoning—inferring, deducing, concluding, and the like—all of which take individual shape via judgments.

Judgment is the individual's individual act of applying the general rules to an individual case, which the general rules cannot do of themselves. Rather, they must be judged appropriate to the case. Judgment reaches beyond the general rules in a way that can never be a mere product of general rules. (Wittgenstein obscured this in saying that it takes a rule to apply a rule. It takes a judge to apply a rule, and while his judgment may be formulated as a rule, that rule itself will still have to be applied by a judge and so be insufficient. But, if a judge is always both necessary and sufficient to apply a rule, then it adds little to say that it takes a rule to apply a rule. Better to say: *it takes a person to apply a rule*.) This reaching beyond to the individual case makes judgment fallible, but at the same time it makes the rational capacity to judge a kind of authority rather than a mere general ability.

The effect of Descartes's emphasis on judgment and thus on individuated reason is also to be seen in the way that Descartes's argument necessarily occurs from within an individual reasoner, a subject. To grasp the crucial nature of judgment to the reasoner, we cannot take the external point of view. From the outside, a reasoner's judgment is itself a fact that can be judged, not only for its validity, but for its other implications. From the inside, however, the reasoner's judgment can be evaluated only by means of other judgments that are not evaluated: the judgment that this judgment should be evaluated, the judgment that it passes or fails evaluation, and so on. In short, from the inside, there is always (at least) one judgment too many. This one (or several) must be trusted for the prior ones to be evaluated. In this way, the subject always presupposes an authority that reaches beyond his competence understood as a general capacity.

This necessary presupposition of authority to make and trust one's judgments doesn't assume that one's judgments are infallible—it is a condition of their being judgments at all. If I "make" a judgment but don't trust it, I am not really judging. Indeed, from within the subject, it is wrong to speak of an authority to make *and* to trust one's judgments as if these were two separate steps. The last judgment, the one that is one too many, is not first made *and then* trusted. That would introduce another judgment, that the earlier one is trustworthy. Rather, to make the judgment *is* to trust it. The subject doesn't confront her current judgment like a fact to be evaluated. She simply judges, makes and trusts and lives inside her judgment. Thus, the subject's assumption of authority to make and trust her judgments is simply the subject's assumption of authority to judge for herself, for the one she is. And, again, this assumption must be rightful, since it is the condition of reasoning and of knowledge.

Finally, that the subject lives inside his judgment is meant to be taken literally. We are rational beings, not merely in that we are beings with the capacity for rationality, but in the deeper sense that our being lies in our enactment of rationality. Here, too, I read Descartes's "I think, therefore I am" as containing more than meets the eye: *In the act(s) of thinking, I exist.* This idea is less strange than it might at first seem. It develops a notion hinted at in the *Nicomachean Ethics*, where Aristotle writes: "a man is said to have or not to have self-control according as his reason has or has not the control, on the assumption that this [his reason] is the man himself," and further, "reason more than anything else *is* man."[7] What this means is that there is no self over and above or under or behind the acts of thinking. The self and its thinking are one: You are what you think. Or the self is just the inside of thinking: You are what thinks you. The self is, so to speak, at stake in its judgments—invested, ventured, even gambled in its acts of thought. My judgments are not a set of lenses between me and the world; they are the very shape of my "I."

Descartes's Discovery Meets the Postmodern Requirements of Argumentation

The subject's authority to judge is not presupposed, so to speak, once and for all. It is implicitly asserted anew with each judgment. It is asserted for the particular rational being that I am, which, Descartes notwithstanding, we can understand as the unitary, conscious, rational, embodied being that I am. It is asserted in person, from the inside, inseparably from the judgments I make, which are inseparable from the self I am. Thus, there is a universal ad hominem argument for this claim: Whoever doubts it, accepts it because he presupposes his own authority to judge for himself that it is doubtful.

Moreover, such a person accepts that his rationality is a necessary and sufficient ground for that authority. So, then, here is another universal ad hominem argument: Every reasoning person accepts that her rationality is a necessary and sufficient ground for her authority to make/

trust her judgments. Notice, in support of this, that it is just this authority that we deny to people we think are insane when we treat their judgments as symptoms rather than as engagements. Indeed, we acknowledge that the self is constituted by this authority when we say of those we label insane that they are really not themselves.

Now, the assumption that rationality is a sufficient condition of one's authority to judge implies as well that whoever is regarded as rational must be regarded as having that authority. Much as a judgment is only a judgment for one who assumes his authority to judge, so can I argue in hope of changing the other's judgment only by assuming her authority to judge. Then, to argue with another, to aim to persuade her by reason, is implicitly to grant her authority to judge. Indeed, to regard her judgments as judgments and not just the output of some mechanical process is to grant her authority to judge for herself. *The assumption of the subject's authority to judge for herself is a necessary presupposition of any operation of rationality at all, and the mutual assumption of each other's authority to judge is the presupposition of any interpersonal rational argument.*

It follows that postmodernists must presuppose their own authority to judge, and that of their counterparts in argument, and ultimately that of all human beings. This puts a new face on the postmodern requirement of ad hominem argument. Where previously it appeared as a kind of *faute de mieux* strategy in light of the impossibility of reaching an indubitable given beyond interpretation, it now appears as part of the recognition of the rationality of one's audience. Because the audience, as rational beings, have as much authority for their judgments as the speaker, the speaker must persuade in a way that grants that equal authority. That means that the speaker's arguments must appeal to the recipients' own judgments and take the form of showing either that a conclusion is entailed by those judgments or that a contrary conclusion is in contradiction with those judgments.[8] That postmodernists do argue this way suggests that they do recognize the authority claimed by their listeners: Otherwise, why bother to convince them by rational ad hominem argument, rather than using trickery or brainwashing or the like?

Postmodern Argumentation and Post-postmodern Liberalism

I think I have shown, strictly by ad hominem argument, that postmodernists must implicitly grant the authority to judge that all rational subjects necessarily claim. However, there is more that one can say about rationality from within the requirements of postmodern argumentation. The subject uses her reason, not simply to reach judgments *period,* but to reach judgments about what to believe and about how to act. And this, too, is presupposed in the exercise of rationality: Whoever reasons must treat reasons *as reasons,* that is, as bestowing on facts a pro or con valence for whatever acts (theoretical or practical) of which the thinking subject is capable. For a reasoner, facts become reasons by becoming grounds for actions appropriate to the nature of those facts. And rational subjects must presuppose this for their exercising their reason to count as reasoning, rather than as just going through the motions. Then, there is an ad hominem argument that all reasoners must, as reasoners, presuppose that they are required to believe and to act in ways that are appropriate to the objects of their reasoning. This conclusion, taken together with what we have said so far about the necessity of recognizing the authority of the subject to judge for himself, brings us in sight of a universal moral principle established wholly within the requirements of postmodern argumentation.

That we must grant that people have authority to judge for themselves what to believe is not in itself a moral principle, since it can be granted even while brainwashing or drugging or coercing the other into believing this or that. The coerced other will still only believe what he judges belief-worthy. However, if there is no logical contradiction between recognizing people's authority to judge for themselves and brainwashing them into believing this or that, there is at least a discordance. To recognize people's authority to judge for themselves in any more whole-hearted way than mere lip service requires that we not force judgments upon their minds. Rather, we must allow them to form their own judgments. In this way, recognition of people's authority to judge for themselves provides moral undergirding for the postmodernist's requirement of universal ad hominem argument.

A similar argument applies to action. There is no logical contradiction in granting people the authority to judge what to believe and then acting toward them in terms of one's own judgments and contrary to theirs, leaving them still believing what they judge belief-worthy. But there is discordance. Since the authority of the subject extends to her judgments about what is of value to her and about how the unitary, conscious, rational, embodied being that she is ought to act, that authority naturally points outward beyond her beliefs to her actions and the fate of her body. (This is "natural" in view of the fact that the subject about which we are speaking is an animal, whose rational capacities have been selected in evolution to govern its body's actions.) Then, to recognize people's authority to judge for themselves in any more wholehearted way than mere lip service requires that we not force our judgments upon their bodies. Rather, we must allow them to extend their authority along its natural course to their actions. And this requires not forcing people to act in ways that they do not themselves judge proper. In this way, recognition of people's authority to judge for themselves provides moral undergirding for the postmodern protest against the oppression of those wrongly excluded from full standing in the human community.

Wholehearted recognition is more than merely not contradicting the claim to authority; it is positively allowing it to operate in its natural, embodied, active way. It does no violence to usage to call such "wholehearted recognition" *respect*, since, as Kant suggested, respect is a kind of stepping back from the other, making way for him.[9] If it can be shown that this wholehearted recognition or respect is the appropriate treatment of rational beings, we will have arrived at a postmodern moral universal: *In light of the nature of human subjects as reasoning beings who naturally claim authority for their own judgments, it is wrong to force our judgments on their minds or on their bodies.*

It might be thought that "appropriateness" is too soft a notion to ground a moral universal. This will certainly seem to be so if appropriateness is understood in the tepid way in which we speak of the requirements of etiquette. However, the appropriateness that I have in mind is the logical relationship between facts and judgments about action that I earlier argued must be presupposed by the very use of reason: Reasoners must presuppose that they are required to treat the objects of their reasoning (in this case, human subjects) in ways that are appropriate to those objects' nature. If it can be shown that there is a form of treatment that is most appropriate to rational beings, then the exercise of reasoning itself presupposes the requirement that they be so treated.

Respect is most appropriate to rational subjects because (*a*) it recognizes wholeheartedly a kind of authority that rational subjects necessarily and rightly claim, (*b*) that authority is claimed by subjects who are embodied beings reasoning to form judgments about reality and about how to act in it, and (*c*) that authority is the only authority in the world that is naturally claimed. Reason (*a*) makes it appropriate to give the subject's claim to authority some normative weight, (*b*) makes it appropriate to extend that weight to the judgments and actions over which the subject makes its claim, and (*c*) makes it inappropriate to give any other claim as great a weight as this one. Together, (*a*), (*b*), and (*c*) make it most appropriate, more appropriate than any other form of treatment, to refrain from imposing judgments on the minds and bodies of rational beings, because it is their nature to assert authority to judge for themselves. I think that is the strongest kind of moral argument one can make—at least in the condition of postmodernism.[10]

If it is wrong to impose judgments on the minds and bodies of rational human beings, on their thoughts and on their actions, then two principles must guide our treatment of them:

> *Principle 1*: People must be treated according to judgments that they freely form and endorse.
> *Principle 2*: People must be protected against violations of principle 1.

We should then treat people according to their own beliefs and according to those principles necessary to make sure that everyone is treated only according to their own beliefs. The result is recognizably a form of liberalism—in fact, a version of the liberal ideal of individual sovereignty—and one that not only meets, but, indeed, arises out of, the requirements of postmodern argumentation. However, since it reinstates universal moral principles with tools that derive from postmodernism's attack on universal moral principles, I call it *post-postmodern liberalism*.

Comments on Levinas, Habermas, and Rawls

To strengthen the case for post-postmodern liberalism, I shall close by suggesting very briefly how it provides what is missing in the important ethical theories of Emmanuel Levinas, Jürgen Habermas, and John Rawls. All three of these thinkers have been attacked by postmodernists. Nonetheless, I don't think it is inaccurate to call these thinkers "postmodern liberals," since they all try to steer clear of the bolts hurled by postmodernism against moral universalism: Levinas by seeking an ethical experience that eludes concepts (which are by nature general) and Habermas and Rawls by building ad hominem argumentation directly into their theories. And they all end up affirming the core notion of liberalism: Individuals are to be at least allowed, and to some degree helped, to live their own lives according to their own lights without violence or oppression from others.

Note that my argument in this section no longer claims to take place within the requirements of postmodern argumentation. In particular, I shall not try to establish my conclusions vis-à-vis Levinas, Habermas, and Rawls in an ad hominem fashion. Rather, I shall argue that the liberalism that has been established in this way supplies something that these three thinkers' doctrines lack and need.

In keeping with the critique of modern or Enlightenment universalism, Levinas maintains that any attempt to define the other individual by means of general principles or concepts must deny his real otherness. "Modernity," writes Levinas, "will subsequently be distinguished by the attempt to develop from the identification and appropriation of being *by* knowledge toward the identification of being *and* knowledge. . . . Identical and non-identical are identified. The labor of thought wins out over the otherness of things and men."[11] Moreover, this elimination of all otherness by thought is of a piece with the "wip[ing] out [of] all otherness by murder."[12]

The real basis of the ethical lies, for Levinas, prior to principles or concepts, in the "proximity of the other," in the encounter with the excess of the otherness of the other, that by which that otherness exceeds our attempts to tame it by capturing it in the net of our concepts. Levinas describes this encounter as "the irruption of the face into the phenomenological order of appearances. . . . The proximity of the other is the face's meaning."[13] "The face . . . is that whose *meaning* consists in saying 'thou shalt not kill.' "[14] And with this comes a responsibility for the other older than concepts: "The Other becomes my neighbor precisely through the way the face summons me, calls for me, begs for me, and in so doing recalls my responsibility. . . . A guiltless responsibility, whereby I am none the less open to the accusation of which no alibi, spatial or temporal, could clear me. . . . A responsibility for my neighbor, for the other man, for the stranger or sojourner, to which nothing in the rigorously ontological order binds me—nothing in the order of the thing, of the something, of number or causality."[15] Says Levinas of his work, "I analyze the inter-human relationship as if, in the proximity with the Other—beyond the image I myself make of the other man—his face . . . *ordains* me to serve him."[16] And elsewhere he writes, "To thematize this relation is already to lose it. . . ."[17]

Now, it is one thing to say that we have a certain awareness of the sheer otherness of other people, quite another thing to say that this awareness has a meaning prior to, and thus unshaped by, our conceptualizing or thematic thinking, and yet a third thing to say that this meaning reveals my real duty not to murder the other, my true moral responsibility for the other. The first of these is unobjectionable. There is certainly some sort of awareness of the otherness of the other, and no doubt it is of moral relevance.

The second claim, however, appeals to exactly the sort of experience of the given—an undeniable intuition of the morally laden "face"—that postmodernism and antifoundationalism reject. Bear in mind that Levinas is saying not merely that other people in travail do sometimes actually call out to us, appeal to us with their sobs or moans or words, and urge upon us a responsibility for them. He is saying that the other, as such and always, without acting or speaking in any way to appeal to us, simply in and via her otherness, calls us to responsibility for her. This is to read a content into the experience of the other which is, quite strictly, an intuition of meaning. Its authority lies in its being a sheer given, not something imposed or added by us. The power of Levinas's vision lies in the notion of an experience of the meaning of otherness that eludes the net of our concepts, and this is just what postmodernism denies is possible. If there is no given, no undeniably true intuition, then the bottom falls out of Levinas's theory.[18]

Moreover, Levinas's claim goes beyond the standard fare of phenomenological description insofar as it "describes," not just what "is," but an "ought." The responsibility to which the face calls me is said by Levinas to be my true responsibility. I am, for Levinas, truly ethically bound to the other. Suppose we suspend the objections raised in the previous paragraphs and accept that we do intuit in the face of the other a call to our responsibility for the other, to our duty not to murder him. That would be a fact. That the other calls me to responsibility doesn't imply that I am responsible, however, any more than that the other says I owe him money implies that I do. Even if the call of the other makes me feel responsible for him, there is still a distance between this feeling and being truly morally responsible for the other. No phenomenological description of facts could ever add up to a real moral duty. The result is that, while Levinas's assertion of the otherness of others is appealing, it and the supposed moral duty it evokes are supported by nothing more than his inescapably mystical pronouncements.

Post-postmodern liberalism can remedy these shortcomings while preserving what is appealing in Levinas's doctrine. We have already seen how post-postmodern liberalism provides a nonmystical route to a moral duty to respect the other. But it also gives us a nonmystical account of the irreducible otherness of the other. Precisely in the difference between the status of the other's judgment for her compared to its existence for me as a fact still to be judged, I confront the irreducible distance between separate subjects. To recognize the way that the other makes/trusts her judgments from within is to see the other from within and yet, since I cannot make/trust her judgments as if they were my own, to fail ultimately to establish strict identity with the being of the other. Her being, then, is not absorbed into my knowledge; rather, the nonidentity of her being with mine is known.

To recognize the other's authority over her judgments, all the while not identifying with those judgments, is to hear the moral call of the other to my responsibility from across the unbridgeable distance between us. And, given that respect is the most appropriate response to beings who naturally claim authority over their judgments, that call does invoke my true moral responsibility. Here, then, without mysticism, and without foundational intuitions, we derive the morally laden otherness of the other from recognition of, and respect for, her as a reasoning subject.

Habermas maintains that anyone who engages in rational justification to others implicitly accepts rational argument's commitment to uncoerced and informed assent from its audience. On these grounds, Habermas contends that the arguer is committed to treating the other according to norms to which the other can uncoercedly and informedly assent.[19] The problem, however, is that, even if the arguer presupposes commitment to persuasion by uncoerced consent, *nothing requires him to shape his actions by the conditions of interpersonal argument.* Put otherwise, even if there are morally laden commitments built into justification to others, these commitments do not require people (*a*) to engage in justification in the first place or (*b*) to conform their actions to their justifications if they do so engage. Requirements (*a*) and (*b*) are separate substantive moral requirements, not provided for by the conditions of justification themselves. Thus Habermas's theory can have no moral claim on anyone who does not believe that he must justify his actions to others before acting or that he must act only in ways that he can justify to others.

The needed substantive moral requirements are provided by post-postmodern liberalism in the notion that wholehearted recognition of people as rational authority-claiming subjects requires that we allow them to form their own judgments and that we refrain from treating them according to judgments they do not themselves make—except where necessary to assure that no one is so treated. Here, then, we derive the obligation to conform to the conditions of argument, regarding both beliefs and actions, from recognition of, and respect for, the nature of human beings as rational subjects.

In *Political Liberalism*,[20] Rawls defends a version of liberalism that is political both in its subject and in its justification. Its subject is the basic structure of society (the main political, economic, and social institutions), thus leaving large areas of "private" or "civil" life subject to citizens' personally held ideals. As for justification, Rawls's liberalism is put forth as a "freestanding view."[21] By this Rawls means that it is not based on a comprehensive philosophical, religious, or moral doctrine that aims to determine all or most of what is valuable in life. Thus it is unlike Mill's liberalism, which was founded on the comprehensive doctrine of utilitarianism, and unlike Kant's, which was founded on his comprehensive doctrine of pure reason. To establish his liberalism as a freestanding view, Rawls hopes to avoid taking a position on any metaphysical issues by starting instead from an idea he finds embedded in our democratic culture: the idea "of society as a fair system of social cooperation between free and equal persons."[22] This way, Rawls's political liberalism is meant to appeal to the holders of a wide range of irreconcilable though reasonable comprehensive doctrines—religious, philosophical, and moral—as long as they can find within their particular doctrines some reasons to join an "overlapping consensus" on the ideas distinctive to liberal democratic culture. As he has recently summarized it in replying to Habermas,

> The central idea is that political liberalism moves within the category of the political and leaves philosophy as it is. It leaves untouched all kinds of doctrines, religious, metaphysical, and moral, with their long traditions of development and interpretation. Political philosophy proceeds apart from all such doctrines, and presents itself in its own terms as freestanding. Hence, it cannot argue its case by invoking any comprehensive doctrines, or by criticizing or rejecting them, so long of course as those doctrines are reasonable, politically speaking. When attributed to persons, the two basic elements of the conception of the reasonable are, first, a willingness to propose fair terms of social cooperation that others as free and equal also might endorse, and to act on these terms, provided others do, even contrary to one's own interest; and, second, a recognition of the burdens of judgment [grounds for expecting that reasonable people will differ irreconcilably in their comprehensive doctrines] and accepting their consequences for one's attitude (including toleration) toward other comprehensive doctrines.[23]

As for the notion of "citizens as reasonable," it is drawn "from the public political culture of a democratic society."[24]

The problem here is that if the concept of the reasonable only holds for those who share a democratic culture, then those who do not share that culture—though they live within its midst as, say, Ku Klux Klanners or other extremists—cannot be said to be unreasonable, only different. Then, the upholders of democratic liberal politics cannot say that the dissenters are wrong, only different. And that means that the relation between the democratic liberal state and the dissenters, particularly when the state uses force to repress the dissenters' "principled" violence, is strictly a power relation rather than a moral one. The dissenters cannot be said to have failed in an obligation owed to the democratic liberal citizens, since the claim for that obligation goes no further than the shared beliefs of those citizens.

Put more generally, a liberal political theory that aims to be "political not metaphysical"[25] cannot generate a moral obligation for those who do not share its liberal political culture. Indeed, even those who do share that political culture only *believe* they are obligated. They are *truly* obligated only if liberal political values are truly worthy of allegiance independent of any comprehensive doctrine and/or if the comprehensive doctrines that teach them that liberal values are worthy are true. However, as a political doctrine, Rawls's theory eschews appeal to, or even judgment about, its own truth (Rawls will only call it reasonable)[26] or the truth of the comprehensive doctrines held by citizens. Thus, political liberalism cannot generate a moral obligation to its own liberal values. It must rest content with the hope that the citizens will fill this in for themselves.

The needed moral obligation is provided by post-postmodern liberalism in the notion that it is most appropriate to the nature of rational beings to treat them only according to the judgments they are prepared to make. Then, it is wrong not to be reasonable in just the way that Rawls and democratic culture have defined it. And there is a moral obligation to be reasonable that goes beyond subscribing to reasonable comprehensive doctrines supportive of reasonable liberal political values. It is an obligation on all rational beings, including the extremists in, but not of, "the public political culture of a democratic society." Of course, this would make Rawls's theory, not just political, but ever so slightly metaphysical.[27]

Notes

This chapter is a revised version of an article originally published in the *Canadian Journal of Philosophy*, supplementary volume 21: *On the Relevance of Metaethics: New Essays on Metaethics*, ed. J. Couture and K. Nielsen (1996): 251–72. I am indebted to Joseph Flay, emeritus professor of philosophy at Pennsylvania State University, and Jonathan Loesberg, professor of literature at

American University, for numerous helpful comments, many of which I have incorporated into this chapter.

1. In *Speech and Phenomena*, Jacques Derrida gives an argument for non-givenness of meaning and thus for the fundamentality of interpretation from within phenomenology itself. He does so by playing Husserl's *Phenomenology of Internal Time-Consciousness* (trans. James Churchill [Bloomington, Ind.: Indiana University Press, 1964; originally published 1928]) off against Husserl's own theory of the intuitive givenness of linguistic meaning. The latter requires there to be an instantaneous grasp of the meaning of a term, while the former shows that there is nothing in consciousness that is instantaneous. Everything in consciousness is elapsing in time, and that implies that the appearance of an instantaneous grasp of meaning is really the product of a gathering up of flowing elements of experience into some meaningful totality, which is to say, interpretation. Nor should the term "elements" here be taken as implying yet other instantaneous givens, since that too is denied by the elapsing nature of consciousness. As far down as we go, all we get are interpretations. See Jacques Derrida, *Speech and Phenomena, and Other Essays on Husserl's Theory of Signs* (Evanston, Ill.: Northwestern University Press, 1973).

2. Zygmunt Bauman, *Postmodern Ethics* (Oxford: Blackwell, 1993), p. 13.

3. John Rawls, *Political Liberalism* (New York: Columbia University Press, 1993).

4. See Jürgen Habermas, "Discourse Ethics," in his *Moral Consciousness and Communicative Action* (Cambridge, Mass.: Massachusetts Institute of Technology Press, 1990), pp. 43–115.

5. René Descartes, *The Philosophical Writings of Descartes* (Cambridge: Cambridge University Press, 1984), vol. 2, pp. 270, 272–73.

6. See Peter Singer, *Rethinking Life and Death* (New York: St. Martin's Press, 1995), p. 180; and A. Trendelenburg, "A Contribution to the History of the Word 'Person,' " *Monist* 20 (1910): 336–63.

7. Aristotle, *Nicomachean Ethics*, trans. David Ross (Oxford: Oxford University Press, 1980), bk. 9, sec. 8; bk. 10, sec. 7 (emphasis in original). For interesting commentary on these passages, their translation, and their significance in Aristotle's ethical theory, see Richard Kraut, *Aristotle on the Human Good* (Princeton, N.J.: Princeton University Press, 1989), pp. 128, 183, 189.

8. All ad hominem arguments appeal to the logical law of noncontradiction, insofar as they aim to show that a given conclusion is either acceptable because compatible with the listener's judgments or unacceptable because incompatible with them. It might seem, then, that the law of noncontradiction is an exception to the requirement of ad hominem argument, since it is presumably held valid independently of the listener's endorsement of it. But this misconceives the role of the law. The law of noncontradiction is not an arbitrary rule that a person can judge appropriate or not. It is the material condition of having a judgment of one's own at all. I simply cannot judge that P, if I also think that not-P. Thus Aristotle used an ad hominem argument for the law itself, holding, in the

Metaphysics, that if one affirms that the same thing can at the same time both be and not be, then this affirmation affirms the truth of its own negation. Further, to deny the law of noncontradiction is to deny that denial. To deny the law of noncontradiction, one must implicitly affirm that the truth of the denial of the law is incompatible with the truth of the affirmation of that same law, and that means that whoever would deny the law of noncontradiction must assume the law's truth to do so. See Aristotle, *Metaphysics*, bk. 11, sec. 5, in *The Complete Works of Aristotle*, ed. J. Barnes (Princeton, N.J.: Princeton University Press, 1991), vol. 2, pp. 1677–78.

9. "[B]y the principle of respect which [people] owe one another they are directed to keep themselves at a distance." Immanuel Kant, "The Metaphysical Principles of Virtue," pt. 2 of *The Metaphysics of Morals*, in *Ethical Philosophy*, trans. James W. Wellington (Indianapolis, Ind.: Hackett, 1983; originally published 1797), p. 113.

10. Given the logical gulf between facts and values, "appropriateness" may be just the relationship that one should expect at the core of a moral doctrine— even one that is not argued within the requirements of postmodern argumentation.

11. Emmanuel Levinas, "Ethics as First Philosophy," in *The Levinas Reader*, ed. Sean Hand (Oxford: Blackwell, 1989), p. 78 (emphasis in original).

12. Ibid., p. 85.

13. Ibid., p. 82.

14. Emmanuel Levinas, *Ethics and Infinity: Conversations with Philippe Nemo* (Pittsburgh, Pa.: Duquesne University Press, 1985), p. 87 (emphasis in original).

15. Levinas, "Ethics as First Philosophy," pp. 83–84.

16. Levinas, *Ethics and Infinity*, p. 97 (emphasis in original).

17. Levinas, "Substitution," in *The Levinas Reader*, ed. Hand, p. 110.

18. Curiously, Bauman bases the positive doctrine of his *Postmodern Ethics* on Levinas's teaching without even considering its apparent violation of this key tenet of postmodernism. See Bauman, *Postmodern Ethics*.

19. See Habermas, "Discourse Ethics."

20. See Rawls, *Political Liberalism*.

21. Ibid., pp. 12–13, inter alia.

22. Ibid., p. 9, inter alia.

23. John Rawls, "Reply to Habermas," *Journal of Philosophy* 92, no. 3 (March 1995): 134 (I have omitted Rawls's references).

24. Ibid., 135.

25. Rawls, *Political Liberalism*, p. 10; see also Rawls, "Justice as Fairness: Political Not Metaphysical," *Philosophy and Public Affairs* 14 (Summer 1985): 223–51.

26. "[P]olitical liberalism, rather than referring to its political conception of justice as true, refers to it as reasonable instead." Rawls, *Political Liberalism*, p. xx.

27. Actually, I think that this would vastly improve Rawls's theory and that it is in any event necessary at other points in the theory as well. Consider the fact that the abortion controversy needs a solution within the nonmetaphysical framework of political liberalism. Rawls is quite sure this is possible, as he points out in a lengthy footnote:

> As an illustration, consider the troubled question of abortion. Suppose . . . that we consider the question in terms of three important political values: the due respect for human life, the ordered reproduction of political society over time, including the family in some form, and finally the equality of women as equal citizens. (There are, of course, other important political values besides these.) Now I believe *any reasonable balance of these three political values will give a woman a duly qualified right to decide whether or not to end her pregnancy during the first trimester.* The reason for this is that at this early stage of pregnancy the political value of the equality of women is overriding, and this right is required to give it substance and force. (Rawls, *Political Liberalism*, p. 243, n. 32 [emphasis mine])

But note right away that Rawls's conclusion about abortion only follows on the assumption that a first-trimester fetus is not among those equal persons who are to be protected by the laws of a liberal state (otherwise, the political value of women's equality would not be overriding). This is clearly a metaphysical, not merely a political, claim.

3

Drug Addiction, Liberal Virtue, and Moral Responsibility

So that there will be no misunderstanding about the argument I am about to make, let me start by saying that I think that the "War on Drugs" is immoral on both consequentialist and deontological grounds. On consequentialist grounds, it is wrong because it produces more harm than the evil it aims to vanquish.[1] This is primarily because making drugs illegal has the effect of driving their prices up dramatically, due to the fact that then only those willing to risk imprisonment will supply the drug. The cocaine used daily by a heavy user could be produced and sold for pennies legally. Illegally, however, it can easily cost one hundred dollars or more a day. The effect of this is to create enormous incentives to poor people to sell the drug, to find new users, and to use deadly violence to settle bad debts or to keep competitors out of their market. (Police attribute about a third of the many murders in Washington, D.C., to the work of drug-trade "enforcers.")[2] This, in turn, means that inner-city communities are so violence-ridden that no one will invest in them and whoever has the talent to escape will do so, with the result that both money and talent flow away from where they are needed most.

Moreover, since the drug trade is the main source of big money and the main entertainment in otherwise hopeless lives, large numbers of inner-city dwellers are involved in it at some level, and thus large numbers get arrested and spend time in prison, further sapping the community of potential resources. (The prison population in the United States has more than doubled over the past decade, fueled in large measure by drug-related convictions.)[3] And this all has a kind of evil multiplier effect: With more violence, there are more strains on medical emergency resources and thus greater health expenses with less resources available for normal uses, such as prenatal health care. With more money tempting people to the drug trade, lives are rendered unstable and unpredictable with negative effects on the health and well-being of children. With more young men in prison, there are fewer eligible husbands and thus more unmarried young mothers. And so on. Thus, though I think that legalizing drugs has its dangers and would probably have some negative consequences, I think that these pale beside the danger and harm produced by the War on Drugs.

Deontologically, I think that the War on Drugs is immoral because I believe that a sane adult has the right to put whatever he wants in his body. The liberalism that underlies the argument that I shall make in this chapter is of the Lockean-Kantian variety that places special weight on the capacity of rational beings to govern their own lives. It holds that the ability of people to shape their own lives according to their own judgments is the necessary condition of their living lives that are truly meaningful to them, lives that they can think of as their own accomplishment and thus in which they can take pride. It is the necessary condition of people living lives that have a worth that reflects their special capacity as rational beings. Thus the right to self-governance (as far as this is compatible with the same right for all), which necessarily includes the right to control one's body, is the condition for the special dignity that humans have and the special respect to which they are entitled. Taking this right away is treating human beings in a condescending and disrespectful manner, as if they were not capable of running their lives, as if their bodies were resources owned by the society.

Sovereignty over one's body is the sine qua non of a free society. Thus, I subscribe to what Kant called the supreme principle of morality, namely, that the freedom of each should be limited only so far as is necessary to make it compatible with the like freedom of all.[4] And I subscribe generally to John Stuart Mill's principle that the society has no right to restrict a sane adult's freedom except to prevent harm to others.[5]

None of this, however, implies that drug addiction is morally acceptable or morally indifferent. Kant thought that allowing bodily desires to master one's mind is a vice.[6] And, while Mill believed that we should use the law *less* to control people's behavior, he believed that we should remonstrate with our fellows *more* about what is really good and evil in life.[7] He clearly felt that what is immoral is a larger category than what can be rightly prohibited. Thus, there will be no inconsistency with the liberal views I have thus far stated when I add that I believe there is a sense, a liberal sense in fact, in which drug addiction is immoral.

To reach this conclusion, I shall sketch a theory of liberal virtue according to which drug addiction (when it possesses certain characteristics that I shall shortly spell out) is a vice. It is a vice that I think sane adults have a right to indulge, though they should not, and one that I think that the state has no right to prohibit, though the state should discourage it. I shall argue, further, that the vice of drug addiction is one for which the addict is responsible, as he is responsible for the actions that result from the addiction. This notwithstanding, I shall go on to argue that insofar as drug addiction results from remediable and unfair social conditions, then society as a whole may share responsibility for the drug addictions in its midst and for the actions that predictably accompany them. This should bring to light a number of disagreements between my view and that of Jan Narveson, even though we both agree that individuals have the moral right to use drugs and that the state has no business waging the War on Drugs.

Strong Addictions and Strong Desires

Narveson treats drug addiction as if it were just like any strong desire. There is nothing special about it, nothing to distinguish it from a strong desire to see operas or boxing matches.[8] I contend that this overlooks a feature that addictions sometimes have which other strong desires lack and which places addictions *with this feature* in a special moral category.

For Narveson, a drug addict is someone who "cannot resist the next dose," and this, according to him, makes the addict no different from someone who cannot resist the next opera, will spend her last penny on opera tickets, and so on.[9] This fails to note, however, that, when we call something an addiction, we normally mean that it is more than simply a strong desire; it is a strong desire of a certain sort: namely, an ongoing, self-perpetuating strong desire, such that (in at least some cases) it would be extremely hard to stop pursuing the desired object *even if one judged it to be contrary to one's interest to continue.* The *International Dictionary of Psychology* lists among the criteria for drug addiction: "having a compulsive inability to resist taking the drug despite the knowledge that it is harmful."[10]

I am not suggesting that all addictions have this property. Indeed, it is currently fashionable to stretch the term addiction way beyond its original home in the pharmaceutical realm, to characterize people's desires for "food, smoking, gambling, buying, work, play, and sex."[11] According to this usage, addiction needn't involve the development of chemical tolerance with its attendant dangers of withdrawal, needn't be to anything harmful in itself, and may even be a beneficial process by which one harnesses oneself to some worthwhile activity like exercise. In the case of drug addiction, however, the implication is normally that the continuation of the practice is contrary to the user's self-interest and, in some sense, overwhelms his ability to pursue his self-interest as he understands it. I think that the extensions of the term to nonchemical substances, nonharmful practices, and even to positive activities feed off (draw pungency from) this primary sense of the term addiction.

In any event, at least some addictions have the property of impelling the addict to continue in spite of his judgment that the desired object is harmful and that he would be better off without it and without the desire for it. Such addictions I will call *strong* addictions. Addictions that would not survive the individual's judgment that they are contrary to his self-interest, I shall call *weak* addictions. (In this category, I place my own addiction to coffee in the morning and to *MacNeil-Lehrer* in the evening.) What I shall say about the moral status of drug addiction is meant to apply only to strong addictions.

When addiction is strong, we can say that the addict's decision to take the next dose is rational in that it gives him some pleasure and forestalls the threatened pains of withdrawal. It may even give him great pleasure—though it is widely noted that the pleasure derived from addictive substances, whether heroin or potato chips, declines over time, while the strength of the desire persists.[12] By contrast, however, the addict's being or remaining addicted is irrational in that the overall amount of pleasure gained is not worth the harm done to his body, mind, work, and/or relationships, *according to the addict's own judgment*. In short, the addiction is rational in the short run and irrational in the long run. Strong addiction, then, has the effect of disabling the individual's capacity to shape his life according to his long-term best interest.

It should be evident that there is a clear and important distinction between the opera lover's strong desire and the junky's strong addiction. The opera lover's desire is itself a gift. She is better off for having the desire because it adds to the pleasure available to her. The dope addict's strong addiction is by contrast a misfortune. He would be better off without it because having it makes his life worse overall than it could have been. To see why this distinction is morally relevant, I want now to sketch a liberal theory of virtue.

Liberal Virtues and Vices

The idea of liberal virtues may strike some readers as odd, even as an oxymoron, since much recent debate has been concerned with the supposed neutrality of liberalism, which is thought by some to be its main selling point as a moral theory, and which seems to rule out favoring any particular set of characterological dispositions over others.[13] I think that this debate is largely otiose, since the neutrality at issue in the debate would not be desirable even if it were possible, which it isn't. It amounts to asking liberalism to be a moral position that doesn't take a moral position. There is an important and distinctive way in which liberalism is neutral, but—as I shall indicate shortly—it is not neutral in a way that rules out favoring certain kinds of character traits over others.

Liberalism's neutrality lies in the fact that it prohibits forcing one sane adult's will on any other sane adult (except when necessary to prevent such forcing). This means that liberalism is not neutral with respect to actions (such as theft or rape) or policies (such as the imposition of a religious orthodoxy) that involve such forcing. If liberalism were neutral on these, it would not be a moral position at all. But, aside from its prohibition on force, liberalism remains neutral in the large sense that it insists on the right of sane adults to adopt any action, lifestyle, and moral view for themselves that they wish.

In this context, it is, in any event, not surprising that the recent resurgence of interest in what is called "virtue ethics" is, in its canonical, MacIntyrean form, offered as an alternative to liberalism.[14] Virtue ethicists aim to develop an ethical theory by starting with some notion of human excellence and showing that the components of an independently determined excellent life include behaviors that are recognizably moral. This means that they must not only develop a standard of human excellence but do so *before* they have a standard of moral behavior. But, without a standard of moral behavior and without an Aristotelian or Christian belief in an ontologically real human teleology, it is, to put it mildly, hard to come up with a standard of human excellence. MacIntyre has found no better alternative than measuring human excellence by the standards found in the culture at the time, but this sort of conventionalism offers little hope for showing that the standards are anything more than conventional prejudices about excellence.

Aristotle is sometimes taken as the model for this sort of conventionalism, since he does normally start analysis by considering (with great respect) prevailing opinions and he does end up accepting as the virtues those that are enshrined in the conventions around him. Nonetheless, Aristotle did not, in my view, think that he was practicing conventionalism of the sort recommended by MacIntyre. He thought that prevailing opinions were likely to contain truth (and not just be prevalent conventions) because he was confident in the human capacity to know reality, and he thought he could see the superiority of virtues like courage over vices like cowardice, as we today think we see the superiority of health over sickness (indeed, as we see health as *health* and not just as an arrangement of bodily components).

The problem, then, for virtue ethics is that, insofar as it aims to derive morality from a standard of human excellence, it must provide a justification of that standard, good reasons for believing that it really is a standard of *excellence* rather than merely a conventional prejudice. But without a natural teleology to fall back on, it seems inevitable that such a justification will have to rely on a moral view—and that will undermine the attempt to derive morality from the standard of human excellence.

By way of illustration, consider the promising suggestion about how to derive morality from human excellence that has been put forth by Michael Slote. Slote considers the possibility that excellence or virtue is a kind of strength or self-sufficiency, which is inherently admirable.[15] Slote is able to account for a surprisingly large number of common moral views by showing how forms of behavior commonly thought to be moral exhibit a kind of strength or self-sufficiency. For example, he accounts for the obligations of fairness—to do one's share in cooperative ventures from which one benefits—as exhibiting one's disposition not to be a parasite, which in turn exhibits one's self-sufficiency rather than dependence, and so on. Fruitful as this approach is, it seems to me that it does not escape the difficult circle within which all virtue ethics operates: We still need to know why strength or self-sufficiency is a *good* trait. Without a natural teleology, there seems no way to do this without appealing to some account of moral goodness—and that will make virtue derivative from a moral theory, just the opposite of the virtue ethicists' goal. Nor will it do to deny that we need to know why strength or self-sufficiency is a good trait, or to claim that it is simply a primitive good or self-evidently admirable. That would effectively reduce morality to a blind attachment, in Slote's suggestion, to something on the order of uncritical affection for John Wayne types, or "Marlboro men."

A liberal theory of virtue differs from the MacIntyrean variety and from what is normally called "virtue ethics" because it does not expect to develop a moral theory by starting from an account of human excellence. Rather, it frankly accepts that human excellence can be identified only from the standpoint of an already existing moral theory and thus that virtue is a derivative, rather than a basic, element of an ethics. A liberal theory of virtue takes the standard of excellence implicit in liberalism. And this, in the Lockean-Kantian version, is found in liberalism's celebration of the capacity of human beings to govern their lives by their own rational judgments.

Since the rights that liberalism thinks people have derive from people's capacity for rational self-government, liberalism is hardly neutral on the worth of this capacity. If this capacity is not taken as extremely valuable, then the argument for rights that effectively provide the space for its exercise is undercut. To the extent that an individual fails to exercise her capacity for rational self-government, and more so to the extent that she purposely weakens that capacity, she can be said to be acting in a way that is unworthy of the rights she has. Or, if the ability to pilot one's life according to one's rational judgments is the source of the special dignity of human life, then one who fails to use, or who positively subverts, this ability is acting in an undignified manner.

Let us call the ability of human beings to govern their lives by their rational judgments "the sovereignty of practical reason." Then, we can say that the liberal virtues are those dispositions that promote the sovereignty of practical reason, and the vices are those dispositions that undermine that sovereignty.

This approach gives us something that is all too often missing in liberal moral theory, namely, a roll for *shame*, as distinct from *guilt*. Guilt—both the status and the feeling—is normally linked to failures in one's duty to others. Shame, by contrast, is normally thought to be appropriate in cases where a person fails to be the sort of person that he or she should be. Thus, a liberal moral theory, with its emphasis on people's right to act as they wish as long as they don't violate the rights of others, seems to have a place only for guilt—the guilt that arises from violating others' rights. If, however, we add to this that liberalism must highly value the capacity for rational self-government, we get a way in which people can fall short of being the sort of people they should be *according to liberalism*. Then, a liberal can consistently hold that someone who fails to use, or who positively subverts, his ability for rational self-government acts in a shameful manner, even if he is guilty of no violation of anyone's rights.[16] I leave aside, until the section on "Responsibility for Vice and Addiction," the question of whether such failure or subversion is voluntary and thus something for which people can be held responsible. I shall continue to speak, in the present section and the next, of people subverting their capacity for self-governance and so on without meaning to take a position on whether they do so freely.

It should be noted in passing that this is not the only way in which one might try to launch a liberal theory of virtue. Separating himself from any conception of liberalism that thinks it is a neutral ideal, William Galston defends a rich and varied list of virtues as liberal.[17] He devotes most of his analysis to instrumental virtues, such as tolerance or law-abidingness, that are necessary means to the preservation of liberal societies. In addition, he mentions approvingly three intrinsic liberal virtues: (*a*) rational self-determination (which he attributes to Locke), (*b*) the ability to act on the moral law (which he attributes to Kant), and (*c*) the development of individuality (which he attributes to John Stuart Mill, Ralph Waldo Emerson, and others). The first of these is the same as the sovereignty of practical reason that I take as central to liberalism. I am not persuaded that the remaining two are appropriate standards, for the following (all too briefly stated) reasons:

The capacity to act on the moral law is part of the capacity to subject one's actions to practical reason—indeed, for Kant it is equivalent to the capacity to subject one's actions to *nothing but* practical reason. Thus, I don't think that the second standard is really a separate standard of virtue; rather, it is a case of the first. As for individuality, while it may be one important excellence that can be realized in liberal societies, my own view is that liberalism insists, first and foremost, that one's choice be one's own—even if it is a choice to conform. Wouldn't a liberal prefer a society of people who conform because they choose to, to one where they are nonconformists because they are conditioned to be that way?

The idea that the virtues are the dispositions that support the sovereignty of practical reason is closer to classical doctrine than may be immediately apparent. For example, this account gives us a way of explaining the so-called "cardinal" virtues: prudence, fortitude, temperance, and justice.[18] *Prudence* is nothing but the sovereignty of practical reason itself, *fortitude* is the ability to hold to one's rationally chosen course of action in the face of hardship and danger, *temperance* is the ability to hold to it in the face of temptation by pleasures close at hand. And, considered as a virtue, *justice* is the disposition to leave others the same space to live according to their rationally chosen course of life that one claims for oneself. One advantage of this explanation of the virtues is that it overcomes the suspicion that at least the first three of the cardinal virtues lack the generality to be *the* virtues. Temperance, for example, seems to be part of a particular (perhaps puritanical) moral system and not something of value to everyone (say, to voluptuaries). But if present pleasures are recognized to have a kind of deceptively strong appeal by virtue of their very nearness, then temperance is the ability to withstand this deceptive appeal and weigh present pleasures by their real value in light of one's overall life aims. Then, temperance is a means to whatever course of life one chooses. Even voluptuaries might be tempted to overrate certain nearby pleasures (say, of security or good reputation), and thus temperance will enable them to hold to their course no less than it will help puritans.

Moreover, this account is akin to Aristotle's, though of course it is not an identical twin. For Aristotle, it will be remembered, the virtues are the components of a *eudaimon,* or happy, life. Indeed, for Aristotle, this claim is tautological. The virtues are the ways of living excellently, and the *eudaimon* life is an excellently lived life. The virtues make up the excellently lived life. Contrary to a common view, Aristotle is not a teleological moral thinker in the sense that, say, Mill is. Aristotle, of course, holds a teleological view of nature, including human nature. But, the virtues are not simply means to happiness. Or, if they are means to it, they are in the sense in which bricks and cement are means to a building, not the sense in which blueprints and trowels are means to a building. For Aristotle, the virtues stand to the happy life as the parts to the whole, and they are means to the end of happiness only in the way that the parts are means to the existence of the whole.

Aristotle arrives at the virtues by arguing that a happy life must be a life in which the distinctive human capacity is exercised excellently. The distinctive human capacity is reason, which in its excellent theoretical use gives us the intellectual virtues and in its excellent practical use gives us the moral virtues. The moral virtues are those ways in which people's appetites are appropriately subjected to their practical reason. A morally virtuous person is one whose desires have been trained to take their cue from reason, rather than simply go all out for satisfaction. Thus, the virtues are dispositions to *measured* passions and *measured* actions. This is how Aristotle arrives at his famous doctrine of the mean.

The mean is not an algorithm for finding virtue; it is a description of the inner life of virtuous persons. Desires or passions in themselves push for total satisfaction. But virtuous acts share with art and athletics the property of being neither too much nor too little. This doesn't mean that the virtues are midway between total satisfaction and none at all, just that they are in between the two, and thus that the desires have been subjected to some kind of rational control. And this is all the doctrine of the mean tells us. It is not, as is sometimes mistakenly thought of Aristotle, some way of figuring out what is virtuous by first identifying excess and defect and then splitting the difference between them. Excess and defect cannot be identified prior to identifying the right amount. Thus Aristotle's mean is not a way of figuring out what virtue is; it is a characteristic of those desires and actions that are already known to be virtuous.

The moral virtues, then, for Aristotle, amount to dispositions in our desires to allow themselves to be governed by rational judgment, to be felt and acted upon in a rationally measured way. To use the terms introduced earlier, we can say that the virtues are dispositions to accept the sovereignty of practical reason over one's desires. The difference between Aristotle's account and the liberal one is that Aristotle emphasizes the substantive outcomes of that sovereignty, the particular virtues that result from the subjection of desires to practical reason. The liberal view, by contrast, focuses on the preconditions, rather than the results, of the sovereignty of practical reason. Where, for example, on the Aristotelian view, temperance is a virtue because it is the attitude that a man of practical wisdom would cultivate, for liberalism, it is a virtue because it is a precondition for the effective exercise of practical wisdom. That the liberal theory identifies as virtues those dispositions that enable and promote the sovereignty of practical reason gives us a way of saying how some addictions are vicious.

Before taking this up, however, we should round out the discussion of the liberal theory of virtue by considering the following question: If liberalism celebrates the sovereignty of practical reason and condemns as vice dispositions that undermine this sovereignty, why doesn't liberalism allow—even demand—that law be used to prevent such vices? After all, if freedom is a value because it enables people to exercise sovereignty over themselves, why should we protect the freedom to subvert this exercise?

To this, I think the liberal has two main replies. The first is that, even if it would be good for me to be forced not to weaken my ability for rational self-governance, it is no other person's right to do this. My fate becomes subject to other people's rights only insofar as I act in ways that harm or endanger others. People do not have general rights to do whatever is good for other people whether they want it or not. The second reply is that it is not good for me, once I have become an adult, to be forced not to weaken my ability for rational self-governance. That is because what makes rational self-governance good for me is that it creates a life that is in an important way *my* life, *my* accomplishment. And this is possible only if the project of rational self-government is *my* project. While society and my parents have the right, indeed the duty, to force upon me as a child the education and rearing needed to make me into an adult capable of self-government, it is not appropriate for anyone to continue such force once I am an adult. To do the latter is to undermine the reality, and thus the worth, of my project of self-governance by stealing that project from me and making it into someone else's project for me. That the project may be subverted because I have surrendered to some vice is part of what makes the project worthwhile when it succeeds. Consequently, the liberal holds that adults have the right to indulge their vices, including vicious addictions, to which we now turn.

Vicious Addictions

As I return now to the moral status of drug addiction, bear in mind that I am speaking only of what I earlier called "strong addiction" and that I am staying neutral for the time being on the question of the addict's freedom. Strong drug addictions are ones in which the desire for the drug overcomes the addict's knowledge that it is harmful and that he would be better off without the drug and the desire for it. For each drug dose considered alone, it may be rational for the addict to indulge, since he gets some pleasure and avoids a real pain (of withdrawal). However, the addict himself can see that the total package is not a good bargain. In the long run, he would gain more from not being addicted than he does from his drugs.

Strong addiction is a vice according to the liberal theory. By becoming addicted, the addict undermines his ability to govern his life in the long run (that is, the whole course of his life) by his rational judgment. This is a vice rather than a single irrational act because it is not merely an act contrary to his self-interest but the undermining of his ongoing ability to govern his life by his rational judgment. The strong addict has (freely or not) created for himself a (more or less) permanent obstacle to his doing what it would be rational for him to do with his life. He commits a kind of treason against the sovereignty of his own practical reason.

Consequently, calling strong addiction a vice is not due to some puritanical repulsion against "unearned pleasure" or some puritanical prejudice in favor of sobriety. Rather, strong addiction is wrong in terms of the addict's own goals. Insofar as (per hypothesis) the addict gets less of what he wants in the long run from being addicted than he would without the addiction, it is in terms of his own goals that the irrationality of his addiction is measured. A strong addiction is something that persists against the addict's own "better judgment." It amounts to a kind of self-betrayal.

This shows us an additional strength of the liberal theory. According to it, vices are dispositions to self-betrayal. This gives the liberal theory of virtue and vice its normative cutting edge. The standard theories put forth by virtue ethicists generally give some list of excellences that virtuous folks realize and vicious ones fail at. But it is far from obvious why failure at an excellence is a moral failure.[19] The burgers one grills on the backyard barbecue do not achieve the excellence of haute cuisine, but this doesn't make backyard chefs vicious. On the liberal theory, by contrast, there is a clear solution to this puzzle. The excellences that the liberal theory identifies as virtues are means to the individual's own ability to live the life that, on reflection, she most wants to live. Failure at those excellences amounts to betrayal of one's own aims, a kind of assault on one's own life.

That the liberal vices are dispositions to self-betrayal gives us a way to redeem (partially) Mill's dubious claim that the liberal principle (that liberty may only be restricted to prevent harm to others) prohibits selling oneself into slavery.[20] Mill contended that a principle protecting liberty cannot protect this particular freedom since it is a freedom to destroy one's liberty. This claim runs into skepticism because the liberal principle is normally thought to protect a sane individual's freedom to end his life. Suicide seems like a sacrifice of more liberty than merely selling oneself into slavery, since even a lifelong slave will have some occasions on which he can make free choices, which is more than a successful suicide will have.

On the liberal theory of virtue, however, we can distinguish suicide from voluntary enslavement. Insofar as suicide is the result of a rational decision about the pains and pleasures of staying alive, it is an expression of the sovereignty of one's practical reason over one's life. In a way, it is the ultimate expression, or one of the ultimate expressions, of that sovereignty, since it places the size of one's very life in one's hands. Selling oneself into slavery, by contrast, amounts to handing over one's sovereignty to another. Suicide ends the self, while voluntary enslavement betrays the self. On these grounds, we can say that while Mill was wrong to hold that people could be rightly prevented from selling themselves into slavery, he was right in expressing a liberal contempt for those who do.

Responsibility for Vice and Addiction

It is generally held that responsibility goes hand in hand with free choice. A person can be responsible only for what she has chosen freely. Since vices are moral failings, and since we tend to think that we can fail morally only if we are responsible for the failure, it would seem that vices must be freely chosen to be (real, *moral*) vices. This fits with the modern tendency to exclude from the moral what people cannot help doing (or being), and to treat the latter as a matter of nonmoral fortune. This tendency is, to be sure, part of the moral egalitarianism of the modern era, since setting aside those things that people cannot help leaves everyone at, so to speak, an equal starting point for being moral or immoral. This view of morality finds its strongest advocate in Kant, but it actually stretches back at least as far as Aristotle, who thought that virtue and vice are necessarily matters of choice.[21]

Aristotle was aware that his view led him into a very difficult tangle. Since he took virtues to be dispositions to act in certain ways (and not primarily as the acts themselves), he realized that once a person has, say, a vicious disposition, his vicious act might be said to be an effect of the force of that disposition, rather than a result of choice. Aristotle's response to this was that vicious dispositions are the result of habituation due to an accumulation of vicious acts in the past, and those acts were products of choice. The vicious man, then, if he doesn't choose his vicious act now, did choose the acts that made him vicious and thus chose to become the sort of person who has vicious dispositions.[22] This is not fully satisfactory, however, since it leaves us wanting to know why such a person chose those early vicious acts, and the answer to that seems to be that he was somehow the sort of person who was prone to make such choices. But, then, it doesn't seem to be possible to say that he chose to become that sort of person, without launching ourselves into an infinite regress.

The alternative to this is simply to say that people are appropriately morally evaluated in terms of the sorts of persons they are, irrespective of how they came to be that way, even if they couldn't help it. This approach was taken most clearly by Nietzsche, who rejected free will as a myth engendered by the weak to make the strong feel guilty about their strength. Nietzsche viewed the whole of Judeo-Christian morality as a revolt of slaves against their masters. The weak slaves succeeded in getting the strong masters to believe that their natural aggressiveness was a moral evil that they had freely chosen and for which they were thus responsible and guilty.

Rejecting the Judeo-Christian view, and the egalitarianism that follows in its wake, as a kind of sickness, Nietzsche strove to recapture an ancient, pre-Judeo-Christian ethic, whose terms of evaluation were "good and bad" rather than "good and evil." *Good and evil* correspond, respectively, to the slaves' valuation of their own weakness (their tendency to turn the other cheek) and their devaluation of the master's strength (his natural predatoriness). *Good and bad*, by contrast, correspond, respectively, to a valuation of the strong and the noble and devaluation of the weak and despicable. With belief in free will dismissed as a myth, this latter ethic is one that explicitly esteems qualities (such as strength) that simply characterize the sort of person someone is, without asserting that he has or even could have chosen to be that sort of person.[23]

Adapting these notions to our present purposes, we have two alternatives, which we can, with a bit of license, call the Aristotelian and the Nietzschean. The Aristotelian insists that vice must be chosen and thus that the vicious must be responsible for their vice, if it is to be vice at all. The Nietzschean holds that a natural disposition (which no one has chosen or is responsible for) can be a vice. I do not think that there is an a priori argument for preferring one of these approaches over the other. The Aristotelian fits our modern temper, but leads to a kind of puzzle when pushed to the extreme. The Nietzschean is clear and coherent, and yet it renders moral evaluation into the sort of evaluation we might make of (subhuman) animals, praising them as, so to speak, good specimens, for qualities, such as speed and grace, that are simply a matter of their makeup.

This last remark might suggest that there is some conceptual obstacle to calling the Nietzschean approach moral, since we do not normally think that moral appraisal is continuous with the sort of evaluations we make of animals. But it is precisely this latter claim that is called into question by Nietzsche's attack on modern morality. Nietzsche is explicitly calling for a redefinition of morality, and thus no conceptual analysis of the term as we define it will settle the issue. Moreover, insofar as dispositions lead people to be better or worse members of society and the like, there is a clear sense in which they are moral dispositions and their evaluation moral evaluation, even if the dispositions themselves are not chosen.

I think, rather, that all we can say is that to take Nietzschean appraisal as the fundamental type of moral appraisal is to mean something different by "morality" than we have come to mean by it in the modern era under the influence of the Judeo-Christian tradition that Nietzsche is at pains to critique. Moreover, the Aristotelian approach does seem to work satisfactorily as long as it is not pushed to the limit, and it is, in any case, more in line with the liberal theory at work in this chapter and this book. I shall therefore assume from here on that vices must be, in some common sense of the term, voluntary to be vices and thus that people with vices must be responsible for those vices. With this said, I shall take up the question of whether drug addictions can be said to be voluntary and drug addicts responsible for their addictions and for the actions those addictions can be said to cause.

In raising this question, it should be noted that the main action that drug addictions cause is that of taking the next dose of drugs. It is generally untrue that drugs cause people to do violent or criminal acts. While PCP may be an exception, addicting drugs normally pacify their users. The most antisocial thing that drug use can be said to cause is lassitude or what is sometimes given the technical name "amotivational syndrome." What causes crime is not drugs but their high price, which, coupled with the strong desire for the drugs, produces a powerful motivation for criminal acts. However, even if one attributes such acts to addiction, there is reason to believe that individuals who commit such acts are responsible for doing so.

Note that in making this claim, though I reach the same conclusion that Narveson does, I do not share his view that the question of responsibility is a pragmatic matter of determining the proper social response to addiction. The pragmatic problem is, of course, enormously important. Nonetheless, its solution depends on a factual question that must be answered first. The factual question is whether the addict could have acted otherwise. I believe that the answer to this is yes. This can be argued for in two ways.

First of all, there is the Aristotelian point, rightly adverted to by Narveson. Even if drug use were to make a person into some kind of blind robot, he would still be responsible for what he does in the robotic state *because he is responsible for having taken the drug in the first place before the robotic state began.* And if it be thought that addiction makes the addict into some kind of blind robot who must take drugs, then he would be responsible for what he does in that robotic state *because he is responsible for having taken the drugs that led him to become an addict, which was before that robotic state began.* A drunk driver may not know what he is doing when he veers off the road and kills a pedestrian. He is thus not responsible in the way that someone is who commits premeditated murder. Nonetheless, the drunk is responsible for the harm he causes because he wasn't drunk when he started drinking, and he is responsible for having started.

But, further, neither drugs nor addiction makes one into a blind robot. Drugs may cloud one's judgment and addiction adds the pain of withdrawal as an incentive to continued use, but neither takes control of one's actions in a way that makes one into an automaton. Even drug-beclouded individuals know the difference between right and wrong and can understand when they are hurting others and so on. And the pain of withdrawal that addicts may fear is surely less than the pain feared by, say, soldiers on a battlefield. If soldiers can still choose to do battle, addicts can hardly be thought to be unable to choose to face the pain of withdrawal.[24]

This may seem to fly in the face of the criterion for addiction that I cited earlier, namely, "having a compulsive inability to resist taking the drug despite the knowledge that it is harmful."[25] This criterion seems to suggest that it is the very nature of addiction that addicts are unable to stop their addictions, which, in turn, would suggest that addicts are not responsible for the continuation of their addictions. Note that even this leaves open the Aristotelian point that addicts are responsible for having started up their addictions (before they became addicts). And, if addicts are responsible for starting up their addictions, they are ultimately responsible for the continuation of their addictions, since in starting up an addiction one starts up something that continues. But, further, it is a mistake to think that the very nature of addiction entails that one can't stop. If that were so, we would have to say of people who do stop their addictions (and many do) that they were never really addicted! It seems more plausible to hold that addictions are very difficult to stop but, for the vast majority of people, not impossible to stop. This, of course, still leaves puzzles not unlike the one to which the Aristotelian view of responsibility for vice leads (and not unlike the related problem of weakness of the will: how people can fail to do what they recognize to be in their best interest). But these puzzles are not unique to the problem of addiction. They haunt all discussions of freedom and responsibility, without rendering these terms senseless.

It might be objected that there is a contradiction between saying that the addict can stop his addiction and saying that his addiction is a liberal vice, because the former implies that he has retained his ability for rational self-governance and the latter that he has surrendered that ability. But this puts the implications too strongly. The psychological truth seems to be that strong addiction is a powerful obstacle to self-control that can, with considerable effort, be controlled. Though the ability for self-governance is retained, it is voluntarily weakened, or, rather, the addict voluntarily increases the forces that w⸴ ˑʳ against it. This is captured in the liberal theory by characterizing vices as *dispositions* that *undermine* the sovereignty of practical reason. Dispositions, like habits, are hard but not impossible to overcome, and undermining something weakens it without necessarily destroying it entirely.

Consequently, given the account of strong addiction that I have set forth, I conclude that individual addicts are (in the vast majority of cases) responsible for their addictions, for their continued drug use and thus for their continued addiction, and for any other actions that addiction may be said to cause. And this means that insofar as the strength of their desire for the drug (or the strength of their fear of withdrawal) keeps them addicted *even though they know they would be better off without the drug or the addiction*, strong addicts can be held responsible for undermining the sovereignty of their practical reason over their lives or for cultivating dispositions that undermine that sovereignty. Then, their addictions are vices according to the liberal theory.

But this is not the whole story. The discussion so far has proceeded on the unstated assumption of what might be called "normal circumstances." Strong addiction is a vice because in choosing it one undermines one's ability to subject one's life over the long run to one's practical reason. This assumes normal circumstances because it omits the possibility that undermining one's ability for self-governance may be one's best act of self-governance—an omission that makes sense in normal circumstances. Given normal conditions, people have enough to gain from subjecting their whole lives to their practical reason, so that it is irrational in terms of their self-interest to surrender the capacity to do so. But the irrationality of choosing strong addiction is not an eternal truth, independent of context. If I was, say, in a concentration camp facing constant pain and fear and small hope of ultimate survival, there would be little to recommend sobriety if drugs were available, and little reason to take the long view of my life and protect my capacity for rational self-governance against the self-induced blandishments of addiction. Then, becoming an addict in a concentration camp would not be irrational. In short, if circumstances are bad enough, then strong addiction might be the best act of rational self-governance available, and then it would not be appropriate to call it a vice.[26]

The general point is that social conditions could be so awful that preserving one's ability to govern one's life over the long run would be of little or no value. Then, strong addiction would be rationally adaptive behavior, making the best out of a bad situation. And if those awful social conditions were unjust, unnecessary, and remediable, then who-ever was responsible for their existence and continuation would be re-sponsible for making what is normally a vice into, not a virtue, but a self-interestedly rational action. It is, of course, still a tragic loss. A life lived in a drug-induced cloud, driven from dose to dose by the lure of immediate pleasure and the fear of immediate pain, is still from a liberal (and just about any other) standpoint an inferior life that can only be "justified" by the extremity of the conditions to which it is a response. It is still a life in which the long-term sovereignty of practical reason—the condition for the unique dignity of human beings—has been sur-rendered, even if under the circumstances surrender is the individual's best alternative.

Note that such circumstances make strong addiction rational in the way that weak addiction is, although by opposite means. In both cases, the pleasures gained from the addiction suffice to make the addiction a rational strategy. But, since (by definition) weak addiction is one that would not survive recognition of its harmfulness, weak addiction is ra-tional because the pleasures are large and the dangers small. By con-trast, strong addiction under awful circumstances is rational because the advantages of preserving long-term self-governance have diminished to a point at which the short-term pleasures of addiction are the best alter-native available.

Further, the individual who surrenders his sovereignty by becoming an addict under awful circumstances makes a choice to do so and thus is *causally* responsible for the addiction. He is not, however, *morally* responsible for it, where this refers to the sort of responsibility for an action that makes one rightly the object of moral blame or praise for it. Moral responsibility for the addict's choice passes to whomever it is who is responsible for creating or maintaining conditions evil and awful enough to make surrender of sovereignty rational. We can reach this in the following way.

Conditions that are so bad must count as intolerable, virtually by definition. But, if someone confronts me with a choice between two alternatives where one is bad but tolerable and the other bad and intoler-able, that person *forces* me to opt for the tolerable alternative. I am forced to hand over my wallet to a gunman though he leaves it to me to choose between my money and my life. If addiction is chosen as a bad but tolerable alternative to (soberly facing and experiencing) intolerable conditions, then it is forced by whomever it is who is responsible for the intolerable conditions. And that implies that the forcer is morally culpable for the addiction and its likely consequences.

I think that this description applies to the situation of at least a substantial number of drug addicts in America's inner cities. They face awful circumstances that are unjust, unnecessary, and remediable, and yet that the society refuses to remedy. Addiction is for such individuals a bad course of action made tolerable by comparison to the intolerable conditions they face. In that case, I think that moral responsibility for their strong addictions, and for the vicious betrayal of human self-governance that these entail, passes to the larger society.

Notes

This chapter is a revised version of an article originally published in *Drugs, Morality, and the Law*, ed. S. Luper-Foy and C. Brown (New York: Garland, 1994), pp. 25–47. Reprinted with permission.

1. For more extensive discussion of the irrationality of the War on Drugs, as well as statistical evidence and citation of sources, see my *The Rich Get Richer and the Poor Get Prison: Ideology, Class, and Criminal Justice*, 4th ed. (Needham, Mass.: Allyn & Bacon, 1995), pp. 31–38; see also "The War on Drugs: Is It Time to Surrender?" *QQ: Report from the Institute for Philosophy and Public Policy* (University of Maryland) (Spring/Summer 1989): 1–5; and Jonathan Marshall, "How Our War on Drugs Shattered the Cities," *Washington Post*, 17 May 1992, p. C1.

2. "Capt. Alfred Broadbent, commander of the District's homicide squad . . . , estimated that as many as a third of last year's 489 homicides were tied to enforcers, an estimate that nearly matches the number of slayings police have classified as drug-related." Pierre Thomas and Michael York, "Enforcers Are D.C.'s Dealers of Death," *Washington Post*, 18 May 1992, pp. A1, A6.

3. See Sharon LaFraniere, "U.S. Has Most Prisoners Per Capita in the World," *Washington Post*, 5 January 1991, p. A3.

4. Immanuel Kant, "The Metaphysical Elements of Justice," pt. 1 of *The Metaphysics of Morals*, trans. J. Ladd (Indianapolis, Ind.: Bobbs-Merrill, 1965; originally published 1797), p. 35.

5. John Stuart Mill, *On Liberty* (Harmondsworth, England: Penguin Books, 1974; originally published 1859), p. 68.

6. Immanuel Kant, *Lectures on Ethics* (Indianapolis, Ind.: Hackett, 1980), pp. 157–59.

7. "Instead of diminution, there is need of a great increase of disinterested exertion to promote the good of others. . . . Human beings owe to each other

help to distinguish the better from the worse, and encouragement to choose the former and avoid the latter." Mill, *On Liberty*, p. 142.

8. Jan Narveson, "Drugs and Responsibility," in *Drugs, Morality, and the Law*, ed. S. Luper-Foy and C. Brown (New York: Garland, 1994), pp. 3–24.

9. Ibid., p. 13.

10. *International Dictionary of Psychology* (New York: Continuum, 1989), p. 9.

11. *Encyclopedia of Psychology* (New York: Wiley, 1984), p. 14.

12. "Over the lifespan of the [addictive] process, the high diminishes. The individual experiences progressively less relief with increasing degrees of tolerance." Ibid., p. 14.

13. For more on this debate and references to the literature, see William Galston, *Liberal Purposes* (New York: Cambridge University Press, 1991). See also Charles Larmore, *Patterns of Moral Complexity* (New York: Cambridge University Press, 1987), for what might be thought of as the position of the Rawlsian camp in this debate.

14. Alisdair MacIntyre, *After Virtue* (Notre Dame, Ind.: University of Notre Dame Press, 1981).

15. Michael Slote, "Agent-Based Virtue Ethics," *Midwest Studies in Philosophy* 20 (1995): 83–101. Slote has expressed some doubts about this particular suggestion, but not about the project of deriving morality from a standard of human excellence.

16. Perhaps this would account for the questionable moral status of professional boxing, with its substantial risk of brain damage.

17. Galston, *Liberal Purposes*, pp. 213–37.

18. For a classical account of the cardinal virtues, see Josef Pieper, *The Four Cardinal Virtues* (Notre Dame, Ind.: University of Notre Dame Press, 1966).

19. This, by the way, is an independent problem for virtue ethicists. Even if they succeed in demonstrating the real excellence of some standard of excellence, they still face the problem of explaining why failing to be excellent is a moral failure, and, indeed, why it is a failure at all for anyone who does not aspire to achieve excellence.

20. Mill, *On Liberty*, p. 173.

21. Aristotle, *Nicomachean Ethics*, trans. David Ross (Oxford: Oxford University Press, 1980), bk. 2, sec. 5; bk. 3, sec. 1–5.

22. Ibid., bk. 3, sec. 5.

23. Friedrich Nietzsche, *The Genealogy of Morals*, in *The Birth of Tragedy and the Genealogy of Morals,* trans. Francis Golffing (New York: Doubleday, 1956; originally published 1887), pp. 159–61, 178–80.

24. I have been influenced on this point by Phillip Scribner's "Do Drugs Deprive Us of Free Will?" in *Drugs, Morality, and the Law*, ed. S. Luper-Foy and C. Brown, pp. 79–110.

25. See note 10 above and accompanying text.

26. The same argument would suffice to show that Mill's contempt for the individual who sells himself into slavery is also appropriate only in normal circumstances. If the circumstances are bad enough, even this might be the best alternative and thus no vice.

4

The Labor Theory of the
Difference Principle

Viewing economic systems in terms of the proportions in which people are laboring for one another is uniquely appropriate to critical moral liberalism, because this way of looking at economic systems enables us to determine whether unjust domination is functioning in them by means of seemingly free exchanges. Accordingly, critical moral liberalism needs a principle of economic justice that specifies the terms under which people are laboring for one another that are fair and reasonable to all alike. I contend that, suitably interpreted, John Rawls's second principle of justice, the so-called difference principle, supplies critical moral liberalism with the needed standard of economic justice. I shall argue that interpreting the difference principle as a principle distributing labor rather than money or goods shows that the difference principle is a fairer standard of economic distribution than the free market and that it is a standard capable of determining the conditions under which capitalist, socialist, and communist economic arrangements are just. I shall show, as well, that so interpreting the difference principle makes good on Rawls's claim that it is a principle of reciprocal advantage, fair to better and worse off alike, and refutes those critics who have claimed that it is biased against the better-off members of society. I call this way of interpreting Rawls's second principle "the labor theory of the difference principle."

On the Alleged Bias of the Difference Principle

The difference principle holds that economic and social inequalities are just only insofar as they are to the greatest benefit of the least-advantaged group in the distribution.[1] A distribution is not fully just, then, as long as it is still possible, either by transfers within the distributive scheme or by replacing that scheme with another, to reduce the shares of the better-off groups in ways that improve the shares of worse-off groups over the long run.[2] Thus the difference principle requires redistribution from the better off to the worse off until that point after which the absolute size of the worse-off shares begins to diminish.[3] This feature of the difference principle has led a number of commentators to suspect that it is lopsided in favor of those at the lower end of society. Thomas Nagel, for example, finds Rawls's theory resting on the presumption "that sacrifice at the bottom is always worse than sacrifice at the top," or "that sacrifices which lessen social inequality are acceptable while sacrifices which increase inequality are not."[4] And R. M. Hare writes, "A maximin strategy would (and in Rawls does) yield principles of justice according to which it would always be just to impose any loss, however great, upon a better-off group in order to bring a gain, however small, to the least-advantaged group, however affluent the latter's starting point. If intuitions are to be used, this is surely counterintuitive."[5]

Against this, Rawls maintains that the difference principle is "a principle of mutual benefit," one under which individuals "do not gain at one another's expense since only reciprocal advantages are allowed."[6] Since it is "one of the fixed points of our considered judgments that no one deserves his place in the distribution of native endowments," the better-off individual is not entitled to claim that he deserves a greater share simply because he is more talented. Thus, he "cannot say that he deserves and therefore has a right to a scheme of cooperation in which he is permitted to acquire benefits in ways that do not contribute to the welfare of others. . . . From the standpoint of common sense, then, the difference principle appears to be acceptable both to the more advantaged and to the less advantaged individual."[7]

Rawls's argument here is not very satisfactory. Even if the better-off or more talented individual is not entitled "to acquire benefits in ways that do not contribute to the welfare of others," it does not follow that he is entitled to acquire benefits only in ways that *maximize* the welfare of others. For example, leaving distributions to the workings of the free market also, in effect, forbids anyone to benefit in ways that do not contribute to the welfare of others, since if the market is really free then only mutually beneficial exchanges will be agreed to, that is, only exchanges that improve the welfare of all parties to the exchange. The difference between the free market and the difference principle is that the former allows any outcome that improves the exchanging parties' welfare relative to its level before the exchange, while the latter allows only that outcome in which the worst-off party's share is the most it can possibly be and the best-off party's is the smallest necessary to achieve this. As such, Rawls's argument does not establish the superiority of subjecting distributions to the difference principle over letting the free market run its course, producing whatever inequalities it may.

Moreover, that the more talented do not deserve their greater talent does not in itself imply that they are entitled to benefit from those talents only in ways that benefit others. No doubt, the fact that people do not deserve their greater talents supports the notion that they are not entitled to benefit from those talents in ways that make others worse off. But why aren't they entitled to benefit from their talents in ways that have no net effect, positive or negative, on others?[8] On the face of it, it seems that Rawls is confusing justice with benevolence and insisting that the more talented have a positive duty to benefit others (regardless of what those others do for or to them) as a condition of the just enjoyment of the benefits of their own greater talents. It does not seem that the existence of such a positive duty is one of the fixed points in our considered judgments. What is more, even if we grant Rawls that people are not entitled to benefit from their talents in ways that do not improve the welfare of others, then this is surely true for both the more and the less talented. Yet the difference principle, in requiring reduction in the shares of the better off in order to maximize those of the worse off, seems to permit the latter to benefit in ways that do not improve the welfare of others. This suggests that the principle that no one should benefit from his abilities in ways that do not benefit others is being applied only to those with greater abilities, and this supports the charge that the difference principle is biased in favor of the least advantaged.[9] Indeed, we seem drawn to the conclusion that, if the principle that no one should benefit from his abilities in ways that do not benefit others is *either* applied evenhandedly to all groups in society *or* replaced with the less questionable principle that no one should benefit in ways that worsen the conditions of others, the difference principle is undermined.

Now, I believe that Rawls can answer these charges, but to do so requires a different interpretation of the difference principle. This different interpretation is not a matter of changing the difference principle per se but of changing our understanding of what the difference principle distributes, and this in turn depends on changing generally our understanding of what is being distributed in economic distributions. In what follows, I shall argue that, for the purpose of assessing the justice

of economic systems, it is appropriate to think of economic distributions as distributions of labor, rather than of goods or of money. Goods
are products of labor, and money is just paper if it is not an effective
claim on other people's labor (in the form of products or services). A
distribution of money is a distribution of titles to other people's labor,
and a particular distribution of income in a society is a quantitative
representation of the proportions in which the members of that society
work for one another. The implications of this conception are quite far
reaching. For example, if we take economic distributions as distributions of goods or money, redistributing from the better-off group to the
worse-off according to the difference principle appears to be imposing
a sacrifice on the former group for the benefit of the latter. Faced with
this, we shall naturally be prone to ask for a justification for taking from
the pockets of the rich to give to the poor. If, however, we understand
an economic distribution as a distribution of titles to the labor of others,
the greater shares of the better off will be seen to be made up, not of
their goods or money, but of *other people's* labor. Then we shall be
prone to ask for a justification for allotting the better off even as great
a share of other people's labor as the difference principle allows them.

I contend that viewing economic distributions as distributions of
labor enables us to see the superiority of the difference principle to the
free market and, I believe, to all alternative principles. Further, it shows
that *either* insisting that the principle that no one benefit from his talents
in ways that do not improve the welfare of others be applied evenhandedly to the more and the less talented *or* replacing this with the principle
that no one benefit in ways that worsen the condition of others supports
the difference principle, rather than undermining it. Moreover, it shows
that, either way, the difference principle is truly a principle of mutual
benefit, the only principle according to which each benefit conferred by
one person on another is matched by a reciprocating benefit. This
should dispose of the notion that the difference principle is biased in
favor of the least advantaged.

Before I proceed, it should be noted that the truth of the labor theory
of the difference principle does not presuppose the truth of the Marxian
labor theory of value, though if the latter is true, it surely supports the
former. The Marxian theory holds that, in a capitalist society, labor is
the "substance" of the exchange value of commodities; it is what actually regulates the proportions in which commodities exchange. The
labor theory of the difference principle rests on the weaker claim that,
for the purpose of morally evaluating alternative distributive systems, it
is appropriate to consider such systems as distributing, neither simply

goods nor money, but the labor that goes into those goods or that can be purchased with that money. This claim is weaker than the Marxian claim in that it asserts nothing about what actually regulates exchange. It would, however, be supported by the truth of the Marxian theory, since if labor is the substance of the value of commodities, then it is surely appropriate to consider distributions as distributions of labor.[10]

In the following section, "What Economic Distributions Distribute," I shall attempt to set forth the case for the appropriateness of viewing economic distributions as distributions of labor for the purpose of moral evaluation. In the section entitled "Justifying Unequal Distributions," I shall demonstrate the implications for the difference principle of viewing the principle as distributing labor, rather than money or goods. In the section on "The Difference Principle as a Principle of Reciprocal Advantage," I shall show how the labor theory of the difference principle enables us to make good on Rawls's claims about the principle. In the final section of this chapter, "Justifying Capitalism, Socialism, and Communism," I shall show how the difference principle enables us to identify the conditions under which capitalist, socialist, and communist standards of distribution match the requirements of justice.

What Economic Distributions Distribute

In Rawls's social contract theory, people must agree on a principle of economic justice while standing in an "original position" behind a "veil of ignorance" that deprives them of knowledge of their personal situation, including their particular moral conceptions. Because the agreement reached in the original position is supposed to establish the fundamental principles of justice, the parties to the agreement cannot consider themselves as already owning some goods, since this would make their agreement parasitic on some prior principle of what people are entitled to, when their agreement is meant to determine this in the first place. This is equally a reasonable constraint on moral thinking about distributive principles outside the original position, since, if we on the outside evaluate such principles from a baseline at which we assume that we already rightly own certain things, then, rather than arriving at a truly fundamental principle of distributive justice, we will arrive at some derivative of the principle that is effectively presupposed in treating our preexisting ownership as a valid baseline.[11]

Now, if we consider the batch of goods that makes up the social product, it is clear that the cost to individuals of that batch is either goods that they already own (for example, raw materials that have gone into production) or the labor that they have contributed to producing those goods (including the labor of obtaining raw materials, and so forth). Since moral philosophical considerations rule out thinking of individuals as already owning some goods, we are left with the recognition that what it costs individuals to produce the social product is their labor. Counting this cost is legitimate in or out of the original position because, even if people own nothing, they know that they have bodies and finite lifespans and thus that, as a matter of fact, the goods in the social product will cost them some quantity of their irreplaceable time and energy, that is, their labor.[12] And counting this cost is appropriate in light of the ideal of individual sovereignty, since time and energy are the basic resources available to individuals to devote to living according to their own judgments.

If the social product is being distributed among those who have produced it, then individuals are not simply receiving the goods that they themselves have produced. Rather, each receives goods that others have labored to produce. It follows that alternative principles of distribution establish, not merely different allocations of things, but different proportions in which individuals work for one another. Since their time and energy are finite, rational individuals will be concerned with how much of that time and energy will be spent serving their own purposes (which, of course, may be benevolent or charitable purposes),[13] and how much will be spent serving others. Consequently, it is appropriate for individuals in or out of the original position to consider alternative distributions as representing different proportions in which individuals labor for one another. Since "laboring for" is a social relation, I shall refer to the fact that economic distributions represent proportions in which individuals labor for one another as the "social dimension" of economic distributions. I contend that it is recognition of the crucial nature of this social dimension to creatures whose time and energy are finite that makes it appropriate to consider economic distributions as distributions of labor for the purpose of morally evaluating those distributions.

Consider that economic distributions might be thought of as distributions of goods, money, or labor. It might seem that little hinges on which one chooses, since each can be exchanged for—and thus be thought to represent—the other two. But, in fact, much hinges on the choice, since focus on money or goods hides, while focus on labor reveals, the social dimension of economic distributions. If we think of a distribution in terms of goods or money, then we shall see it as a matter of the relative size of each individual's share, how much money or goods each has. The relations between shares will be either quantitative (if one has more, another has less) or psychological (those with less may feel envious of those with more, and those with more may feel superior to those with less). What we shall not see is that, where one person possesses a good produced by another, the labor of that other has been put at the possessor's disposal. And where the goods produced by some group of cooperating individuals are distributed among them unequally, some will have more of other people's labor at their disposal than others have at theirs. The same can be said of money. If one person earns one hundred thousand dollars a year and others earn ten thousand a year, this is more than a difference in the size of each individual's share. It means as well that, in return for one year of his labor, the first person can have ten of the others work for him (provide him with products or services) for a year. This is not to say that such unequal distributions cannot be justified—rather, it is to say clearly what it is that must be justified if such unequal distributions can. I shall refer to the fact that focus on money or goods hides the social dimension of economic distributions as the "money illusion," although it should be clear that this refers equally to goods or money.[14]

Having said this much, I do not mean to suggest that it is never appropriate to consider the size of the shares of goods that individuals end up with as a result of different distributive principles. Rather, my claim is that this consideration is appropriate at a different and later point in the moral evaluation of such principles. Obviously, if economic distributions were *only* a matter of labor, that labor would be pointless. What makes it rational for individuals to contribute their labor to the social product is that they receive goods in return. Consequently, the size of the shares in goods that result from alternative distributions is an appropriate consideration in determining which among the alternatives it would be rational for all to choose. Thus I contend that the appropriate way for individuals in or out of the original position to evaluate alternative distributive principles is to view them as different systems of the proportions in which individuals labor for one another and then to consider the shares of goods that each such system yields in order to determine which it would be most rational for all to accept.

Justifying Unequal Distributions

Consider how the problem of arriving at a just economic distribution appears in light of the conclusions of the previous section. First of all, it is clear that we cannot approach this problem assuming that people with greater talents automatically deserve greater rewards. Rawls maintains that it is "one of the fixed points of our considered judgments that no one deserves his place in the distribution of native endowments" and thus that it is incorrect to think that those with greater gifts are more worthy and for that reason deserve greater rewards.[15] This is, to be sure, one of the fixed points of my considered judgments, but I am not as confident as Rawls is that this view is widely shared. The point, however, can be made much more directly and without dubious appeal to such "fixed points." Once we recognize that the substance of economic rewards is other people's labor, then it is obvious that the simple fact that A has greater talent than B is no reason to assert that A deserves some portion of B's labor. Nor can we assume, in the fashion of the defenders of the free market, that any exchange reached voluntarily by A and B is just. This puts the cart before the horse. It assumes in advance that the free market is the standard of justice, when what is needed is a determination of the standard of justice against which we could determine whether the free market did or did not yield just results. Moreover, since those with greater talent will probably be able to hold out for better terms than those with less talent, taking free market exchanges as our standard has the effect of smuggling the notion that greater talents deserve greater rewards back into our conception of a just distribution. Furthermore, we know that exchanges that broadly count as voluntary are affected by the relative power, wealth, or need of the exchangers, all of which factors may be arbitrary from the point of view of justice and thus may lead to unjust distributions if allowed to function. Thus neither greater rewards to greater talents nor free market exchanges will assuredly result in a just economic distribution. Nor, of course, am I claiming that either assuredly results in the reverse. Rather, the question of what constitutes a just distribution must be asked from a position of neutrality on these matters. From such a position, we can ask whether greater rewards to greater talents and free market exchanges are just.

If an economic distribution is a system of proportions in which individuals work for one another, we can find a just distribution by asking for reasonable terms for the exchange of labor (in one form or another) between persons. For this, we must first find some measure of labor that is independent of the laborer's level of talent. If we build the laborer's level of talent into the measure of his labor, then we will build into our reasonable terms for the exchange of labor the assumption that more talented labor automatically deserves greater reward. This not only violates our neutrality on this issue, but it again puts the cart before the horse, since what we want is a baseline against which we can determine if and when more talented labor does deserve a greater reward, that is, a claim on a greater share of the labor of less-talented others. Nor does such a baseline bias us against greater rewards for the greater talents. The point is that we cannot determine whether it is reasonable for some quantity of skilled labor to exchange for (earn title to) a greater quantity of unskilled labor, unless we have a quantitative measure of labor that is indifferent to whether it is skilled or not.

Two quantitative measures of labor that are indifferent to level of talent are *time labored* and *effort expended*. These give us not only an objective measure of labor independent of talent, but also a measure of the worth of labor to the laborer that is independent of his or her talent. That is, though individuals may differ in their natural gifts, they are alike in that their labor is a definite quantity of their total lifetime spent and a definite quantity of their total life energy expended—neither of which can be replaced. Moreover, while both these measures are independent of talent or natural gifts, neither is independent of the training that goes into developing talents or gifts. Such training is also measurable in time or effort and can be thought of as factored into the time labored or effort expended in any given exchange. For reasons of simplicity, let us select time labored as our standard since it is more easily measured than effort expended. However, what I shall say about time labored could be said equally of effort expended or even of some combination of time and effort expended.

If we measure labor in terms of time labored, we shall naturally judge unequal distributions against a baseline distribution in which the goods or money each person receives represents an amount of time labored by others that is equal to the amount of time that she has labored herself. It may appear that the selection of this as our baseline biases the discussion because it has the effect of requiring deviations from equality to be justified in a way that equality itself need not be. But this starting point is not biased, because it is not selected on the basis of a presumption in favor of equality. It is selected, rather, by subtracting the effect of talent on the measure of labor so that we can have a non-question-begging way of considering the claim that more-talented labor deserves greater rewards. Moreover, since time labored includes time invested in training, all that is subtracted is the effect of natural gifts themselves. Since our standard then includes what people do with their natural gifts while subtracting the effect of those gifts themselves, we subtract only that which in no way results from the individual's own choices or actions. That is, we subtract only that for which the claims of desert are dubious. On the other hand, the amount of time a person labors for others is the result of her own choices and actions and thus unquestionably a ground of desert (if anything is). If more talented labor is entitled to greater rewards, these rewards will be produced by other people's labor. Thus it is reasonable to test the dubious claim that greater talent deserves greater rewards against a baseline in which all that counts is what does result from individuals' choices and actions, that is, time labored.

If we assume (again for simplicity's sake) that everyone works the same amount of time, we can say that in the equal distribution that is our baseline, everyone contributes and receives the products of the same time labored, say t hours.[16] Put otherwise, we can represent this distribution as a series of exchanges between everyone and everyone else in which each gives and receives t hours labored, in the form of services or products. If an equal distribution can be represented as such a series of exchanges, it can be represented even more simply as an exchange between any two members of society selected at random. Assume that we select A and B, who are exchanging t for t and thus ending up with equal shares. Against this baseline, A asserts that she is more talented than B and thus entitled to something better than an equal share. A claims that her t hours of labor given to B should bring $t + n$ hours of labor from B to her in return. The question of whether an unequal distribution is just, then, comes down to whether and when it would be reasonable for A and B to exchange t hours of A's labor for $t + n$ hours of B's labor. This is, in effect, how the question of justifying economic inequality arises in Rawls's version of the social contract, and the analysis in the remainder of this chapter can be viewed as an application of the social contract to the problem of economic justice.[17]

We must remember that A and B are to be thought of, not as traders bringing goods from distant zones, but as members of a single economic system, a cooperative scheme in which what each gives and gets affects the total amount produced and thus the absolute value of everyone's share. In this light, it will be reasonable for B to contribute $t + n$ hours of labor to A in return for A's t hours of labor, if the result is to increase output in a way that makes B better off than he was when he was giving and receiving t hours. And, of course, it must make B better off in an amount greater than the output of n alone, since he could conceivably have worked the additional n hours for himself and added the resultant output to what he received when all were giving and receiving t.

Thus it will be rational for B to contribute $t + n$ hours of labor to A where the result is to increase B's share by m (a quantity of *goods,* not labor, as A's labor for B is still t), where m is the surplus over B's share when he and A contributed t, plus what B could produce for himself with n. Presumably, this could happen where giving B's $t + n$ to A worked as an incentive to bring out A's greater talents in a way that raised overall output and increased B's share by m. We can say that it would be rational for A and B to exchange t hours of A's labor for $t + n$ hours of B's, whenever the increment of n hours to A is sufficient to encourage her to devote her talents to the cooperative venture in a way that results in an increment to B of m goods.

A numerical example will help here. Imagine that a society has only two groups, those with greater than average talents, the As, and those with average abilities, the Bs. We can then think of the economic distribution in this society as an exchange of labor between an A and a B as representatives of their groups. Assume that As produce loaves of bread and Bs produce cups of sugar and that the average level of output in the society is one loaf or one cup per hour labored. Assuming that without a special incentive As produce at the average level, an equal distribution (for a day's labor) looks like table 1.

Table 1. Equal Distribution

	A	B
Measured in labor time	8 hours	8 hours
Measured in goods	8 loaves	8 cups

In this case, A and B each contribute eight hours of their labor to each other, in the form of an exchange of eight loaves for eight cups. A receives one cup for an hour of her labor, and B receives one loaf for an hour of his.

Assume now that with some incentive A can double her output, and that the minimum increment that will function as an incentive to bring out this heightened productivity voluntarily is a 50 percent increase in what she earns per hour. Nothing less makes enough of a difference to A. Since B always works at the average level of productivity, this will require B to work proportionately 50 percent longer. Since this is the minimum incentive that A will accept and the lowest increase in productivity she gives in return, we can refer to this case as that of the lowest minimum incentive. Under it, the resulting distribution would be

Table 2. Lowest Minimum Incentive

	A	B
Measured in labor time	8 hours	12 hours
Measured in goods	16 loaves	12 cups

In this case, A trades eight hours of her labor for twelve hours of B's (the t for $t + n$ in our previous discussion), in the form of an exchange of sixteen loaves for twelve cups. In this case, the range of inequality is that A earns 150 percent of what B earns, that is, A receives, for a day's labor (based on an eight-hour workday), money sufficient to purchase a day and a half of B's labor. Here A receives one and one-half cups for an hour of her labor and B receives one and one-third loaves for an hour of his. The exchange, for A, is reasonable *ex hypothesi,* that is, we set it at the minimum incentive that A would find reasonable to bring forth her more productive efforts voluntarily. The exchange is reasonable for B because he receives an additional one-third loaf for every hour of his work over and above what he had in the equal distribution (the m in our previous discussion).

Let us assume further that A can produce even more than sixteen loaves in a day. Her maximum productivity is twenty-four loaves. For this, the minimum incentive that she will accept is a 100 percent increase in what she earns per hour (compared to equal distribution). Since B always works at the average level of productivity, this incentive will require B to work proportionately 100 percent longer (compared to equal distribution). Since this incentive is the minimum that A will accept for her new level of productivity, and since this is her highest level of productivity, we can refer to this case as that of the highest minimum incentive. Under it, the resulting distribution would be

Table 3. Highest Minimum Incentive

	A	B
Measured in labor time	8 hours	16 hours
Measured in goods	24 loaves	16 cups

In this case, A trades eight hours of her labor for sixteen hours of B's, in the form of an exchange of twenty-four loaves for sixteen cups. In this case, the range of inequality is that A earns twice what B earns, that is, A receives, for a day's labor, money sufficient to purchase two days of B's labor. Here, A receives two cups for an hour of her labor and B receives one and one-half loaves for an hour of his. Once again, for A, the exchange is reasonable *ex hypothesi*. It is reasonable for B because he receives an additional one-half loaf for every hour of his work over and above what he had in the equal distribution (a higher *m* than in table 2).

Now it should be clear that, though sixteen cups is the minimum that A will take for the twenty-four loaves she produces in a day, there is a range above sixteen that she could ask for which would still leave B better off than he was under equal distribution. So, for example, if A were to demand twenty-three cups in return for her twenty-four loaves, B would have to work twenty-three hours to get the twenty-four loaves, and thus he would end up earning $1\frac{1}{23}$ loaves for each hour labored, which is still better than the one loaf per hour he received under equal distribution. Thus, assuming that sixteen cups is A's bottom line, were A to offer her twenty-four loaves to B on the free market, B would find it rational to pay anywhere from sixteen to twenty-three cups in return. Thus we can say that were these exchanges left to the market, the resultant distribution would be indeterminate in this range since any trade of twenty-four loaves for anything between sixteen and twenty-three cups would be beneficial to A and B. (I am assuming that, wherever the trade is set within this indeterminate range, all the effects of market forces—competition, supply and demand, and so on—have already done their work, and no further reduction in prices can be expected.)[18] Under the free market, the resulting distribution would be

Table 4. Free Market Range

	A	B
Measured in labor time	8 hours	16 to 23 hours
Measured in goods	24 loaves	16 to 23 cups

In this case, A trades eight hours of her labor for anywhere from sixteen to twenty-three hours of B's in the form of an exchange of twenty-four loaves for anything from sixteen to twenty-three cups. The maximum range of inequality that could result from these exchanges would have A earning $2\frac{7}{8}$ as much as B; A would receive, for a day's labor, money sufficient to purchase $2\frac{7}{8}$ days (twenty-three hours) of B's labor. For A, any of these exchanges are reasonable *ex hypothesi;* they start at her minimal acceptable incentive and improve from there. Any of these exchanges are reasonable for B because he receives at least $1\frac{1}{23}$ loaves per hour, which is still more than the one loaf an hour he receives under equal distribution. (I am momentarily ignoring table 2 to keep matters simple. If it were included, that would only change the range of possible mutually beneficial market exchanges, not the point being made.)

Now, of the four cases discussed, it should be clear that the difference principle requires the third, where A and B exchange twenty-four loaves for sixteen cups. This is the case in which the inequality between the best-off and the worst-off representative persons, A and B, is reduced to the minimum (sixteen hours of B's labor in return for eight hours of A's) compatible with maximizing the worst off's share (B gets twenty-four loaves, or one and one-half per hour). Were the inequality reduced further, A would not produce twenty-four loaves a day, and thus B's share would decline. Were the inequality to be increased, B would be giving more than sixteen hours to A. Thus B's share (per hour) would decline, and, in any event, the inequality would be more than is necessary to maximize B's share. Using the notation introduced earlier, we can say that the difference principle permits inequalities, exchanges of t for $t + n$ hours of labor, where n is the smallest increment that will produce the largest m for the worst-off person in the distribution. In the third case, n is eight hours of B's labor and m is the surplus of half a loaf per hour that B gets over what he would have in an equal distribution.

The Difference Principle as a Principle of Reciprocal Advantage

Consider now how the objection that the difference principle is biased in favor of the worse off and against the better off arises, and how it is cast in new light by viewing economic distributions as distributions of labor. If A could have gotten twenty-three cups for her twenty-four loaves on the market and the difference principle allows her only sixteen cups, then this does seem a lopsided affair, since no limitation is placed on B's share, and especially since the exchange of twenty-three cups for twenty-four loaves would also have improved B's position. Moreover, if our distributive system operates on a free market basis with taxation and transfer payments used to bring distributions in line with the difference principle, A will first have gotten her twenty-three cups and then the government will come along, forcibly confiscate seven of these, and transfer them back to B. This, of course, looks, at best, like Robin Hood stealing from the rich to give to the poor and, at worst, like forcing A to labor for B on terms not of her choosing.[19]

This is, indeed, how the redistribution ordered by the difference principle looks if we think of an economic distribution as a matter of individuals' shares in money or goods. If, instead, we view the distribution as a matter of individuals' shares in other people's labor, things take on an entirely different cast. In this light, the seven cups that A might get on the market (above the sixteen allowed by the difference principle) represent seven additional hours of B's labor for A. What gives A the right to have B labor these additional seven hours for her? We cannot simply say that she has this right because B would agree to it on the free market, because that assumes in advance that free market exchanges are just, which is what we are trying to determine. Such exchanges may simply reflect A's greater power to hold her products off the market, and this may be a power that is unjust or that produces unjust outcomes. To stay neutral on the question of the justice of market exchanges, we must ask what benefits B derives from working these additional seven hours for A. The answer is none. This labor produces no benefits for B that he could not already have working sixteen hours to produce the sixteen cups that *(ex hypothesi)* A would have accepted for her twenty-four loaves.

Considering economic distributions as distributions of labor, it becomes clear that in limiting A to sixteen cups from B, the difference principle is not confiscating seven cups from A. It is prohibiting A from obtaining additional labor from B without benefiting B in return. B's labor beyond the sixteen hours necessary to produce sixteen cups *results in no additional benefit for B*. If, on the market, A can get more than sixteen hours of labor from B *without conferring additional benefits on B*, then this must reflect A's favorable market position, due to B's need or A's greater talent, facts that are arbitrary from the standpoint of justice. This is what the difference principle prohibits.

This is also why the difference principle is truly a principle of mutual benefit. In setting the distribution at twenty-four loaves for sixteen cups, it assures that A and B are benefited for all of the labor that each contributes to the other. A is benefited; *ex hypothesi,* sixteen is the minimum she would find reasonable compensation for producing her twenty-four loaves. B, on the other hand, in producing the sixteen cups, does only that much additional labor (above the baseline of equal exchanges) for which he receives benefits in return. For A to ask for more is to ask B to work for her additionally for no additional compensation. This is (or should have been) Rawls's answer to the better-off representative man to show that he "has no grounds for complaint" when his share is limited by the difference principle. He cannot complain because the only limit on his greater share is that every increment of greater-than-equal labor that others contribute to him must make those others better off as well. This is how Rawls could show that the difference principle is "a fair basis on which those better endowed . . . could expect others to collaborate with them."[20]

This also enables us to see clearly the difference between the difference principle and free market exchanges. We can represent the range of inequality in our example by the fraction *(t + n)/t,* since A's income is *(t + n)/t* times B's (that is, A is paid for *t* hours of her labor enough money to purchase the products of *t + n* hours of B's labor). Such inequalities are reasonable if they produce a surplus *m* for B over what B could have gotten for his *t + n* hours under conditions of equality. We can think of an unequal distribution, then, as an exchange in which B contributes *n* to A in return for A's *m* to B. The free market allows any exchange of *n* for *m* that leaves both parties better off than before the exchange. (In our example, this means that *n* can vary between eight and fifteen hours of B's labor, above the eight hours represented by *t.*) The difference principle allows only the *smallest n* that will encourage A to produce *m* in return (this *n* is eight hours in our example). If a larger *n* will produce a larger *m,* then the difference principle requires this larger *n.* (This is why the difference principle requires the third rather than the second of the cases in our example.) The difference between free market exchanges and the difference principle, then, is this: The market requires only that the *total n* yield a surplus of *m* to B. The difference principle requires that *every unit of n* from B to A yield a unit of *m* for B. Thus the market would allow *n* to go to fifteen hours because this total still leaves B with a surplus (an additional 1/23 loaf per hour). But the difference principle limits *n* to eight hours because the units of *n* beyond this yield no additional unit of *m* to B.[21] Here lies the superiority of the difference principle to free market exchanges.

The "money illusion" obscures the nature of this limit. It makes the difference principle appear as confiscating A's money (or goods) and giving them to B, when in fact the principle is limiting B's labor for A. It is this illusion that leads to the error of thinking that the difference principle simply imposes sacrifices on the better off for the benefit of the worse off. Once the money illusion is dispelled, the share of the best off is seen to be constituted by the labor of others. Limiting this share is not imposing a sacrifice on the best off; it is making sure that those whose labor constitutes this share receive compensation in return and give no extra labor that does not receive such compensation. On the other hand, the best-off's share is allowed to rise to that point necessary to make it reasonable for her to work voluntarily in the ways that benefit those whose labor constitutes that share. This shows, I believe, more clearly than Rawls has been able to, that the difference principle is a principle of reciprocal advantage.

Earlier, I maintained that viewing the difference principle as distributing labor rather than money or goods would show that the defense of the difference principle is compatible, first, with insisting that both more-talented and less-talented persons benefit from their talents only in ways that benefit others and, second, with the less controversial notion that persons should not benefit from their talents in ways that worsen the condition of others. Now we can see that the difference principle's compatibility with both of these precepts appears problematic only when distributions are taken as distributing money (and what holds of money, holds equally of goods). It is only when the difference principle is thought of as taking the more-talented person's money and giving it to the less talented that the difference principle seems to require only of the more talented that they benefit in ways that improve others. Viewing the difference principle as distributing labor, however, we see that when it "takes" the more-talented person's money it is in reality limiting her share of the less-talented person's labor, and it is limiting it at the point at which both persons benefit from their talents only on terms that benefit others: The more talented gets her greater-than-equal share $(t + n)$ only insofar as she gives a compensating benefit (m) to the less talented. And the less talented receives this benefit only insofar as he gives his greater-than-equal labor time in return. All that the difference principle does when it "takes" money from the more talented is limit the n hours of labor by the less talented for the more to that point after which no further benefit is contributed in return from the more talented to the less. This only prevents the more talented from earning additional increments of n without conferring additional benefits on those whose labor constitutes n. On the other hand, by allowing n to rise as high as is necessary to maximize m, the difference principle insists that the less talented receive benefits only in return for exercising their talents in ways that benefit the more talented as much as is necessary to make it reasonable for them to produce and contribute m in return. Thus both groups are able to benefit from their talents only insofar as they benefit others.

As for the second precept referred to above—that no one should benefit from their talents in ways that worsen the condition of others—it is again only the money illusion that makes it appear that the difference principle confuses benevolence with justice and imposes a positive duty on the more talented to benefit others as a condition of their (the more talented group's) reaping the benefits of their own greater talents. If the difference principle distributes labor rather than money, then it is not insisting that the more talented give some of their money away to the less—it is insisting that the more talented take no more labor from the less talented than they give benefits for in return. Inasmuch as the difference principle prevents the more talented from benefiting in ways that cost the less talented more labor without benefiting them in return, the difference principle is preventing the more talented from benefiting in ways that worsen the condition of the less talented.

These challenges to the difference principle can be met because viewing economic distributions as distributions of labor brings to light the social nature of economic distributions, the way in which the benefits of one person are the burdens of another. Focus on money or goods, by contrast, makes economic distributions appear as relations between separate individuals, each of whom starts with some quantity of benefits unrelated to the burdens of others. Viewing economic distributions as distributions of money is seeing them occurring among the separate islands of an archipelago. Requiring a rich islander to give his money or goods to a poor islander across the sea then appears as forcing charity in the guise of justice. Viewing economic distributions as distributions of labor, by contrast, has the effect of draining the water from the archipelago and revealing how the islands are connected as peaks of an unbroken landmass. From this view, the wealth of rich "islanders" is seen connected to, indeed, constituted by, the labor of poor ones. Requiring the rich person to give his money to the poor then appears only as limiting the rich person's control over the poor one's labor—and this brings the issue clearly out of the realm of charity and into that of justice.

Justifying Capitalism, Socialism, and Communism

It should not be thought that the interpretation of the difference principle I have given here implies that the principle can operate only between people who are actually contributing their labor to the social product, nor does it imply that greater rewards must flow directly and exclusively to those with greater talents.[22] Note that reference to greater talent implies here no belief in the greater inherent worth of some than others. Greater talent is defined internally to any ongoing economic system. It represents any above-average capacity to produce more of the things that people desire in that system. Now, once a system with the rationale

I have outlined got going, there would be no particular limit on the size of $t + n$ relative to t, as long as a suitably large m were returned to the worse off. If $t + n$ became so large that an individual could not himself spend it in his lifetime or did not wish to, he could give or bequeath some of it to others, who might not have to work at all. As long as this magnitude of $t + n$ were necessary to evoke the m, this distribution would still be justified according to the difference principle. Moreover, as long as it were reasonable for the worse off to contribute their $t + n$ to those with greater talents in return for m, it would be reasonable for them as well to contribute their $t + n$ to a scheme that yielded them m even if this meant that the $t + n$ did not end up in the hands of those whose talents went into m. That is, once economic distributions are seen as distributions of labor, any distribution that satisfies the difference principle, by minimizing inequality between the best- and the worst-off groups and maximizing the share of the worst-off group (and, à la the lexical difference principle,[23] the shares of all groups in between), is a distribution in which no one labors more for others than is necessary to yield him benefits in return. Thus any such society is truly one in which people labor for one another on mutually beneficial terms.

These last remarks show the conditions under which a capitalist economy would be one in which people labor for one another on terms that are fair to better and worse off alike. Since the free market is open ended in its outcomes, it might spontaneously yield the distribution required by the difference principle. More likely, this would have to be achieved by government intervention in the form of redistributive taxation and welfare policies, aimed at reducing inequalities and improving the share of the worse off until the point of diminishing returns. Nevertheless, the result would still be essentially a capitalist economy, perhaps of the sort seen in recent years in Sweden. (Indeed, Rawls spends considerable time in *A Theory of Justice* describing the institutions of just such a modified capitalist economy.)[24]

This conclusion might appear to confirm Marxist suspicions that the difference principle is just an ideological justification of capitalism, albeit clothed in the garments of the welfare state. But this would be a mistake. The fact is that the difference principle is neutral as to capitalist, socialist, and communist systems of distribution. Which system is just, according to the principle, depends strictly on empirical conditions. That is, under appropriate conditions, the difference principle leads to the distributive standard associated with socialism and, under yet other conditions, to the standard associated with communism, as these standards have been enunciated by Marx in *The Critique of the*

Gotha Program.[25] There, Marx introduced two standards of distribution, one for the first phase of communism as it emerges after capitalism and one for the second, or higher, phase that emerges when productivity is so great that scarcity is, for all intents and purposes, overcome. Following a long tradition, I shall refer to the first phase as "socialism" and the higher phase as "communism."

Marx's distributive standard for socialism is identical to what we identified earlier as the baseline of equal exchanges of labor time. At this stage, Marx wrote, the laborer "receives a certificate from society that he has furnished such and such an amount of labour . . . , and with this certificate he draws from the social stock of means of consumption as much as costs the same amount of labour. The same amount of labour which he has given society in one form he receives back in another."[26] Marx's distributive standard for communism is the famous slogan, "From each according to his ability, to each according to his needs."[27]

Recall that the difference principle allows deviation from the baseline of equal exchanges of labor time, when incentives are needed to draw forth the more productive labor of the more talented members of society so as to maximize the share of the rest. Since the calculation of labor time at the baseline of equal exchanges includes time spent training and developing one's talents, such incentives in effect reward people for their possession of greater-than-average natural abilities. I say "in effect" because people are rewarded, not merely for possessing greater talents, but for using them in ways that improve the shares of others. Nevertheless, since this amounts to unequal rewards for equal amounts of labor, its resultant effect is to bestow greater rewards on those who happen to have greater talents. For reasons outside of their control, those with lesser abilities have no chance to receive these greater rewards. Now, Rawls himself recognizes that fortune in the distribution of natural abilities is arbitrary and thus inappropriate as a ground for greater reward.[28] This is what leads him to require that the incentives work to the benefit of the rest of society, not just the more talented ones. Nevertheless, since fortune in the distribution of natural abilities is an arbitrary ground, allowing such incentives must still be viewed as a necessary accommodation to human nature as it is, necessary since the alternative would seem to be overt and substantial coercion (if it is even possible at all to organize production efficiently by means of such coercion).[29]

If the difference principle justifies this accommodation when it is necessary to maximize the share of the worst off, it follows that the accommodation is no longer justified when no longer necessary. In short, if history brought us to a point at which either people were so enlightened as to no longer need inequalities as incentives for more productive labor or production were so efficiently organized that what everyone would do in exchange for an equal share were enough to maximize the share of the worst off, inequalities would no longer be necessary to maximize that share and thus no longer be allowed under the difference principle. What would remain as the standard of just distribution would be the baseline of equal exchanges of labor time, Marx's socialist principle. It follows that, under the difference principle, the question of whether economic justice requires capitalism or socialism is answered by determining if the conditions obtain in which incentives are no longer necessary to maximize the share of the worst off.[30]

Much the same can be said of the question of whether economic justice requires socialism or communism. Marx's communist principle is a more perfect principle of equality than his socialist principle. That is, the socialist principle countenances inequalities that the communist principle does not. Since the difference principle requires reducing inequalities down to that point necessary to maximize the share of the worst off, it leads from capitalism to socialism when capitalist inequalities are no longer necessary, and it leads from socialism to communism when socialist inequalities are no longer necessary. This is hard to see because the socialist principle appears to be a perfectly egalitarian principle, while the communist principle no longer requires equal shares at all. This has led some commentators to take Marx's move from the socialist to the communist principle to reflect abandonment of egalitarianism.[31] Marx's reasons for the move, however, indicate that just the reverse is the case. Since misinterpretations of this move are so widespread, it will repay us to quote Marx's explanation of it at length. Having stated the socialist principle of equal reward for equal time labored, Marx wrote,

> [T]his *equal right* is still stigmatized by a bourgeois limitation. The right of the producers is *proportional* to the labour they supply; the equality consists in the fact that measurement is made with an *equal standard,* labour.
>
> But one man is superior to another physically or mentally and so supplies more labour in the same time, or can labour for a longer time; and labour, to serve as a measure, must be defined by its duration or intensity, otherwise it ceases to be a standard of measurement. The *equal* right is an unequal right for unequal labour. It recognizes no class differences, be-

cause everyone is only a worker like everyone else; but it tacitly recognizes unequal individual endowment and thus productive capacity as natural privileges. *It is, therefore, a right of inequality in its content, like every right.* Right by its very nature can consist only in the application of an equal standard; but unequal individuals (and they would not be different individuals if they were not unequal) are measurable only by an equal standard in so far as they are brought under an equal point of view, are taken from one *definite* side only, for instance, in the present case, are regarded *only as workers* and nothing more is seen in them, everything else being ignored. Further, one worker is married, another not; one has more children than another, and so on and so forth. Thus, with an equal performance of labour, and hence an equal share in the social consumption fund, one will in fact receive more than another, one will be richer than another, and so on. To avoid all these defects, right instead of being equal would have to be unequal.[32]

It is probably this last statement that has led commentators to think that Marx's move from the socialist to the communist principle is a move away from egalitarianism. But this overlooks the nature of those defects in the socialist principle that the communist principle is meant to avoid. As the quote indicates, those defects are the inequalities that result from measuring naturally unequal (that is, differently endowed) people by an equal standard. Interestingly enough, those are the same sort of defects that led from the capitalist to the socialist principle, namely, rewarding people more because of their greater natural endowments or, as Marx has it, allowing these endowments to function as "natural privileges." The communist principle avoids those defects because it makes each person his own standard: each person's productive contribution is measured against his own abilities, and his share in consumption is measured against his own needs. Thus, though what each contributes and receives is a different amount, all have their unique abilities equally taxed and their unique needs equally satisfied. Compared to this, the socialist principle is still a principle that allows inequalities.

For Marx, it is the effective conquest of scarcity that allows transcendence of the socialist principle, with its defects, and movement to the communist: When "all the springs of cooperative wealth flow more abundantly—only then can . . . society inscribe on its banner: From each according to his ability, to each according to his needs!"[33] The substantial overcoming of scarcity makes this possible because, with abundance, it is no longer necessary to force people to labor by making how much they consume depend on how much they labor. Once it is no longer necessary to do this, it is no longer necessary to measure people's contributions and rewards by a common measure. And once it is no longer necessary to do this, it is possible to avoid the inequalities that result from measuring differently endowed people by an equal standard, and instead allow each to be his own standard.

Rather than the difference principle being a justification of capitalism at the expense of socialism and communism, all three turn out to be "cases" of the difference principle: The difference principle requires socialism over capitalism when historical conditions are such that incentives are no longer necessary to maximize the share of the worst off, and it requires communism over socialism when historical conditions are such that it is no longer necessary to tie consumption to production and measure each by a common standard. It follows that, under the difference principle, the argument among defenders of capitalist, socialist, and communist distributive principles comes down to determining which of these historical conditions obtain. If my argument—that the difference principle is really a principle of reciprocal advantage, fair to all producers alike—is valid, then this determination should settle the question of economic justice.

This conclusion, it must be noted, holds of economic distributions considered in abstraction from their accompanying social, legal, and political arrangements. For critical moral liberalism, the justice of real social systems will depend, not only on the justice of their economic distributions, but on the effect of the totality of economic, social, legal, and political arrangements on people's ability to live according to their own judgments. The determination of economic justice constitutes only a part of this more complex problem.

Notes

This chapter is a revised version of an article originally published in *Philosophy and Public Affairs* 12, no. 2 (Spring 1983): 133–59. Copyright 1983 by Princeton University Press. Reprinted with permission.

1. John Rawls, *A Theory of Justice* (Cambridge, Mass.: Harvard University Press, 1971), pp. 60, 302. As Rawls presents it, the difference principle applies to all social and economic inequalities (other than inequalities in liberty, which are prohibited by his first principle of justice). I shall treat it strictly as a principle of economic distribution.

2. "A scheme is unjust when the higher expectations [that is, the expectations of the better-off groups in the distribution], one or more of them, are excessive. If these expectations were decreased, the situation of the least fa-

vored would be improved. How unjust an arrangement is depends on how excessive the higher expectations are." Ibid., p. 79. Note that any unequal distribution can be altered in a way that immediately benefits those with smaller shares. If, however, the greater shares of the better off are functioning successfully as incentives to bring out higher productivity, then the reduction in inequality will have the long-term effect of decreasing the absolute size of the smaller shares and will be ruled out by the difference principle. Further, if the worst-off share in one distributive system is smaller than in another system, then, all things being equal, it is still possible to improve the worst-off share in the first system, and redesign of the first system along the lines of the second is thus required by the difference principle.

3. Speaking of the conditions under which inequality in the life prospects of members of an entrepreneurial and a working class would be just, Rawls writes, "The inequality in expectation is permissible only if lowering it would make the working class even more worse off." Ibid., p. 78.

4. Thomas Nagel, "Rawls on Justice," in *Reading Rawls,* ed. Norman Daniels (New York: Basic Books, 1975), p. 13.

5. R. M. Hare, "Rawls' Theory of Justice," in *Reading Rawls,* ed. Daniels, p. 107; see also Robert Paul Wolff, *Understanding Rawls* (Princeton, N.J.: Princeton University Press, 1977), pp. 173–74.

6. Rawls, *Theory of Justice,* pp. 102, 104.

7. Ibid., p. 104.

8. Some renderings of the difference principle— particularly what Rawls calls the "lexical difference principle" (ibid., pp. 82–83)—suggest that once the worse-off shares have been maximized, the better-off shares can be improved, as long as this does not worsen the shares below them. Thus it might seem that the difference principle does allow people to benefit from their greater talents in ways that do not worsen the shares of others, or that have no net effect on those shares. But note that this occurs only *after* the smaller shares have been maximized, and of course they have been maximized, if need be, at the expense of the larger shares. Thus the only terms on which the difference principle allows people to benefit from greater talents in ways that do not worsen, or have no net effect on, the shares of others is when there is no further way that those greater benefits can be reduced to improve the shares of those who are worse off.

9. Robert Nozick, for example, imagines the more-talented members of society responding to the less-talented members' proposal that they cooperate according to the difference principle. "How generous these proposed terms are might be seen by imagining that the better endowed make the almost symmetrical proposal: 'Look, worse endowed: you gain by cooperating with *us.* If you want our cooperation you'll have to accept reasonable terms. We propose these terms: We'll cooperate with you so long as *we* get as much as possible. . . .' If these terms seem outrageous, as they are, why don't the terms proposed by those worse endowed seem the same?" Robert Nozick, *Anarchy, State, and Utopia* (New York: Basic Books, 1974), p. 195.

10. It is my view that the widespread rejection of the labor theory of value by English-speaking scholars is the result of misconceptions about the theory shared by Marxists and non-Marxists alike. A book that goes very far toward rectifying these misconceptions is John Weeks's *Capital and Exploitation* (Princeton, N.J.: Princeton University Press, 1981). Though the labor theory of the difference principle and the Marxian theory are independent, it is, I believe, an implication of my argument that those who are sympathetic to the labor theory of value should be sympathetic to the difference principle, and vice versa.

11. It is striking how frequently this feature of the problem of establishing fundamental principles of distributive justice is overlooked in the scholarly literature. For example, both Hare's and Nagel's criticisms of the difference principle, quoted in the text accompanying notes 4 and 5 above, take the difference principle to be imposing sacrifices or losses on the better off. But this presupposes that something that the better off are entitled to is to be taken from them, when the difference principle aims to determine what they are entitled to in the first place. So accustomed are we to the fact of individual ownership that it appears as a fact of nature. Once it is recognized as a human institution, evaluation of it must occur from a baseline that does not presuppose its acceptance in any form.

12. If we imagined that distributive principles were established at the beginning of human history, before any system of property was established, it would be obvious that the only cost to human beings of any batch of goods is the labor that goes into them. Depletion of finite natural resources might also be reckoned a cost, but this would impose a limit on the absolute size of any generation's shares under any distributive principle. It would not affect the issue of the relative size of individuals' shares, over which the difference principle and its competitors primarily contend. Consequently, we can ignore this cost for our purposes.

13. Note that I am not assuming that individuals are only or primarily interested in themselves. My point is only that they are naturally and rationally concerned with how much of their finite time and energy will be devoted to their own purposes, *whatever those purposes may be*, altruistic or otherwise. Even the purposes of altruists are *their own* purposes, and if they are sincere about their altruistic purposes, they will care about how those purposes will be served. It is necessary to add this parenthetical qualification to protect my argument against the charge (often leveled, mistakenly I believe, against Rawls) that the difference principle is tied to the dubious conception of human nature as primarily self-interested or egoistic.

14. "[I]t is . . . this money-form of the world of commodities that actually conceals, instead of disclosing, the social character of private labour, and the social relations between the individual producers." Karl Marx, *Capital* (New York: International Publishers, 1967; originally published 1867), vol. 1, p. 76. I believe that Rawls recognizes, at least obliquely, the importance of what I have

called the social dimension of economic distributions, when he contrasts the understanding of economic distributions upon which the difference principle rests with that which leads to an "allocative" conception of justice. "By contrast," he writes, "the allocative conception of justice seems naturally to apply when a given collection of goods is to be divided among definite individuals with known desires and needs. The goods to be allotted are not *produced* by these individuals, nor do these individuals stand in any existing *cooperative* relations." Rawls, *Theory of Justice*, p. 88 (emphasis mine).

15. Rawls, *Theory of Justice*, p. 104.

16. Marx proposed just such a distribution for the first stage of communism (what Marxists generally call socialism). Karl Marx, "Critique of the Gotha Program," in *Marx-Engels Reader*, ed. Robert C. Tucker, 2d ed. (New York: Norton, 1978), p. 530. Interestingly, Marx allowed that labor might be measured either by time ("duration") or by effort ("intensity") in establishing equality. Actually, Marx held that the worker will receive back for his labor an amount of goods produced by an equal amount of labor, *after deductions* for general costs of administration, public goods (for example, schools, health services), and funds for those unable to work have been made. Ibid., pp. 529–30. Since we can think of these deductions as purchasing either goods or insurance for everyone, they can be taken as an indirect return to individuals of labor equal to what they contribute, and thus as not altering the fundamental principle.

17. In Rawls's version of the contracting situation, the original position, the "parties start with a principle establishing equal liberty for all, including equality of opportunity, as well as an equal distribution of income and wealth. But there is no reason why this acknowledgment should be final. If there are inequalities in the basic structure that work to make everyone better off in comparison with the benchmark of initial equality, why not permit them?" Rawls, *Theory of Justice*, p. 151.

18. Defenders of the free market (at least in the textbook version) are likely to balk at this assumption, holding that, under conditions of perfect competition, the selling price will always be the lowest the seller will accept, since otherwise someone will undersell her. This assumes as well, however, that power, need and other factors—arbitrary or dubious from the standpoint of economic justice—are not functioning to permit all sellers to sell above what they would be satisfied with, when that is precisely what has to be determined.

19. "Taxation on earnings from labor is on a par with forced labor." Nozick, *Anarchy, State, and Utopia*, p. 169, see also p. 172.

20. Rawls, *Theory of Justice*, p. 103.

21. This is not the only way that distributions resulting from the free market can be criticized as unjust. Elsewhere, I have argued that allowing unlimited accumulations of property (such as may result from free market exchanges) poses threats to the freedom of the propertyless and thus belies the libertarian capitalist's commitment to individual freedom. See my "The Fallacy of Liber-

tarian Capitalism," *Ethics* 92 (October 1981): 85–95. In my view, that article and the present chapter represent, respectively, a political and an economic refutation of libertarian capitalism as a principle of justice.

22. Cf. Nozick, *Anarchy, State, and Utopia,* p. 189. Nozick takes Rawls's difference principle to imply that individual contributions to the social product can be isolated, so that incentives can be given to the correct persons. On my interpretation of the difference principle, it is not at all clear that this follows. More importantly, I think that treating the difference principle as a matter of distributing shares of other people's labor provides a way that Rawls could answer Nozick's general criticisms of the principle. See ibid., pp. 183ff. All of Nozick's criticisms assume that cooperation between the better- and worse-off groups (or individuals) is a matter of exchanging the products of, rather than the labor of, each. Since the better off are the better endowed, they produce more. If the difference principle requires exchanges of products to result in maximizing the share to the worst off, it seems again lopsidedly unfair to the better off. But Nozick's way of looking at it brings the principle of greater rewards for greater talents into the results through the back door. Once this principle is suspended (it should result from our theory of justice, rather than being presupposed by it), then exchanges between better- and less-endowed persons are exchanges of quantities of labor measured by time (or effort). Seen this way, the difference principle no longer appears lopsided, as I have argued.

23. Rawls, *Theory of Justice,* pp. 82–83.

24. Ibid., pp. 258–84.

25. See note 16 above. For an earlier version of this argument in a different context, see my "The Possibility of a Marxian Theory of Justice," *Canadian Journal of Philosophy,* supplementary volume 7: *Marx and Morality,* ed. K. Nielsen and S. Patten (1981): 307–22. There, considering the historical evolution of standards of justice, I maintain that "the difference principle expresses from within morality, the so-called 'dialectic' of the forces of production and the relations of production. The forces of production are reflected in the capacity to raise the standard of living of the least advantaged and the relations of production are reflected in the changing range of acceptable inequalities." Ibid., p. 320.

26. Marx, "Critique of the Gotha Program," p. 530.

27. Ibid., p. 531.

28. Rawls, *Theory of Justice,* p. 104.

29. Reasons for making this compromise with human nature as it is, may be moral or practical. For Rawls, they are mainly moral: The lexical priority of the first principle of justice guaranteeing equal maximum liberty to all probably rules out overtly forcing people to work when there is some way to obtain their work voluntarily by means of incentives. For Marxism, the reasons are mainly practical: The increase in productivity that accompanies the succession of modes of production in history—from slavery to feudalism to capitalism—is paralleled by a decreasing reliance on overt force in the workplace. See, for

example, Marx, *Capital*, vol. 1, p. 737. Though capitalism is, for Marxism, still coercive, its greater productivity is probably linked to the fact that work is done for perceived self-interest, rather than under the gun or whip.

30. It might seem that a Marxist can never regard capitalism as just, since capitalism is an exploitative arrangement in that the profits of capitalists are constituted out of the unpaid surplus labor of workers. But the Marxian concept of exploitation is, in the first instance, a scientific concept, not a moral concept. Thus, though exploitation would appear to be at least prima facie unjust, it is possible that some degree of exploitation may be justified if it is necessary to raise the level of the forces of production to that point at which a nonexploitative society is possible. It is in such terms that Marx speaks of capitalism: "It is one of the civilizing aspects of capital that it enforces this [extraction of] surplus labour in a manner and under conditions which are more advantageous to the development of the productive forces, social relations, and the creation of a new and higher form than under the preceding forms of slavery, serfdom, etc." Ibid., vol. 3, p. 819, see also p. 441, where Marx speaks of capitalism's "historical mission." It seems, then, compatible with Marxian theory to hold that capitalism, exploitative as it is, is justified to the extent that it is historically necessary to develop the forces of production, and that means to raise the level of well-being of the worst-off members of society.

31. Wood, for example, writes that Marx criticizes equal right "by showing how it necessarily leads to a defective mode of distribution even in its socialist form. To do away with these defects [Marx] says one must 'wholly transcend the narrow horizon of bourgeois right' represented by all principles of equality. Marx alludes to Louis Blanc's slogan 'from each according to his abilities, to each according to his needs' precisely *because this is not in any sense a principle of 'equality.'* " Allen Wood, "Marx on Right and Justice: A Reply to Husami," *Philosophy and Public Affairs* 8, no. 3 (Spring 1979): 292 (emphasis mine).

32. Marx, "The Critique of the Gotha Program," pp. 530–31 (emphasis in original).

33. Ibid., p. 531. Note that the "effective conquest of scarcity" does not mean the total elimination of scarcity or, for that matter, of work. It means the reduction of scarcity to that point at which the desire to labor is itself sufficient to motivate whatever work remains necessary for the satisfaction of everyone's needs. Thus it coincides, for Marx, with the point at which "labour has become not only a means of life but life's prime want." Ibid.

5

The Constitution, Rights, and the Conditions of Legitimacy

I am not an advocate for frequent changes in laws and constitutions, but laws and institutions must go hand in hand with the progress of the human mind. As that becomes more developed, more enlightened, as new discoveries are made, new truths discovered and manners and opinions change, with the change of circumstances, institutions must advance also to keep pace with the times.

Thomas Jefferson

Must We Choose between Protecting Rights and Keeping Government Legitimate?

For much of the twentieth century, the United States Supreme Court has functioned as a forum for determining the fundamental rights possessed by American citizens, and as a court of last resort for the protection of those rights. The Court has, as courts generally have, claimed to *find* these fundamental rights in the law, in particular in the provisions of the Constitution. But this claim is dubious. The Court's recent "findings" have emerged in two waves of constitutional interpretations that are, to say the least, *creative*. The first wave, beginning in 1925 with *Gitlow v. New York,* was characterized by increasing application to state governments of the provisions of the Bill of Rights by interpreting the Fourteenth Amendment to require such application. This first wave was the basis for the second: beginning in 1954 with *Brown v. Board of Education,* the Supreme Court has more or less openly read new meanings into the terms of the Constitution and issued rulings desegregating public facilities, shoring up the rights of criminal suspects, enhancing the protection of free expression, and carving out a constitutional right to privacy with important implications for contraception, abortion, and unconventional sexual practices.[1]

Even among those who believe that these rulings recognize rights we do have morally and should have legally, a troubling question has been raised. It seems undeniable that virtually none of these decisions can be considered to be part of what the framers of the Constitution thought they were doing when they designed the articles and amendments upon which the Court has relied in making those decisions. If this is so, then it follows that the Court has effectively revised the Constitution to reach its decisions, and it is far from clear that it has any right to do that. Writes Michael Perry:

> In the modern period of American constitutional law—which began in 1954, with *Brown v. Board of Education*—the United States Supreme Court has played a major and unprecedented role in the formulation of human rights. Most first amendment doctrine regarding political and religious liberty; most equal protection doctrine regarding racial, sexual, and other forms of discrimination; all due process doctrine concerning rights pertaining to contraception, abortion, and sexual behavior . . . reflect not value judgments . . . made and embodied in the Constitution by the framers, but value judgments made and enforced by the Court against other, electorally accountable branches of government. Thus, in America the status of constitutional human rights is almost wholly a function, not of constitutional interpretation, but of constitutional policy-making by the Supreme Court.[2]

In response to this, continues Perry, there has emerged "a major debate in contemporary constitutional theory. Many theorists contend that constitutional policy making by the Supreme Court is illegitimate . . . on the ground that it is fundamentally inconsistent with our societal commitment to democracy."[3] Later, we shall have occasion to consider Perry's own defense of the Court's constitutional policymaking. For the moment, it is important to get clear on what the problem is.

At issue here is not the Court's authority to invalidate laws on the basis of their incompatibility with the Constitution. That authority, though not without its detractors, is arguably implicit in Article 3, which establishes the Constitution as the "supreme law of the land." A law can be the supreme law of the land only if it supersedes all other laws of the land. For one law to supersede another law means that, when the two laws conflict, the superseded law is rendered nugatory— literally overruled—by the superseding one. If we make the plausible assumption that the Constitution should be read as establishing the institutions necessary to achieve its stated goals, then we can read it as establishing an institution capable of determining when a law is over-ruled by the Constitution. Since determining which law is valid when two conflict is the traditional business of courts, and since the other two institutions of government—the legislature and the executive—are directly involved in the making of laws, the Supreme Court is the natu-ral candidate for the job of determining the constitutionality of the laws made subsequent to the Constitution.[4] But this does not show that the Court has the right to make the kind of constitutional decisions it has made of late.

The reason is that the argument just sketched justifies no more than the right of the Court to determine the compatibility or incompatibility of laws with the Constitution. And that, in commonsense terms, implies "the Constitution *as it was understood by its framers.*" By "common-sense terms," I mean that, if you and I understand ourselves bound by a contract we drew up and signed fifty years ago, we will normally think that we are bound now to what we thought we were binding ourselves to then *and not to what the language in our contract might mean today that it did not mean then.* In the same way, determining what the Consti-tution requires will normally be understood as determining what was required when it was written and ratified—that is, "as it was understood by its framers." To be sure, since the Constitution includes twenty-six amendments, it was not written and ratified at a single time. Moreover, not only is the understanding of the authors relevant, that of the ratifiers is as well. Thus, by "framers" I mean those who wrote the original Constitution, those who wrote the subsequent amendments, and those who participated, even from the sidelines, in debating and eventually ratifying the original Constitution and then each amendment that even-tually became part of the Constitution. The problem of the Court's deci-sions since *Gitlow* and *Brown* is that these decisions clearly read the Constitution in terms that go beyond the understanding of the framers.

There is wide agreement among scholars that the authors and ratifiers of the Fourteenth Amendment did not understand it to apply the Bill of Rights to the states. Moreover, the framers surely would not have understood the Constitution to outlaw racially segregated schooling, since the authors and ratifiers of the original document explicitly coun-tenanced much worse (namely, slavery) and the generation that adopted the Fourteenth Amendment was quite content with "separate but equal" public facilities for the races.[5] Nor can the framers be thought to have understood the Constitution to include a right to privacy that would prohibit the state from interfering with a married couple's right to use contraceptives or with a pregnant woman's right to have an abortion, since the framers lived at a time when such matters were taken as legitimately subject to legal regulation.[6]

Following Perry, let us say that, when the Court tests the constitutionality of a law in light of an interpretation of the framers' understanding of the Constitution, the Court engages in "interpretive review" and, when it tests the constitutionality of a law by going beyond the framers' understanding, the Court engages in "noninterpretive review."[7] For reasons already indicated, I assume that interpretive review is acceptable. It is noninterpretive review that raises the problem.

Those who object to noninterpretive review are not simply knee-jerk antiquarians who want to bind our current fate to the wishes and understandings of the people who set up our form of government two centuries ago. The issue is, rather, that a constitution is supposed to be a set of limits on the exercise of governmental power, such that power exercised within these limits is legitimate and power exercised outside these limits is not. If the Constitution is supposed to limit the exercise of governmental power, then the limits in the Constitution must exist in advance of the exercise of governmental power. This implies that the nature of the limits must be thought of as established when the Constitution was written and ratified—and the same for the content of the limits that are spelled out in the amendments subsequently adopted. And this implies that, where the plain language of the document is unclear, ambiguities must be cleared up by reference to the understanding of its authors and their contemporaries. If, instead, the intentions of the framers are left behind and the Constitution freely renovated by the Court, then, since the Court is an organ of the government, the Constitution becomes the product of the exercise of governmental power, rather than a limit on the exercise of governmental power.

This is all the more troubling since the Court lacks the other feature that is widely accepted as rendering the exercise of power legitimate, namely, accountability to the electorate. The Court is not electorally accountable in the way that the executive and legislative branches are. Indeed, the Court is intentionally designed to be insulated from electoral politics. The worry about the Court's right to go beyond the framers' understandings is then based on the notion that there are two ways in which a governmental institution can exercise legitimate power. It can either do what the Constitution *as it was written* says it can do, or it can do what the electorate directly empowers it to do.[8] Since neither will justify decisions of the sort made since *Brown,* we appear to face a dilemma: We seem forced to choose *either* holding to the understandings and intentions of the framers, at the cost of forgoing valuable recent (and potential future) decisions that expand and more effectively secure our rights, *or* setting the Constitution free from those origins at the risk of losing the very fixity and independence that enables a constitution to protect us from the exercise of illegitimate power. "The stakes," as Perry notes, "are very high indeed."[9] Must we choose between securing our rights and keeping our government legitimate?

In what follows, I shall argue that this "dilemma" is a false one. The appearance of a real dilemma comes from assuming that the conditions of legitimacy are given once and for all. Then government either holds to those conditions or does not, and, where those conditions do not already provide for all our rights, we shall have to choose between rights and legitimacy. I shall argue that, since legitimacy is a moral notion, we cannot take for granted that any existing formulation of its conditions is complete. Consequently, to be legitimate a government must do more than merely keep within some identified set of conditions—it must be continually monitoring the conditions of its legitimacy and effectively correcting existing formulations of these conditions as needed. Thus, I shall contend that a legitimate government is not simply one that keeps to a preestablished recipe for legitimacy but one that has built into it an institutional mechanism for continually reflecting on the conditions of its legitimacy and for effectively translating the results of that reflection into law. I maintain that a Supreme Court able to engage in noninterpretive constitutional review is *part* of such a mechanism.

Further, I contend that chief among the conditions of legitimate government is respect for, and protection of, the fundamental rights possessed by human beings. If a legitimate government is one that is continually and effectively monitoring the conditions of its legitimacy, then it is one that is continually reflecting on the question of what rights people truly possess and building its answers to this question into its practice. If this is so, then the Supreme Court's "discovery" of new rights in the Constitution may be a condition of the continuing legitimacy of our government, rather than a violation of it. Moreover, I maintain that while this leaves much to the judgment of the justices of the Court, it does not give them carte blanche to revise the Constitution according to their personal moral views. The reason for this is that the question of the conditions of legitimacy is a particular question with a particular shape that constrains the kinds of arguments that can be made for answers and thus ultimately constrains the kinds of answers that can be persuasive. I contend that the question of the conditions of legiti-

macy is essentially the question at the heart of the social contract theory, namely: What basic rights would rational human beings with differing, or potentially differing, moral beliefs insist upon as a condition
of subjecting themselves to governmental power that may enforce rules
with which they do not agree?

The argument I shall present for these propositions is far from complete. The area is large and the issues complex and controversial. Spelling out the details of the entire argument would require space far beyond that available to me here. Faced with the alternatives of setting
forth the details of a part of the argument and sketching out roughly the
shape of the whole, I have opted for the latter.

The Constitution as Paper, Practice, and Promise

Justices (and commentators) who hold that we should interpret the Constitution in terms of the framers' understandings and intentions have
been called "strict constructionists," and those who hold that the Constitution should be interpreted in terms of evolving moral and social
conceptions have been called "loose constructionists." For simplicity's
sake, I shall use these labels, but only with the caution that they are
misleading. The fact is that it is not possible to choose either alternative
without having some theory of what the Constitution *is*, what its point
is, what its source of obligatoriness is, and so on. To the so-called loose
constructionist justices who think that the Constitution is an organic,
living thing, waiting to be reinterpreted by each generation, their rulings
that go beyond the intentions of the framers result from strict interpretations of the Constitution, *given what they think the Constitution is.* And
the so-called strict constructionist justices, who hold that the Constitution must be interpreted in light of the original intentions, should not be
thought of as taking the Constitution *as it is.* Rather, they read it in light
of their own theory of what the Constitution is, namely, that it is a
document recording a particular agreement about how power should be
exercised that was hammered out two hundred years ago in Philadelphia. At heart, the disagreement between the so-called strict and loose
constructionists is a disagreement, not between strictness and looseness,
but between two theories of what the Constitution is. To understand the
conflict between so-called strict and loose constructionists, then, we
must pose the question: what *is* the Constitution?

At first glance, the answer is easy. The Constitution is a bunch of
words on a few sheets of paper (originally parchment, of course), set

down in 1787 and ratified a couple of years later. Let's call this the Constitution as *paper*. But this is not enough, since a constitution that exists only as paper is not a real constitution, in the sense that it fails to do any constituting. For that, the paper constitution must play an important role within the system of behaviors that constitutes government. Strictly speaking, that role is not correctly described as "limiting those behaviors," since words on paper alone cannot limit anything. Rather, there must be a social practice in which reference to those words is generally effective in getting governmental behavior limited to the range permitted by those words. Let's call this the Constitution as *social practice,* or, for short, the Constitution as *practice.* It should be clear from the case of Great Britain that one can have a constitution as practice without a constitution as paper, and, I suspect, equally clear from the case of the former Soviet Union that one can have the paper without the practice.

It is not satisfactory to leave matters here. The reason is that neither as paper nor as practice nor as both does the Constitution do what we expect of constitutions. As I said earlier, a constitution is supposed to be a set of limits such that power exercised within those limits is legitimate. We can understand the proposition "power exercised within constitutional limits is legitimate" in two ways, either as a tautology or as a synthetic statement. As a tautology, power exercised within constitutional limits is legitimate because legitimacy means no more than "within constitutional limits." But tautologies are empty, as can be seen from the fact that, so understood, a constitution that said no more than "Do whatever the dictator orders" would render the dictator's power just as legitimate as governmental power hemmed into the space between people's rights by a constitution such as ours. Since I take it that we mean more by legitimate than this, the proposition "power exercised within constitutional limits is legitimate" must be synthetic. The term "legitimate" must add something that is not already present in the notion of constitutional limits. What it adds is (at least) the notion of moral obligatoriness. Legitimate power means (at least) power with which we are morally obligated to comply. This obligation need not be thought of as binding us absolutely or as supplanting our own judgment about how to behave.[10] Rather, that an exercise of governmental power—say, the making of a law—is legitimate is something that a rational individual should recognize as a moral consideration weighing heavily in favor of compliance—possibly, but not easily, outweighed by conflicting moral considerations.

Governmental power, then, is not legitimate only because kept within *just any* set of constitutional limits. Rather, the limits must be good enough to make power exercised within them legitimate. Put otherwise: That power is limited is a factual claim, but that the power so limited is legitimate is a moral claim. If legitimacy entails moral obligatoriness, then a constitution only does what we expect of a constitution to the extent that its limits are those that render power exercised within them morally obligatory.

Since the obligation at issue in legitimacy is a moral one, it follows that neither the fact that the Constitution exists on paper nor that it governs an ongoing practice can supply this obligation-creating function. For that, the Constitution's limits must promise something of a moral nature, something that is sufficient to establish an obligation owed in return. Thus the Constitution is something else besides paper and practice. Let's call this the Constitution as *moral promise* or, for short, the Constitution as *promise*. Now, since this promise is a moral one, we cannot take for granted that any given set of constitutional limits succeeds in making good on the promise. And this, as we shall see, has far-reaching implications for our understanding of the conditions of legitimate power and thus of the role of the Supreme Court.

The Moral Promise and the Conditions of Legitimate Power

As we have seen, those who question the legitimacy of noninterpretive review by the Supreme Court assume generally that there are two ways in which exercises of governmental power are legitimate, namely, either the exercises are subject to the electoral process or they are provided for in the Constitution. But this view is inadequate on several grounds.

First of all, there is nothing inherently legitimating about the electoral process. If anything, the electoral process is the problem, not the solution. Thinkers like John Locke, who so profoundly influenced the formation of our governmental system, were deeply concerned to show how the electoral process could be legitimate. The point is this. The problem of the legitimacy of governmental power arises most strikingly with respect to those against whose wishes or actions that power is exercised. Subjecting power to the electoral process means allowing the voting public to determine whether or not a particular exercise of power is acceptable. This renders governmental power legitimate by subjecting it to the choices of those who are governed by it, since people are normally bound by what they agree to and not oppressed by what they choose. However, since there will rarely be unanimity, the outcome of the electoral process will normally reflect the choices of the majority. But this entails that the policies that emerge from the electoral process will be imposed on the dissenting minority against its wishes. Then, rather than answering the question of legitimacy, this will raise the question with respect to those dissenters. Why are the exercises of power approved by the majority against the wishes of (and potentially prohibiting the desired actions of) the minority obligatory with respect to the minority? Why are such exercises of power not simply a matter of the majority tyrannizing the minority?

These questions not only point up the error of taking electoral accountability as an independent source of legitimacy; they also suggest that it is mistaken to think of electoral accountability and constitutional provision as alternative sources of legitimacy. Rather, the Constitution *with its provisions limiting the majority's ability to exercise power* is the answer to the question of why decisions voted by a majority are binding on the minority who disagree. We shall look more closely at the details of this answer shortly. For the moment, it suffices to note that, insofar as the Constitution hedges majority rule in a way that establishes the obligation of the minority to go along with the majority, the Constitution makes good on the moral promise and keeps the exercises of governmental power legitimate. But, and this is crucial, this works only to the extent that the Constitution really does keep the promise and really does limit power in ways that establish the obligatoriness of governmental power for all citizens. It must be an open question whether our Constitution actually succeeds.

Here, then, we see the deeper inadequacy of the notion that legitimacy is provided by either electoral accountability or constitutional provision. Electoral accountability renders power legitimate only within a constitutional framework. And that works only if the constitutional framework is the right framework, that is, if it contains limits on majority power that are good enough to render that power obligatory on all citizens. Rather than legitimacy being a matter of meeting one of two existing conditions, legitimacy is a matter of whether the Constitution actually makes good on the moral promise. Let us then consider how a constitution keeps the moral promise.

There are two ways in which a constitution might keep this promise, which we can call "formal" and "substantive." *Formally*, the limits set forth in a constitution will establish obligations on us *if we have agreed to be governed by power exercised within those limits*. This is "formal" because it does not depend on the content of the limits: Any limits to which we agree will be thought binding on us. Consequently, any exercise of power within limits to which we have agreed will be binding on us and thus legitimate. *Substantively,* the limits in a constitution will establish obligations on us *if those limits conform to a valid moral conception of the rightful exercise of governmental power.* This is "substantive" because it depends exclusively on the content or substance of the limits: If they conform to a valid moral conception of the rightful exercise of governmental power, they—and power exercised within them—will bind us morally whether or not we have agreed to them. I shall say more about this in a moment, once we see why the formal approach won't work for us.

The *formal* approach won't work for our Constitution for the simple and obvious reason that we didn't agree to it. We weren't there at the time, and by no stretch of the imagination could those who were there have had the right to agree for us. Further, only a fraction of those who were there were even eligible to vote—women, blacks, and many of the poor having been excluded. And among those who did vote—as the debates between the Federalists and the Antis testify—not everyone agreed. The majorities by which the Constitution was approved in the state ratifying conventions were often quite slim—a mere ten votes in Virginia, and only three votes in New York![11] The bald fact is that the number of people who actually agreed to the Constitution is surely no more than a fraction of a percent of all the Americans who have lived at any point between 1787 and now, all of whom are thought morally bound by the system the Constitution establishes. And there is no plausible way to claim that the agreement of that fraction of a percent represents the agreement of us all.

Nor will it do to claim that, by choosing to stay here and enjoy the benefits of the Constitution, we tacitly agree to the conditions of those benefits and thus to the Constitution itself. Tacit agreements are real enough, but their existence depends on a number of conditions. First of all, it must be plausible to construe our being here as choosing to stay here. And for that, we must have the real possibility of leaving (which requires, not only the legal freedom to leave, but the financial means) and the real possibility of getting in somewhere else—possibilities that not everyone here does have.

Moreover, even if we are here because we choose to stay, problems still remain. The tacit agreement argument works by the notion that, in accepting some benefit X, we accept the conditions necessary to make X possible. But that means that, in accepting the benefits linked to our Constitution, we accept only those aspects of the Constitution that are actually necessary to produce those benefits. Then, it remains an open question how much of the existing Constitution we are tacitly agreeing to. Further, if the benefits produced by our Constitution could be improved by altering the Constitution, then accepting the existing benefits doesn't amount to accepting the existing Constitution, since, if given a real choice, we would opt for other benefits under another constitution. In short, even after we meet the requirements for construing being here as choosing to stay here and enjoying the benefits of the Constitution, we can make the tacit agreement argument work only if the benefits are optimal and the existing Constitution is the necessary condition of those optimal benefits. This means that the tacit agreement argument forces us to consider the substance of the Constitution's limits.

We turn, then, to the *substantive* way in which the Constitution might establish legitimate exercises of governmental power. To this question, our own system gives an answer that stems from John Locke. In outline, it is the following: If some form of government can be thought of as something that it would be rational for human beings to choose over other forms or over no government at all, then such government cannot be thought of as tyrannical or oppressive. Moreover, since that form of government will provide benefits (the ones that make it rational to choose it) only on the condition that people generally comply with its laws, rational human beings must recognize that they are obligated to comply with its laws as the necessary price of obtaining and enjoying the benefits. What are the benefits? The Lockean answer is that (over and above the increased productivity and security against foreign invasion that cooperation brings) the decisive benefits are the basic rights that government protects for citizens. Since these rights are to be protected generally, they must be protected against the government itself, and consequently they provide the boundaries within which government is properly limited. Thus, if the government is limited in ways that respect everyone's rights sufficiently to make it rational for everyone to choose this form of government over others or none at all, then government is legitimate in the sense of obligatory upon everyone. A constitution that limits government in ways that ensure sufficient protection of everyone's rights keeps the moral promise.

Within this set of limits, the outcomes of majority decisions will be binding on everyone and thus on the minority who dissent. This is so because even the most legitimate government will have to reach decisions when citizens disagree about which decision is best. In such cases, it is unavoidable that some will be disappointed, since even "not deciding" will effectively amount to deciding upon some policy that some citizens will like and others will not. The question is how best to arrive at decisions in such cases. It is here that majority rule is recommended, not because majorities are more likely to be right than minorities, but because what a majority approves of has fewer dissenters than what a minority approves of. Remember that electoral accountability renders government power legitimate by subjecting it to the wishes of the governed. The real virtue of majority rule is simply that it is not minority rule. And this is clearest with simple majority rule, since requiring two-thirds allows a minority of one-third-plus-one to decide for the rest, and requiring unanimity allows one person to decide for all, and so on.

If governmental activity is limited in a way that leaves it unable to tread upon the basic rights of all citizens, then, when the government rules in ways from which some dissent, the dissenting minority can recognize that this is just an inevitable feature of group decision making rather than something that subjugates them to the will of others. Government so limited is legitimate. If this is true (and I shall assume henceforth that it is), it follows that government is legitimate to the extent that it protects people's basic rights *sufficiently* to defeat the suspicion that those who dissent from governmental actions are subjugated by those actions.

I have emphasized the term "sufficiently" in the last sentence because much hinges on this. Simply paying lip service to people's basic rights won't defeat the suspicion of subjugation. Nor will it do to protect some basic rights and allow others to be trampled. Moreover, and this is crucial to my entire argument, *we cannot be satisfied that any actual inventory of basic rights is sufficient, since any such actual inventory that fallible and limited human beings come up with may miss some basic right that is essential for protection against subjugation.* To be sure, we can identify some of the basic rights with considerable certainty. For instance, protection against subjugation seems surely to require that people have freedom of movement, of expression, and of religion, as well as rights to habeas corpus and representative republican government, all of which our Constitution currently places safely beyond the reach of the majority. I, for one, believe that it requires generally that government not become an engine for the imposition of some people's moral views on others. Thus, I believe that the commitment to keep exercises of power nonsubjugating goes beyond at least what the current Supreme Court believes the Constitution to require, since this commitment would, for example, require prohibiting laws against homosexual sodomy even if there were no right to privacy in the Constitution at all.[12] But, whatever we can determine right now to be required, the fact is that we cannot say once and for all what are the subjugating exercises of governmental power. The simple fact is that we are forever learning that arrangements once taken as natural and neutral are actually oppressive. And this fact has enormous implications for the reality of the Constitution as promise.

Merely subjecting government to some supreme law of the land won't guarantee fulfillment of this promise, since law itself can be a means to subjugation. Not even establishing a supreme law that appears fair will suffice, since appearances can deceive. It is always possible that some existing set of laws, generally thought fair, amounts to no more than a level of subjugation to which we are inured so that we don't notice it. Laws that established property qualifications on holding office, or that limited the vote to men, are examples of laws that were once thought by many to be fair, but are no longer. But this means that while the reality of the Constitution as paper can be found by reading the text, and the reality of the Constitution as practice can be found by studying the actual workings of the government, the reality of the Constitution as moral promise can be found only by the process of moral argument rooted in an ongoing reflection on the conditions of nonsubjugating governance.

This implies that, rather than thinking of legitimate government as government operating within given limits, we need to think of legitimate government more dynamically, that is, as government that continually and effectively monitors its own legitimacy. This amounts to thinking of legitimate government as government that continually and effectively monitors the adequacy of its recognition of basic rights. Insofar as doing this amounts to making good on the Constitution as moral promise, a legitimate government is one that includes an institutional arrangement by means of which the Constitution is treated as a living thing, to be reinterpreted in light of our best understanding of the rights to which people are entitled as this understanding evolves.

To be sure, this monitoring need not necessarily be done by the Supreme Court. Perhaps the amendment process set forth in the Constitution is enough to do the job, as the strict constructionists generally maintain. The conflict between the strict and loose constructionists is not a conflict between those who think of the Constitution as paper and those who think of it as moral promise. Rather, since both sides think that the Constitution is obligatory and sufficient to establish the legitimacy of power exercised within its terms, the two alternatives are better seen as two theories of the Constitution as moral promise. The so-called strict constructionists emphasize the fact that to make good on the moral promise, the Constitution must provide relatively rigid limits on power fixed in advance and thus not be open to revision by reinterpretation. And the nearest we can come to reading the Constitution as containing limits fixed in advance is by trying to read it as it was understood by those who wrote it. For the strict constructionists, the amendment process that the framers spelled out must suffice for correcting the conditions of legitimacy.

The problem with this proposal, however, is that the amendment process leaves it to the very holders of power (and the majority behind them) to determine the conditions of the legitimacy of their own power—when it is precisely the Constitution that is supposed to do that for them. The amendment process cannot suffice for the Constitution as promise, since the promise is precisely that the laws that represent the will of the majority not subjugate the minority whose will is otherwise. The moral promise can be kept only if the Constitution keeps the majority from acting in ways that subjugate the minority. The amendment process cannot satisfy this, since it leaves to the same majority that passes laws that are potentially subjugating the determination of whether they are subjugating. And this is a problem, not because of the venality of the majority, but because the very strength of conviction that leads the majority to think some law is necessary will lead them as well to think that that law is the very opposite of subjugation. This naturally turns us toward the Supreme Court as the appropriate place for the debate about how the Constitution should be interpreted so as to fulfill its moral promise.

The Supreme Court, the Constitution, and the Social Contract

Once we see that the Constitution does its job only to the extent that it puts forth the conditions of nonsubjugating governance, and once we see that this, in turn, requires respect for basic rights *sufficient* to defeat the suspicion of subjugation, there is no alternative but to allow the Constitution to be interpreted in light of our developing understanding of the basic rights that must be protected. If allowing this interpreting means that to some extent the Constitution inevitably becomes the product of governmental power rather than the limit on it, there is much to recommend putting this unavoidable task of interpretation in the hands of the Supreme Court. This is because, as Hamilton recognized in *Federalist* 78, since the Supreme Court controls neither the purse nor the sword, it is the "least dangerous" branch.[13]

To be sure, my argument up to this point supports the views of the loose constructionists. However, I think that it is necessary to understand the implications of the argument in a way that does justice to the wisdom of the strict constructionist position. I shall suggest such an understanding shortly.

In my view, the so-called loose constructionist judges who produced the revolutionary decisions of the past three decades were making good on the Constitution as moral promise. They were spelling out the conditions that we currently understand as necessary to make the power of government nonsubjugating. More aware than the framers about the social-psychological effects of institutional arrangements, we can see how separate but equal public facilities relegate part of society to diminished power over their fates compared to the rest; more aware of the pressures on, and disabilities of, suspects of crimes, we can see how ignorance of rights can undermine the power of suspects to play their proper role in defending themselves against the power of the state; more aware of the pervasive influence of self-righteous moral vigilantes, we can see how lack of a firm boundary around private life can render individuals unable to control the terms of their intimate life and reproduction.

But, it will be objected, doesn't this defense of the loose constructionist view amount to an open invitation to the justices of the Supreme Court to read their personal moral views into the Constitution? I think not, for two reasons. The first is that the question of legitimacy is a distinct one, and it shapes the kinds of arguments that can be put forth in defense of constitutional rulings. Those arguments must show that a given right is a necessary condition of nonsubjugating government. For this, I believe, the Court is forced back onto the *contractarian* foundations of the Lockean rights doctrine. In order to ask the question of the conditions of legitimacy, once we are no longer content to rest with any previously given answer, we must ask, what rights would rational men and women with differing or potentially differing moral beliefs insist on as a condition of putting their fates in the hands of government that may make and enforce rules against their wishes?

My point here is easily misunderstood. I am not saying that the Court is entitled to interpret the Constitution in terms of "social contract" theory because this was the theory subscribed to by the framers and implicitly built into the Constitution by them. Nor am I saying that the Court should opt for "social contract" theory because it is the best, or currently the most satisfactory, moral theory. I think both these claims are largely true but beside the point. My claim is that once government undertakes to monitor the conditions of its own legitimacy understood as the conditions under which governmental power is obligatory, there is effectively no satisfactory way to engage in this monitoring, other than by posing the question that social contractarians pose.

The reason (all too briefly put) is that what it would be rational for human beings to agree with does not subjugate them. With existing answers to moral questions no longer taken for granted, we cannot find what does not subjugate by asking for what people actually agree to. People are shaped by existing moral beliefs and therefore may agree to arrangements that, in fact, do subjugate them. What remains, then, is to look for nonsubjugating governance by asking what it would be rational for people to agree with. Moreover, since we seek the conditions of legitimate governance among people whose moral views do (or may) differ, we cannot simply assume the truth of any controversial moral view in answering the question of legitimacy—even if it is the moral view of the majority. To do so may in effect license the subjugation of the minority who hold a different moral view. Consequently, if we understand the question of legitimacy as that of finding the conditions of nonsubjugating governance among people who do or may differ in their moral views, the general shape of that question is: What rights would rational men and women with differing, or potentially differing, moral beliefs insist on as a condition of putting their fates in the hands of a government that may make and enforce rules against their wishes? And this question will limit the kinds of evidence and arguments that can count toward an answer (for example, by ruling out appeal to disputed moral beliefs).

It is likely to be countered that the social contract is only one among many moral visions and thus my proposal amounts to enshrining one moral belief at the expense of others. This objection is a welcome one because it points to the real virtue of the social contract. The social contract is a way of determining what form of government is nonsubjugating among people who have (or may have) differing moral visions. To be sure, the outcome of asking what people with (possibly) differing moral visions would agree to will be different from what people with one moral vision would agree to. Thus, one can say that the social contract is also one moral vision among others. So be it. It remains the case that what is unique about this vision is that it aims to eliminate subjugation among the holders of disparate visions, and this feature, I contend, uniquely recommends treating the social contract as *the* moral vision embodied in our Constitution—once the Constitution is understood as moral promise. After all, the moral promise is offered to one and all, irrespective of their moral vision.

The second reason that allowing the Court to make good on the Constitution as moral promise doesn't invite the justices to read their own moral views into the Constitution brings us to the wisdom in the strict constructionist view. The strict constructionists are generally right in thinking that at least one of the ways in which the moral promise is kept is by providing a kind of fixity to the rules that make up the Constitution. Their mistake is that they see no alternative between adherence to the original intentions and tyranny. Here too, the social contract provides guidance. Insofar as our social contractarian question is aimed at protecting people's basic rights, it should be thought of, not only as identifying those rights, but as identifying as well the safeguards appropriate to a real human (and, therefore, fallible) institution that will decide on those rights. Here, then, it seems to me that part of the answer to the social contractarian question will be the requirement that judges do not simply give their own personal answers about what our basic rights are. Rather, there should be a general structure into which their answers must be fit. In particular, judges should be required to show that their answers, however novel, are plausible renderings of the text of the Constitution in light of the historically evolving culture of judicial interpretation, of which the current Supreme Court is only the most recent voice. In effect, judges should defend novel judicial interpretations of the Constitution as if they were explaining to earlier judges how these innovations are now needed to maintain continuity with the constitutional project shared by current and past judges.

The "dilemma" of rights versus legitimacy we met at the outset is a false one. The real dilemma that we face is that the conditions of legitimacy are in conflict. Both the loose and the strict constructionists have wisdom on their side. Government is kept legitimate by continually monitoring the conditions of legitimacy, *and* government is kept legitimate by holding it within conditions that cannot easily be overturned or revised. Requiring justices to show that their interpretations are continuous with the written Constitution and the history of its interpretation serves to constrain their decisions within the terms in which the reflection on the conditions of legitimacy has slowly evolved over the course of our history. Among other things, this has the effect of spreading the discussion of the conditions of legitimacy out over time. Instead of allowing the justices to come up with their own specific answers ex nihilo, this requires that they fit their answers into the discussion as it has evolved over the history of the Court. Rather than a mere fiction, the convention of requiring the justices to link their decisions to the Constitution as it has been interpreted by the Court before them serves to limit the possible novelty of the decisions of any particular Court by requiring that those decisions at least plausibly fit into the constitutional culture that has evolved to that point. Indeed, I think that it is precisely because our Constitution has been interpreted in this way over the years that the novel interpretations seem still to be continuous with the original spirit of the document.

The Constitution may be interpretable in many ways, but not in just any way one wants. It cannot plausibly be interpreted in ways that deny that citizens have important rights against government, that deny that elected officials must be effectively accountable to the public, or that assert the existence of rights wholly discontinuous with the rights enumerated in the Bill of Rights. We are sometimes so struck by our disagreements that we think that all we have are disagreements. But our disagreements over the Constitution are shaped by, and contained within, the moral vocabulary of the Constitution, and thus they are disagreements about those things on which we have agreed to disagree. Disagreements over whether the Constitution requires desegregated public facilities, Miranda warnings, or noninterference with a pregnant woman's decision to abort are disputes that are *all in the family,* as the constitutional family has matured since its birth. They are worlds apart from disputes over whether we should censor the press, own slaves, outlaw unpopular religions, or abolish private property. The Constitution projects a moral culture, and this itself, even if it doesn't constrain us to one single outcome, constrains us nevertheless and thus does the work of limiting governmental power—even the Supreme Court's power as it reinterprets the Constitution.

Before proceeding, it will be worth pausing to consider Michael Perry's defense of noninterpretive review by the Supreme Court in human rights cases, since his position may easily be confused with the one I have put forth here. Recall that noninterpretive review means that, when testing the constitutionality of a law, the court reaches beyond the framers' understanding of what the Constitution prescribes. Perry claims that, while there is no constitutional justification for the practice of noninterpretive review (and, of course, no justification in terms of electoral accountability), there is a *functional* justification. Noninterpretive review, Perry believes, serves a function good and important enough to our polity to justify its continuance.

> The basic function of that practice is to deal with those political issues that are also fundamental moral problems in a way that is faithful to the notion of moral evolution (and, therefore, to our collective religious self-understanding)—not simply by invoking established moral conventions (as elec-

torally accountable institutions are prone to do) but by seizing such issues as opportunities for moral reevaluation and possible moral growth.[14]

In short, Perry claims that we as a people are committed (on quasi-religious grounds) to the notion that there are right answers to moral questions and thus that any existing answer provided by accepted moral conventions may be wrong. Consequently, he holds that we are committed to the search for answers that are better than those currently accepted. Electorally accountable officials, however, are loath to stray from accepted conventions because this may end up costing at the polls. The Supreme Court, precisely because it is insulated from electoral politics, serves the function of enabling us as a people to make good on the commitment to search for better answers to moral problems than those provided by existing moral conventions.

Now, I agree with Perry that the fallibility of existing moral beliefs is part of the justification for noninterpretive review. Where we differ is that Perry takes the Supreme Court as a kind of general agent of moral growth, reviewing—and, where necessary, revising—our moral conventions. My view is that the Court's assignment is narrower and more focused. I take it, not as a general agent of moral growth or as a general reviser of moral conventions, but as an institution aimed at providing answers to a specific moral question, namely: What are the conditions of legitimate exercises of power? Which question, I have argued, is equivalent to another: What basic rights would rational human beings insist upon as a condition of agreeing to government that may enforce rulings against their wishes? For example, I take it that, on abortion, Perry would have the Supreme Court serve as a forum for the general assessment of existing moral beliefs about abortion. On my view, the Court would address the narrower question of whether it would be rational for people with differing moral beliefs about abortion to subject themselves to a government with the power to prohibit the pregnant women among them from having abortions.

Though there is much to recommend Perry's view, I think the view I have defended has three important advantages over his. First of all, by narrowing the focus of the moral question we take the Court to be answering, my proposal has the virtue of making the Court's actions more structured and less open ended and, to that extent, reducing the danger of the Court itself becoming an engine of oppression. By contrast, Perry's view leads him to have to admit that the source of the decisions in noninterpretive review will be "the judge's own moral vision."[15] Second, since my proposal is based on satisfying the conditions of legitimate government, it has its source in the very value that those who question noninterpretive review explicitly endorse. By contrast, Perry's view requires believing the rather speculative claim that we Americans are somehow committed to moral reevaluation to such an extent that we must assign this job to some institution of government.

Third, Perry's view does not, as far as I can see, explain why the outcome of the Court's moral reevaluation should be legally binding on the legislature and the citizenry. Why wouldn't it suffice for the Court to issue its judgments on an advisory basis? (We are, after all, also committed to the notion that there are true answers to scientific questions and thus that there may be better answers than those provided by existing scientific beliefs. Nonetheless, we do not empower some scientific institution to make binding decisions about what scientists may believe.) If we are, as Perry claims, truly committed to moral growth and the search for better answers than those given by our existing moral conventions, it would seem that nonbinding judgments on such matters, issued by the highest court of the land, would have considerable influence on legislators and voters *without raising the specter of the Court's exercising power beyond constitutional or electoral mandate.* On my view, by contrast, the Court's decisions must be legally binding precisely because they are decisions about the conditions of legitimate governance by the other branches, conditions whose determination cannot be left up to those branches. Unless the Court's decisions are legally binding, a necessary condition of legitimacy, namely, a built-in mechanism for, not only monitoring, but effectively correcting the conditions of legitimacy, is lacking. I think, by the way, that it is because Congress at least dimly perceives that its own legitimacy is bound up with the effectiveness of the Supreme Court's reflection on the conditions of legitimacy that so little use has been made by Congress of the enormous power granted to it over the Court by Article 3 of the Constitution.

Institutions, Arguments, and the Moral Conversation

Recently, a group of legal writers identified broadly as "the critical legal studies movement" (CLSM) has reinvigorated the notion— propounded earlier in this century by the "legal realist" school—that law is made by judges. Renewing the critique of the picture of judges deciding cases by "finding" the appropriate statute and "deducing" its implications for the case at hand, the CLSMers have argued that our law is incurably indeterminate with respect to particular outcomes in particular cases, such that judges invariably have to make political-moral choices in deciding any case. One target of this argument is the claim that either the Constitution itself or any widely acceptable theory of constitutional interpretation sets forth our fundamental rights with sufficient specificity to determine judicial decisions about our rights.[16] The implication is that such decisions will also reflect judges' political-moral choices.

Needless to say, this poses a substantial challenge to the proposal that I have tried to defend here. I have argued that a legitimate state is one that includes an institutional mechanism for monitoring and correcting the conditions of legitimacy and that the Supreme Court's engaging in noninterpretive review is *part* of that mechanism. I have argued further that this does not simply leave matters to the personal moral views of the judges, because the question of the conditions of legitimacy—the question of the basic rights that must be safeguarded if governmental power is to be nonsubjugating—is a determinate question. This question has the shape of the contractarian test of rational agreement, and this constrains the types of arguments that can be adduced for rights and thus the range of outcomes. At the same time, the outcomes are constrained from the other side by the practice of requiring judges to defend their decisions as interpretations of the Constitution. If, however, after all is said and done, constitutional decisions about basic rights come down to political-moral choices by judges, this seems to leave the project of monitoring and correcting the conditions of legitimacy to the whimsy of the sitting justices—and this would appear to deprive our rights of precisely that fixity and independence necessary for them to function as real limits on governmental action.

I shall close this essay by defending my proposal against this critique. In general, my view is that, while the CLSMers are right in maintaining that there is a range of indeterminacy in Supreme Court judgments about basic rights, they are wrong about the implications of that indeterminacy. They are wrong because they fail to see that human institutions cannot have the kind of determinacy that, say, good arguments possess regarding their outcomes. Accordingly, the CLSM critique applies a standard of determinacy that no institutional framework could, or should, match. The result is that the CLSMers fail to see that the institutional ways in which Supreme Court decisions are constrained suffice to provide as much determinacy as is needed.[17]

Some of the indeterminacy to which the CLSMers point is the inevitable product of the fact that laws are expressed in general terms that must be interpreted when applied to individual cases, at least in any cases controversial enough to be brought as far as the high court. And some of the indeterminacy to which they point is the product of the fact that our own society is not of one mind about the ultimate values that the law ought to embody. The first type of indeterminacy is the sort that haunts familiar constitutional phrases such as "due process," "cruel and unusual punishment," "equal protection," and, of course, such legal perennials as "harm" and "reasonable." The second type reflects the fact that we want the law to respect free choice *and* serve the general welfare, to protect people from unwanted interference *and* support the value of community, to respect precedent *and* adapt to new circumstances, to be knowable in advance *and* flexible enough to be tailored to individual circumstances, and, of course, to do justice *and* be merciful. Not only are all of these pairs of tendencies conflicting, but also we are unable to agree about the final priorities when these pairs come into conflict. Accordingly, any actual judicial decision will necessarily have to stake out positions on the meanings of the tricky legal phrases and cut a course across opposing moral tendencies in the law, in ways that are inherently disputable and about which reasonable men and women will disagree.

However, rather than defeating the project of legitimate governance, these kinds of indeterminacy are, it seems to me, unavoidable aspects of real institutions, operated by real people. Institutions are not arguments. They do not start from self-evident premises and proceed syllogistically to inescapable conclusions. They are actual deployments of real human beings who are required to use judgment in evaluating evidence and arguments and to make and defend decisions that cannot wait until every conceivable objection has been heard and assessed. We cannot ask of such institutions that they proceed according to some algorithm that would yield a single unique answer to every problem. Consequently, while the CLSMers (and the legal realists before them) are right about the indeterminacy of the legal system, the implication of this is not that legal decisions are simply up for grabs. Once we see that indeterminacy is an inescapable feature of real institutions, we see as well that it can be controlled only institutionally—that is, we need institutional arrangements that narrow the range of possible outcomes to an acceptable range and that subject indeterminate judgments to broad challenge and review. The general point is that legal indeterminacy cannot be eliminated theoretically—but it can be tamed institutionally. The line between the indeterminate and the arbitrary cannot realistically be drawn in advance. Rather, that line has to be actively policed. As we already knew, eternal vigilance is the price of free institutions.

Here we would do well to remember the multiplicity of institutional arrangements that circumscribe the activities of the Supreme Court. Legally, there is the amendment process (by means of which a sufficient majority of citizens can literally remake the Constitution as they see fit), there is the power of Congress to determine the jurisdiction of the Supreme Court (by means of which a majority in Congress can set virtually any controversial issue off limits to the Court), there is the power of the president and Congress to appoint the justices of the Court (which effectively limits the Court membership to judges whose views are within the range broadly acceptable to the electorate), and, of course, there is the power of impeachment (whose infrequent use is, in my view, less a testimony to the difficulty of carrying it off than to how well-behaved the Court has generally been). Beyond this, there are the press and the professional community of lawyers and law professors who subject the Court's actions to intense scrutiny and sophisticated assessment, in light of the general requirement of continuity with the written Constitution and the history of its interpretation. And there is ultimately the need for the acquiescence of the government officials who must enforce the Court's decisions and of the general public who must generally support that enforcement. When I said earlier that the Supreme Court's engaging in noninterpretive review is *part* of an institutional mechanism for monitoring and correcting the conditions of legitimacy, it was this larger interacting complex of institutions and practices that I had in mind as the *whole* of which the Court is part.

It is comparatively easy to look down from the heights of theory and sketch out one's pet theory for how a government should be organized. It is quite a bit harder to design an actual institutional complex that—subject to human frailty and unanticipated circumstances—is actually likely to realize any given set of moral ideals over time. This was the goal of the authors of our Constitution. They were practical political philosophers concerned, not with drawing beautiful Platonic republics in the air, but with designing a real republic that—given people's actual capabilities and foibles—would not be likely to decay into tyranny for ages to come.

None of this guarantees that our or any other set of institutions will always come up with the right answers, that they will always identify and protect our real basic rights. But that is an impossible requirement. It would be like insisting that the criminal trial system be designed so that no innocent person would ever be found guilty and no guilty person ever be acquitted. What we can do is design institutions that actually keep alive a wide-ranging public and professional moral conversation about the nature of our basic rights and that effectively translate the conclusions of that conversation into legal reality. If it be granted that a legitimate state is one that includes an institutional mechanism for effectively monitoring and, where necessary, correcting the conditions of its legitimacy, then a mechanism must be designed such that it is actually likely to keep alive and effective the ongoing moral conversation, though it be operated by mere mortals and though it reflect the conflicts in that conversation that have not yet been resolved. If, even now, someone were to sit down and try to come up with such a design for real people, I find it hard to imagine that he or she would come up with anything appreciably better than a written rights-guaranteeing Constitution interpreted by a politically insulated Supreme Court that is wedged between an elected government and a free and fractious populace.

Notes

This chapter is a revised version of an article originally published in *Constitutionalism: The Philosophical Dimension*, ed. A. Rosenbaum (Westport, Conn.: Greenwood, 1988), pp. 127–49. Reprinted with permission.

1. *Gitlow v. New York*, 268 U.S. 652 (1925); *Brown v. Board of Education*, 347 U.S. 483 (1954).

2. Michael J. Perry, *The Constitution, the Courts, and Human Rights* (New Haven, Conn.: Yale University Press, 1982), p. 2.

3. Ibid., pp. 2–3.

4. Cf. ibid., pp. 15–16, 172 n. 21.

5. Ibid., pp. 61–65, 194 n. 26; see also William E. Nelson, *The Fourteenth Amendment: From Political Principle to Judicial Doctrine* (Cambridge: Mass.: Harvard University Press, 1988).

6. Forrest Macdonald, *Novus Ordo Seclorum: The Intellectual Origins of the Constitution* (Lawrence, Kans.: University Press of Kansas, 1985), pp. 15–16, 17 n.

7. Perry, *Constitution, Courts, and Human Rights*, p. 10.

8. For a sampling of authorities who have argued to this effect, see ibid., pp. 28–29 and accompanying notes.

9. Ibid., p. 92.

10. One author who maintains that the putative obligation in the concept of legitimacy is absolute is Robert Paul Wolff, in *In Defense of Anarchism* (New York: Harper & Row, 1970). I have argued against this extreme claim (and the anarchism to which Wolff contends it leads for those who accept their responsibility to make their own moral choices) in my *In Defense of Political Philosophy* (New York: Harper & Row, 1972).

11. Zechariah Chafee, Jr., *How Human Rights Got into the Constitution* (Boston: Boston University Press, 1952), p. 4.

12. Thus I disagree with the Court's ruling in the case of *Bowers v. Hardwick*, 478 U.S. 186 (1986), and I agree broadly with the conclusions of David A. J. Richards concerning the appropriateness of reading the Constitution as implicitly containing some version of John Stuart Mill's principle that the state has the right to limit the freedom of sane adults only to prevent harm to others. David A. J. Richards, *Sex, Drugs, Death, and the Law* (Totowa, N.J.: Rowman & Littlefield, 1982), pp. 1–83. While my conclusions converge generally with Richards's, note that he reaches them by a different route than I do. He starts by arguing that the Constitution implicitly embodies a commitment to the notion of individual rights against government. My argument starts from the claim that the Constitution (as moral promise) embodies an implicit commitment to establish the conditions of legitimate, nonsubjugating governance, and moves from there to the notion of rights against government. One consequence of this difference is that, while Richards is willing to appeal to a variety of foundations for a rights-based moral theory of the Constitution, of which contractarianism is one such foundation, my emphasis on the centrality of the question of legitimacy leads me—for reasons soon to be presented—to emphasize the unique appropriateness of contractarian theory for constitutional interpretation.

13. *Federalist* No. 78, in Alexander Hamilton, James Madison, and John Jay, *The Federalist Papers*, ed. Clinton Rossiter (New York: New American Library, 1961), p. 465.

14. Perry, *Constitution, Courts, and Human Rights,* p. 101.

15. Ibid., p. 123.

16. I refer here generally to Paul Brest, "The Fundamental Rights Controversy: The Essential Contradictions of Normative Constitutional Scholarship," *Yale Law Journal* 90 (1981): 1063–1109; Duncan Kennedy, "The Structure of Blackstone's Commentaries," *Buffalo Law Review* 28 (1979): 205–382; Robert Unger, *The Critical Legal Studies Movement* (Cambridge, Mass.: Harvard University Press, 1986); and the essays in David Kairys, ed., *The Politics of Law* (New York: Pantheon, 1982).

17. I have developed this argument in a different context in my "Law, Rights, Community, and the Structure of Liberal Legal Justification," in *Justification: Nomos XXVIII*, ed. J. R. Pennock and J. W. Chapman (New York: New York University Press, 1986), pp. 178–203.

Part II

Practice

6

Privacy, Intimacy, and Personhood

The summer 1975 issue of *Philosophy and Public Affairs* featured three articles on privacy, one by Judith Jarvis Thomson, one by Thomas Scanlon in response to Thomson, and one by James Rachels in response to them both.[1] Thomson starts from the observation that "the most striking thing about the right to privacy is that nobody seems to have any very clear idea what it is" and goes on to argue that nobody should have one—a very clear idea, that is. Her argument is essentially that all the various protections to which we feel the right to privacy entitles us are already included under other rights, such as "the cluster of rights which the right over the person consists in and also . . . the cluster of rights which owning property consists in."[2] After a romp through some exquisitely fanciful examples, she poses and answers some questions about some of the kinds of "invasions" we would likely think of as violations of the right to privacy:

> Someone looks at your pornographic picture in your wall-safe? He violates your right that your belongings not be looked at, and you have that right because you have ownership rights—and it is because you have them that what he does is wrong. Someone uses an X-ray device to look at you through the walls of your house? He violates your right not to be looked at, and you have that right because you have rights over your person analogous to the rights you have over your property—and it is because you have these rights that what he does is wrong.[3]

From this she concludes that the right to privacy is "derivative" and therefore that "there is no need to find the that-which-is-in-common to all rights in the right to privacy cluster and no need to settle disputes about its boundaries."[4] In other words, we are right not to have any very clear idea about what the right is, and we ought not spin our wheels trying to locate some unique "something" that is protected by the right to privacy. Now, I think Thomson is wrong about this—and, incidentally, so do Scanlon and Rachels, although I am inclined to believe they think so for the wrong reasons.

Thomson's argument is a large non sequitur balanced on a small one. She holds that the right to privacy is "derivative" in the sense that each right in the cluster of rights to privacy can be explained by reference to another right and thus without recourse to the right to privacy. This is the little non sequitur. The easiest way to see this is to recognize that the possibility of such an explanation is quite consistent with the notion that the other rights (that is, the rights over one's person and one's property) are—in whole or in part—expressions of the right to privacy and thus *they* are "derivative" from *it*. If all the protections we include under the right to privacy were specified in the Fourth and Fifth Amendments, this would hardly prove that the right to privacy is "derivative" from the right to be secure against unreasonable search or seizure and the privilege against self-incrimination. It would be just as plausible to assert that this is evidence that the Fourth and Fifth Amendment protections are "derivative" from the right to privacy.[5]

Now, all of this would amount to mere semantics, and Professor Thomson could define "derivative" however she pleased, if she didn't use this as an argument against finding (indeed, against even looking for) the "that-which-is-in-common" to the cluster of rights in the right to privacy. This is the large non sequitur. Even if the right were derivative in the sense urged by Thomson, it would not follow that there is nothing in common to all the protections in the right-to-privacy cluster or that it would be silly to try to find what they have in common. Criminology is probably derivative from sociology and psychology and law and political science in just the way that Thomson holds privacy rights to be derivative from rights to person and property. This hardly amounts to a reason for not trying to define the unifying theme of criminological studies—at least, a large number of criminologists do not think so.[6] In other words, even if privacy rights were a grab bag of property and personal rights, it might still be revealing, as well as helpful, in the resolution of difficult moral conflicts to determine whether there is anything unique that this grab bag protects that makes it worthy of distinction from the full field of property and personal rights.

I shall argue that there is indeed something unique protected by the right to privacy. And we are likely to miss it if we suppose that what is protected is just a subspecies of the things generally safeguarded by property rights and personal rights. And if we miss it, there may come a time when we think we are merely limiting some personal or property right in favor of some greater good, when in fact we are really sacrificing something of much greater value.

At this point, I shall leave behind all comments on Thomson's paper, since if I am able to prove that there is something unique and uniquely valuable protected by the right to privacy, I shall take this as refutation of her view. It will serve to clarify my own position, however, to indicate briefly what I take to be the shortcomings of the responses of Scanlon and Rachels to Thomson.

Scanlon feels he has refuted Thomson by finding the "special interests" that are the "common foundation" for the right(s) to privacy.

> I agree with Thomson that the rights whose violation strikes us as invasion of privacy are many and diverse, and that these rights do not derive from any single overarching right to privacy. I hold, however, that these rights have a common foundation in the special interests that we have in being able to be free from certain kinds of intrusions. The most obvious examples of such offensive intrusions involve observation of our bodies, our behavior or our interactions with other people (or overhearings of the last two), but while these are central they do not exhaust the field.[7]

Now, on first glance, it is certainly hard to dispute this claim. But the claim is nonetheless misleading. Scanlon's position is arresting and appears true because it rests on a tautology, not unlike the classic "explanation" of the capacity of sedatives to induce sleep by virtue of their "dormative powers." The right to privacy *is* the right "to be free from certain kinds of [offensive] intrusions." Scanlon's position is equivalent to holding that the common foundation of our right to privacy lies in our "privatistic interests."

In sum, Scanlon announces that he has found the common element in rights to privacy: rights to privacy protect our special interest in privacy! Thomson could hardly deny this, although I doubt she would find it adequate to answer the questions she raised in her essay. What Scanlon has not told us is *why* we have a special interest in privacy, that is, a special interest in being free from certain kinds of intrusions; and *why* it is a legitimate interest, that is, an interest of sufficient importance to warrant protection by our fellow citizens.[8] I suspect that this is the least that would be necessary to convince Thomson that there is a common foundation to privacy rights.

James Rachels tries to answer precisely the questions Scanlon leaves unanswered. He asks, "Why, exactly, is privacy important to us?"[9] He starts his answer by categorizing some of the interests we might have in privacy and finds that they basically have to do with protecting our reputations or the secrecy of our plans or the like. Rachels recognizes, however, that

> reflection on these cases gives us little help in understanding the value which privacy has in *normal* or *ordinary* situations. By this I mean situations in which there is nothing embarrassing or shameful or unpopular in what we are doing, and nothing ominous or threatening connected with its possible disclosure. For example, even married couples whose sex-lives are normal (whatever that is), and so who have nothing to be ashamed of, by even the most conventional standards, and certainly nothing to be blackmailed about, do not want their bedrooms bugged.[10]

In other words, Rachels recognizes that if there is a unique interest to be protected by the right(s) to privacy, it must be an interest simply in being able to limit other people's observation of us or access to information about us—even if we have certain knowledge that the observation or information would not be used to our detriment or used at all. Rachels tries to identify such an interest and to point out why it is important.

His argument is this. Different human relationships are marked—indeed, in part, constituted—by different degrees of sharing personal information. One shares more of himself with a friend than with an employer, more with a lifelong friend than with a casual friend, more with a lover than with an acquaintance. Rachels writes that "however one conceives one's relations with other people, there is inseparable from that conception an idea of how it is appropriate to behave with and around them, and what information about oneself it is appropriate for them to have." It is "an important part of what it means to have a friend that we welcome his company, that we confide in him, that we tell him things about ourselves, and that we show him sides of our personalities which we would not tell or show to just anyone." And, therefore, Rachels concludes, "because our ability to control who has access to us, and who knows what about us, allows us to maintain the variety of relationships with other people that we want to have, it is, I think, one of the most important reasons why we value privacy."[11]

Rachels acknowledges that his view is similar to that put forth by Charles Fried in *An Anatomy of Values*. Since, for our purposes, we can regard these two views as substantially the same, and since they amount to an impressive argument about the basis of our interest in privacy, it will serve us well to sample Fried's version of the doctrine.

[P]rivacy is the necessary context for relationships which we would hardly be human if we had to do without—the relationships of love, friendship, and trust.

Love and friendship . . . involve the voluntary and spontaneous relinquishment of something between friend and friend, lover and lover. The title to information about oneself conferred by privacy provides the necessary something. To be friends or lovers persons must be intimate to some degree with each other. Intimacy is the sharing of information about one's actions, beliefs or emotions, which one does not share with all, and which one has the right not to share with anyone. By conferring this right, privacy creates the moral capital which we spend in friendship and love.[12]

The Rachels-Fried theory is this. Only because we are able to withhold personal information about—and forbid intimate observation of—ourselves from the rest of the world can we give out the personal information—and allow the intimate observations—to friends and/or lovers who constitute intimate relationships. On this view, intimacy is both signaled and constituted by the sharing of information and allowing of observation *not shared with or allowed to the rest of the world*. If there were nothing about myself that the rest of the world did not have access to, I simply would not have anything to give that would mark off a relationship as intimate. As Fried says,

The man who is generous with his possessions, but not with himself, can hardly be a friend, nor—and this more clearly shows the necessity of privacy for love—can the man who, voluntarily or involuntarily, shares everything about himself with the world indiscriminately.[13]

Presumably, such a person cannot enter into a friendship or a love because he has literally squandered the "moral capital" that is necessary for intimate emotional investment in another.

Now, I find this analysis both compelling and hauntingly distasteful. It is compelling, first of all, because it fits much that we ordinarily experience. For example, it makes jealousy understandable. If the value—indeed, the very reality—of my intimate relation with you lies in your sharing with me what you don't share with others, then if you do share it with another, what I have is literally decreased in value and adulterated in substance. This view is compelling also because it meets the basic requirement for identifying a unique interest at the heart of privacy. That requirement is, as I have already stated, that the interest be an important interest in simply being able to restrict information about, and observation of, myself regardless of what may be done with that information or the results of that observation.

The view is distasteful, however, because it suggests a market conception of personal intimacy. The value and substance of intimacy—like the value and substance of my income—lies, not merely in what I have, but essentially in what others do *not* have. The reality of my intimacy with you is constituted, not simply by the quality and intensity of what we share, but by its unavailability to others—in other words, by its scarcity. It may be that our personal relations are valuable to us because of their exclusiveness rather than because of their own depth or breadth or beauty. But it is not clear that this is necessary. This may be a function of the historical limits of our capacity for empathy and feeling for others. It may be a function of centuries of acculturation to the nuclear family with its narrow intensities. The Rachels-Fried thesis, however, makes it into a logical necessity by asserting that friendship and love *logically* imply exclusiveness and narrowness of focus.

As compelling as the Rachels-Fried view is, then, there is reason to believe it is an example of the high art of ideology: the rendering of aspects of our present possessive market-oriented world into the eternal forms of logical necessity. Perhaps the tip-off lies precisely in the fact that, on this theory, jealousy—the most possessive of emotions—is rendered rational. All of this is, not itself an argument against the Rachels-Fried view, but rather an argument for suspicion. However, it does suggest an argument against that view.

I think the fallacy in the Rachels-Fried view of intimacy is that it overlooks the fact that what constitutes intimacy is, not merely the sharing of otherwise withheld information, but the context of caring that makes the sharing of personal information significant. One ordinarily reveals information to one's psychoanalyst that one might hesitate to reveal to a friend or lover. That hardly means one has an intimate relationship with the analyst. And this is not simply because of the asymmetry. If two analysts decided to psychoanalyze one another alternately—the evident unwisdom of this arrangement aside—there is no reason to believe that their relationship would necessarily be the most intimate one in their lives, even if they revealed to each other information they withheld from everyone else, lifelong friends and lovers included. And this wouldn't be changed if they cared about each other's well-being. What is missing is that particular kind of caring that makes a relationship not just personal but intimate.

The kind of caring I have in mind is not easily put in words, and so I shall claim no more than to offer an approximation. Necessary to an intimate relationship such as friendship or love is a reciprocal desire to share present and future intense and important experiences together, not merely to swap information. Mutual psychoanalysis is not love, or even friendship, so long as it is not animated by this kind of caring. This is why it remains localized in the office rather than tending to spread into other shared activities, as do love and friendship. Were mutual psychoanalysis animated by such caring, it might indeed be part of a love or friendship—but then the "prime mover" of the relationship would not be the exchange of personal information. It would be the caring itself.

In the context of a reciprocal desire to share present and future intense and important experiences, the revealing of personal information takes on significance. The more one knows about the other, the more one is able to understand how the other experiences things, what they mean to him, how they feel to him. In other words, the more each knows about the other, the more both are able to really share an intense experience instead of merely having an intense experience alongside one another. The revealing of personal information, then, is not what constitutes or powers the intimacy. Rather, it deepens and fills out, invites and nurtures, the caring that powers the intimacy.

On this view—in contrast to the Rachels-Fried view—it is of little importance who has access to personal information about me. What matters is who cares about it and to whom I care to reveal it. Even if all those to whom I am indifferent and who return the compliment were to know the intimate details of my personal history, my capacity to enter into an intimate relationship would remain unhindered. So long as I could find someone who did not just want to collect data about me, but who cared to know about me in order to share my experience with me, and to whom I cared to reveal information about myself so that person could share my experience with me, and vice versa, I could enter into a meaningful friendship or love relationship.

On the Rachels-Fried view, it follows that the significance of sexual intimacy lies in the fact that we signal the uniqueness of our love relationships by allowing our bodies to be seen and touched by the loved one in ways that are forbidden to others. But here, too, the context of caring that turns physical contact into intimacy is overlooked. A pair of urologists who examine each other are no more lovers than our reciprocating psychoanalysts. What is missing is the desire to share intense and important experiences. And to say this is to see immediately the appropriateness of sexual intimacy to love: in sexual intimacy, one is literally and symbolically stripped of the ordinary masks that obstruct true sharing of experience. This happens, not merely in the nakedness of lovers, but even more so in the giving of themselves over to the physical forces in their bodies. In surrendering the ordinary restraints, lovers allow themselves to be what they truly are—at least as bodies— intensely and together. (Recall Sartre's marvelous description of the *caress.*)[14] If this takes place in the context of caring—in other words, if people are making love and not just fucking—their physical intimacy is an expression and a consummation of that caring. It is one form of the authentic speech of loving.

Finally, on this view—in contrast to the Rachels-Fried view—the un- savory market notion of intimacy is avoided. Since the content of inti- macy is caring, rather than the revealing of information or the granting of access to the body usually withheld from others, there is no neces- sary limit to the number of persons one can be intimate with, no logical necessity that friendship or love be exclusive. The limits, rather, lie in the limits of our capacity to care deeply for others, and of course in the limits of time and energy. In other words, it may be a fact—for us at this point in history, or even for all people at all points in history—that we can enter into only a few true friendships and loves in a lifetime. But this is not an inescapable logical necessity. It is only an empirical fact of our capacity, one that might change and might be worth trying to change. It might be a fact that we are unable to disentangle love from jealousy. But this, too, is not an a priori truth. It is rather an empirical fact, one that might change if fortune brought us into a less possessive, less exclusive, less invidious society.

This much is enough, I think, to cast doubt on the relationship be- tween privacy and friendship or love asserted by Rachels and Fried. It should also be enough to refute their theory of the grounds on which the right to privacy rests. For if intimacy may be a function of caring and not of the yielding of otherwise withheld information, their claim to have established the necessity of privacy for important human rela- tionships must fall. I think, however, that there is another equally funda- mental ground for rejecting their position: it makes the right to individ- ual privacy "derivative" from the right to social (that is, interpersonal) relationships. And I mean "derivative" in a much more irreversible way than Thomson does.

On the Rachels-Fried view, my right to parade around naked alone in my house, free from observation by human or electronic peeping toms, is not a fundamental right. This right is derived from the fact that, with- out the ability to keep myself from being observed when naked and alone, I could not reveal my body to the loved one in that exclusive way that is necessary to intimacy on the Rachels-Fried view. This strikes me as bizarre. It would imply that a person who had no chance of entering into social relations with others, say a catatonic or a perfectly normal person legitimately sentenced to life imprisonment in solitary confinement, would thereby have no ground for a right to privacy. This must be false because it seems that if there is a right to privacy, it belongs to individuals regardless of whether they are likely to have friends or lovers, regardless of whether they have reason to amass "the moral capital which we spend in friendship and love." What the forgoing suggests is that even if the Rachels-Fried theory of the relationship of privacy and intimacy were true, it would not give us a fundamental interest that can provide the foundation for a right to privacy for all human individuals. I believe, however, that such a fundamental interest can be unearthed. Stanley I. Benn's theory of the foundation of privacy comes closer to the view that I think is ultimately defensible.

Benn attempts to base the right to privacy on the principle of respect for persons. He, too, is aware that utilitarian considerations—for example, prevention of harm that may result from misuse of personal information—while important, are not adequate to ground the right to privacy.

> The underpinning of a claim not to be watched without leave will be more general if it can be grounded in this way on the principle of respect for persons than on a utilitarian duty to avoid inflicting suffering. That duty may, of course, reinforce the claim in particular instances. But respect for persons will sustain an objection even to secret watching, which may do no actual harm at all. Covert observation—spying—is objectionable because it deliberately deceives a person about his world [that is, it transforms the situation he thinks is unobserved into one which is observed], thwarting, for reasons that *cannot* be his reasons, his attempts to make a rational choice. One cannot be said to respect a man as engaged on an enterprise worthy of consideration if one knowingly and deliberately alters his conditions of action, concealing the fact from him. The offense is different in this instance, of course, from A's open intrusion on C's conversation [with D]. In that case, A's attentions were liable to affect C's enterprise by changing C's perception of it; he may have felt differently about his conversation with D, even to the extent of not being able to see it as any longer the same activity, knowing that A was now listening.[15]

Benn's view is that the right to privacy rests on the principle of respect for persons as choosers. Covert observation or unwanted overt observation deny this respect because they transform the actual conditions in which the person chooses and acts, and thus make it impossible for him to act in the way he set out to act, or to choose in the way he thinks he is choosing.

This, too, is a compelling analysis. I shall myself argue that the right to privacy is fundamentally connected to personhood. However, as it stands, Benn's theory gives us too much—and, though he appears to know it, his way of trimming the theory to manageable scale is not very helpful. Benn's theory gives us too much because it appears to establish a person's right never to be observed when he thought he wasn't being observed and never to be overtly observed when he didn't wish it. This would give us a right not to have people look at us from their front windows as we absent-mindedly stroll along, as well as a right not to be stared in the face. To deal with this, Benn writes,

> it cannot be sufficient that I do not *want* you to observe something; for the principle of respect to be relevant, it must be something about my own person that is in question, otherwise the principle would be so wide that a mere wish of mine would be a prima facie reason for everyone to refrain from observing and reporting on anything at all. I do not make something a part of me merely by having feelings about it. The principle of privacy proposed here is, rather, that any man who desires that he *himself* should not be an object of scrutiny has a reasonable claim to immunity.[16]

Benn goes on to say that what is rightly covered by this immunity are one's body and those things, such as possessions, which the conventions of a culture may cause one to think of as part of one's identity.

But this begs the question. Benn has moved from the principle that respect for me as a person dictates that I am entitled not to have the conditions in which I choose altered by unknown or unwanted observation, to the principle that I am entitled to have those things (conventionally) bound up with my identity exempt from unknown or unwanted observation. But the first principle does not entail the second, because the second principle is not merely a practical limitation on the first; it is a moral limitation. It asserts that it is wrong (or, at least, significantly worse) to have the conditions in which I choose altered, when things closely bound up with my identity are concerned. This follows only if the first principle is conjoined with another that holds that the closer something is to my identity, the worse it is for others to tamper with it. But this additional principle is, after all, just an abstract version of the right to privacy itself. And since Benn has not shown that this additional principle follows from the principle of respect for persons as choosers, his argument presupposes what he seeks to establish. It is quite strictly a *petitio principii*.

In sum, then, though we have moved quite a bit further in the direction of the foundation of privacy, we have still not reached our destination. What we are looking for is a fundamental interest, connected to personhood, that provides a basis for a right to privacy to which all human beings are entitled (even those in solitary confinement) and that does not go so far as to claim a right never to be observed (even on crowded streets). I proceed now to the consideration of a candidate for such a fundamental interest.

Privacy is a social practice. It involves a complex of behaviors that stretches from refraining from asking questions about what is none of one's business to refraining from looking into open windows one passes on the street, from refraining from entering a closed door without knocking to refraining from knocking down a locked door without a warrant.

Privacy can in this sense be looked at as a very complicated social ritual. But what is its point? In response, I want to defend the following thesis. *Privacy is a social ritual by means of which an individual's moral title to his existence is conferred.* Privacy is an essential part of the complex social practice by means of which the social group recognizes—and communicates to the individual—that his existence is his own. And this is a precondition of moral personhood. To be a person in the moral sense, an individual must recognize not just his actual capacity to shape his destiny by his choices. He must also recognize that he has an exclusive moral right to shape his destiny. This in turn, presupposes that he believes that the concrete reality which he is, and through which his destiny is realized, belongs to him in a moral sense.

And if one takes—as I am inclined to—the symbolic interactionist perspective, which teaches that "selves" are created in social interaction rather than flowering innately from inborn seeds, to this claim is added an even stronger one: privacy is necessary to the creation of *selves* out of human beings since a self is, at least in part, a human being who regards his existence—his thoughts, his body, his actions—as his own. I use "self" and "person," here, correlatively.[17] Roughly speaking, a self is the subjective reality of a human being with the moral status of a person.

Thus the relationship between privacy and personhood is a twofold one. First, the social ritual of privacy seems to be an essential ingredient in the process by which "persons" are created out of prepersonal infants. It conveys to the developing child the recognition that this body to which he is uniquely "connected" is a body over which he has some exclusive moral rights. Second, the social ritual of privacy confirms, and demonstrates respect for, the personhood of already developed persons. I take the notion of "conferring title to one's existence" to cover both dimensions of the relationship of privacy to personhood: the original bestowal of title and the ongoing confirmation. And, of course, to the extent that we believe that the creation of "selves" or "persons" is an ongoing social process—not just something that occurs once and for all during childhood—the two dimensions become one: privacy is a condition of the original and continuing creation of "selves" or "persons."

To understand the meaning of this claim, it will be helpful to turn to Erving Goffman's classic study, "On the Characteristics of Total Institutions."[18] Goffman says of total institutions that "each is a natural experiment on what can be done to the self."[19] The goal of these experiments is *mortification of the self,* and in each case total deprivation of privacy is an essential ingredient in the regimen. I have taken the liberty of quoting Goffman at length, since I think his analysis provides poignant testimony to the role that elimination of privacy plays in destruction of the self. And thus, conversely, he shows the degree to which the self requires the social rituals of privacy to exist.

> There is another form of mortification in total institutions; beginning with admission a kind of contaminative exposure occurs. On the outside, the individual can hold objects of self-feeling—such as his body, his immediate actions, his thoughts, and some of his possessions—clear of contact with alien and contaminating things. But in total institutions these *territories of the self are violated.* . . .
> There is, first, a violation of one's informational preserve regarding self. During admission, facts about the inmate's social statuses and past behavior—especially discreditable facts—are collected and recorded in a dossier available to staff. . . .
> New audiences not only learn discreditable facts about oneself that are ordinarily concealed but are also in a position to perceive some of these facts directly. Prisoners and mental patients cannot prevent their visitors from seeing them in humiliating circumstances. Another example is the shoulder-patch of ethnic identification worn by concentration-camp inmates. Medical and security examinations often expose the inmate physically, sometimes to persons of both sexes; a similar exposure follows from collective sleeping arrangements and doorless toilets. . . . In general, of course, the inmate is never fully alone; he is always within sight and often earshot of someone, if only his fellow inmates. Prison cages with bars for walls fully realize such exposure.[20]

That social practices that penetrate "the private reserve of the individual"[21] are effective means to mortify the inmate's self—that is, literally, to kill it off—suggests (though it doesn't prove) that privacy is essential to the creation and maintenance of selves. My argument for this will admittedly be speculative. However, in view of the fact that this argument escapes the shortcomings of the views we have already analyzed, fits Goffman's evidence on the effects of deprivation of privacy, fulfills the requirement that privacy be based on a fundamental human interest worthy of protection, provides the basis for a right to privacy to which all human beings are entitled, and yet does not claim a right never to be observed, I think it is convincing.

If I am sitting with other people, how do I know this body that is connected to the thoughts I am having is *mine* in the moral sense? That is, how do I know that I have a unique moral right to this body? It is not enough to say that the body is connected to my consciousness, since that simply repeats the question or begs the question of what makes these thoughts *my* consciousness. In any event, connection to my consciousness is a factual link, not a moral one. In itself, it accounts for why I am not likely to confuse the events in this body (mine) with events in that body (yours). It does not account for the moral title that gives me a unique right to control the events in this body, a right I don't have in respect to the events in that body.

Ownership in the moral sense presupposes a social institution. It is based upon a complex social practice. A social order in which bodies were held to belong to others or to the collectivity, and in which individuals grew up believing that their bodies were not theirs from a moral point of view, is conceivable. To imagine such an order does not require that we deny that for each body only one individual is able to feel or move it. Such a social order is precisely what Goffman portrays in his description of total institutions, and it might be thought of as displaying the ultimate logic of totalitarianism. Totalitarianism is the political condition that obtains when a state takes on the characteristics of a total institution. For a society to exist in which individuals do not own their bodies, what is necessary is that people not be treated as if entitled to control what the bodies they can feel and move do, or what is done to those bodies—in particular, that they not be treated as if entitled to determine when and by whom that body is experienced.

This suggests that there are two essential conditions of moral ownership of one's body: the right to do with one's body what one wishes, and the right to control when and by whom one's body is experienced. This, in turn, reflects the fact that things can be appropriated in two ways: roughly speaking, actively and cognitively. That is, something is "mine" to the extent that I have the power to use it, to dispose of it as

I see fit. But, additionally, there is a way in which something becomes "mine" to the extent that I know it. What I know is "my" knowledge; what I experience is "my" experience. Thus it follows that if an individual were granted the right to control his bodily movements although always under observation, he might develop some sense of moral ownership of his physical existence.[22] However, that ownership would surely be an impoverished and partial one compared to what we take to be contained in an individual's title to his existence. This is because it would be ownership only in one of the two dimensions of appropriation, the active. Ownership, in the sense we know it, requires control over cognitive appropriation as well. It requires that the individual have control over whether or not his physical existence becomes part of someone else's experience. That is, it requires that the individual be treated as entitled to determine when and by whom his concrete reality is experienced. Moral ownership in the full sense requires the social ritual of privacy.

As I sit among my friends, I know this body is mine because, first of all, I believe—and my friends have acted and continue to act as if they believe—that, unlike with any other body present, I am entitled to do with this body what I wish. Second, but also essential, I know this body is mine because I have in the past taken it, unlike any other body present, outside of the range of anyone's experience but my own, I can do so now, and I expect to be able to do so in the future. What's more, I believe—and my friends have acted and continue to act as if they believe—that it would be wrong for anyone to interfere with my capacity to do this. In other words, they have treated and continue to treat me according to the social ritual of privacy. And since my view of myself is, in important ways, a reflection of how others treat me, I come to view myself as the kind of entity that is entitled to the social ritual of privacy. That is, I come to believe that this body is mine in the moral sense.

I think the same thing can be said about the thoughts of which I am aware. That there are thoughts, images, reveries and memories of which only I am conscious does not make them mine in the moral sense—any more than the cylinders in a car belong to it just because they are in it. This is why ascribing ownership of my body to the mere connection with my consciousness begs the question. Ownership of my thoughts requires a social practice as well. It has to do with learning that I can control when, and by whom, the thoughts in my head will be experienced by someone other than myself and learning that I am entitled to such control—that I will not be forced to reveal the contents of my consciousness, even when I put those contents on paper. The contents of my consciousness become mine because they are treated according to the ritual of privacy.

It may seem that this is to return full circle to Thomson's view that the right to privacy is just a species of the rights over person and property. I would argue that it is more fundamental. The right to privacy is the right to the existence of a social practice that makes it possible for me to think of this existence as mine. This means that it is the right to conditions necessary for me to think of myself as the kind of entity for whom it would be meaningful and important to claim personal and property rights. It should also be clear that the ownership of which I am speaking is surely more fundamental than property rights. Indeed, it is only when I can call this physical existence mine that I can call objects somehow connected to this physical existence mine. That is, the transformation of physical possession into ownership presupposes ownership of the physical being I am. Thus the right to privacy protects something that is presupposed by both personal and property rights. Thomson's recognition that there is overlap should come as no surprise. The conclusion she draws from the existence of this overlap is, however, unwarranted. Personal and property rights presuppose an individual with title to his existence—and privacy is the social ritual by which that title is conferred.

The right to privacy, then, protects the individual's interest in becoming, being, and remaining a moral person. It is thus a right that *all* human individuals possess—even those in solitary confinement. It does not assert a right never to be seen even on a crowded street. It is sufficient that I can control whether and by whom my body is experienced in some significant locales and that I have the real possibility of repairing to those locales. The right to privacy protects my capacity to enter into intimate relations, not because it protects my reserve of generally withheld information, but because it enables me to make the commitment that underlies caring as *my* commitment uniquely conveyed by *my* thoughts and witnessed by *my* actions.

Notes

This chapter is a revised version of an article originally published in *Philosophy and Public Affairs* 6, no. 1 (Fall 1976): 26–44. Copyright 1976 by Princeton University Press. Reprinted with permission.
    1. Judith Jarvis Thomson, "The Right to Privacy," *Philosophy and Public*

Affairs 4, no. 4 (Summer 1975): 295–314; Thomas Scanlon, "Thomson on Privacy," *Philosophy and Public Affairs* 4, no. 4 (Summer 1975): 315–22; and James Rachels, "Why Privacy is Important," *Philosophy and Public Affairs* 4, no. 4 (Summer 1975): 323–33.

2. Thomson, "Right to Privacy," 295, 306.

3. Ibid., p. 313.

4. Ibid.

5. This reversibility of "derivative"-ness is to be found in Justice Douglas's historic opinion on the right to privacy in *Griswold v. Connecticut.* He states there that "specific guarantees in the Bill of Rights have penumbras, formed by emanations from those guarantees that help give them life and substance." The right to privacy, he goes on to say, is contained in the penumbras of the First, Third, Fourth, Fifth, and Ninth Amendment guarantees. Surely the imagery of penumbral emanations suggests that the right to privacy is "derivative" from the rights protected in these amendments. But later Douglas states that the Court is dealing "with a right of privacy older than the Bill of Rights," which along with other language he uses, suggests that the rights in the Bill of Rights are meant to give reality to an even more fundamental right, the right to privacy. 381 U.S. 479 (1965).

6. See, for instance, Herman and Julia Schwendinger, "Defenders of Order or Guardians of Human Rights?" *Issues in Criminology* 5, no. 2 (Summer 1970): 123–57, especially the section entitled "The Thirty-Year-Old Controversy," pp. 123–29.

7. Scanlon, "Thomson on Privacy," 315.

8. I think it is fair to say that Scanlon makes no claim to answer these questions in his essay.

9. Rachels, "Why Privacy Is Important," 323.

10. Ibid., 325.

11. Ibid., 327–29.

12. Charles Fried, *An Anatomy of Values: Problems of Personal and Social Choice* (Cambridge, Mass.: Harvard University Press, 1970), p. 142. It might be thought that in lifting Fried's analysis of privacy out of his book, I have lifted it out of context and thus done violence to his theory. Extra weight is added to this objection by the recognition that when Fried speaks about love in his book (though not in the chapter relating privacy to love), he speaks of something very like the caring that I present as a basis for refuting his view. For instance: "There is rather a creation of love, a middle term, which is a new pattern or system of interests which both share and both value, in part at least just because it is shared." Ibid., p. 79. What is in conflict between us, then, is not recognition of this, or something like this, as an essential component of the love relationship. The conflict, rather, lies in the fact that I argue that recognition of this factor undermines Fried's claim that *privacy* is *necessary* for the very existence of love relationships.

13. Ibid., p. 142.

14. "The Other's flesh did not exist explicitly for me since I grasped the Other's body in situation; neither did it exist for her since she transcended it toward her possibilities and toward the object. The caress causes the Other to be born as flesh for me and for herself . . . , the caress reveals the flesh by stripping the body of its action, by cutting it off from the possibilities which surround it; the caress is designed to uncover the web of inertia beneath the action—i.e., the pure 'being-there'—which sustains it. . . . The caress is designed to cause the Other's body to be born, through pleasure, for the Other—and for myself." Jean-Paul Sartre, *Being and Nothingness*, trans. Hazel E. Barnes (New York: Philosophical Library, 1956), p. 390.

15. Stanley I. Benn, "Privacy, Freedom, and Respect for Persons," in *Today's Moral Problems*, ed. Richard Wasserstrom (New York: Macmillan, 1975), p. 8 (emphasis in original).

16. Ibid., p. 10 (emphasis in original).

17. For purposes of this discussion, "self" and "person" both refer to an individual who recognizes that he owns his physical and mental reality in the sense that he is morally entitled to realize his destiny through it, and thus that he has at least a strong presumptive moral right not to have others interfere with his self-determination.

18. Erving Goffman, *Asylums* (New York: Anchor Books, 1961), pp. 1–124.

19. Ibid., p. 12.

20. Ibid., pp. 23–25 (emphasis mine).

21. Ibid., p. 29.

22. I am indebted to Professor Phillip H. Scribner for pointing this out to me.

7

Driving to the Panopticon: A Philosophical Exploration of the Risks to Privacy Posed by the Information Technology of the Future

[T]he major effect of the Panopticon [is] to induce in the inmate a state of conscious and permanent visibility that assures the automatic functioning of power.

Michel Foucault

If we can never be sure whether or not we are being watched and listened to, all our actions will be altered and our very character will change.

Hubert Humphrey

Experience should teach us to be most on our guard to protect liberty when the government's purposes are beneficent.

Louis Brandeis

Intelligent Vehicle Highway Systems (IVHS) is a joint government and private sector project aimed at applying information technology to highway transportation in order to make highway travel safer, speedier, and more efficient. The short-term goal, already partially realized, is to use computers to track vehicles and provide drivers with information concerning road conditions and optimal routes. The long-term goal, currently in the experimental stage, is to use computers to take over the driving itself. The project, however, is not without its risks. According to the IVHS America Legal Issues Committee, "IVHS information systems [will] contain information on where travelers go, the routes they

169

use, and when they travel. This information could be used to disadvantage individuals, and should be secure."[1] This is from a list of what the Privacy Task Group of the Legal Issues Committee calls, interestingly, " 'Strawman' Privacy Principles." I hope that my title, "Driving to the Panopticon," makes clear that I don't regard the threat to privacy posed by Intelligent Vehicle Highway Systems as a strawman at all. Nor do I think that the committee's vague reference to use of information to individuals' disadvantage does any more than begin to hint at the nature of that threat.

The "panopticon" was Jeremy Bentham's plan for a prison in which large numbers of convicts could be kept under surveillance by very few guards.[2] The idea was to build the prison cells in a circle around the guard post. All the prisoners would be silhouetted against light coming into the cells from windows on the outside of the circle. Their movements would be visible to a single guard in the center. The French philosopher Michel Foucault used Bentham's panopticon as an ominous metaphor for the mechanisms of large-scale social control that characterize the modern world.[3] He contended that it became, perhaps subconsciously, the model for institutions in nineteenth-century Europe and America. "Is it surprising," asked Foucault, "that prisons resemble factories, schools, barracks, hospitals, which all resemble prisons?"[4]

As Bentham realized and Foucault emphasized, the system works even if there is no one in the guardhouse. The very fact of general visibility—being see*able* more than being seen—will be enough to produce effective social control.[5] Indeed, awareness of being visible, wrote Foucault, makes people the agents of their own subjection.

> He who is subjected to a field of visibility, and who knows it, assumes responsibility for the constraints of power; he makes them play spontaneously upon himself; he inscribes in himself the power relation in which he simultaneously plays both roles; he becomes the principle of his own subjection.[6]

Foucault went on to stretch the panopticon metaphor beyond architecture to characterize the practices of conventional medicine, psychology, and sex education, all of which he thought subject us to increasing social control because they create a world in which the details of our lives become symptoms exposed to a clinical gaze—even if no one is actually looking.[7] I want to stretch the panopticon metaphor yet further, to emphasize, not just the way it makes people visible, but the way that it makes them visible *from a single point*.

An intriguing and illuminating feature of the suspicion about the threat to privacy posed by IVHS is that the information that would be accumulated by it is public. Wherever we drive, we drive in the public world and thus we are normally subject to unobjectionable public observation. Courts have held that normal observation by police officers in or from public places does not intrude on a person's private affairs. This has been specifically applied to "the following of an automobile on public streets and highways,"[8] even when the following was done by tracking a beeper planted on an object in the driver's possession. In Unites States v. Karo, the Supreme Court held that "while in [their] vehicles on public roads . . . , [t]he defendants had no privacy interest in what could have been visually observed in these public places."[9]

If there is a threat to privacy from IVHS, it comes from the fact that—as readers of detective fiction well know—by accumulating a lot of disparate pieces of public information, you can construct a fairly detailed picture of a person's private life. You can find out who her friends are, what she does for fun or profit, and from such facts others can be inferred, whether she is punctual, whether she is faithful, and so on. Richard Wasserstrom observes, in an article first published in 1978, that the information already collected in data banks at that time, if gathered together, could produce a "picture of how I had been living and what I had been doing . . . that is fantastically more detailed, accurate, and complete than the one I could supply from my own memory."[10]

There is, then, something to learn about privacy from the sort of threat that IVHS represents: namely, that privacy results, not only from locked doors and closed curtains, but also from the way our publicly observable activities are dispersed over space and time. If we direct our privacy-protection efforts at reinforcing our doors and curtains, we may miss the way in which modern means of information collection threaten our privacy by gathering up the pieces of our public lives and making them visible from a single point. This is why the panopticon is a more fitting metaphor for the new threat to privacy than, for example, that old staple, the fishbowl.

But a threat to privacy is only worrisome insofar as privacy is valuable or protects other things that are valuable. No doubt privacy is valuable to people who have mischief to hide, but that is not enough to make it generally worth protecting. However, it is enough to remind us that whatever value privacy has, it also has costs. The more privacy we have, the more difficult it is to get the information that society needs to stop or punish wrongdoers. Moreover, the curtain of privacy that is traditionally brought down around the family has often provided cover for the subjugation and abuse of women and children. Privacy is not a free lunch. To believe, as I do, that privacy is essential to a free society is to believe that it is worth its costs. But, then, freedom itself is not a free lunch. A free society is a dangerous and often chaotic one. Let us, then, look at the value of privacy.

By *privacy*, I understand the condition in which other people are deprived of access to either some information about you or some experience of you. For the sake of economy, I will shorten this and say that *privacy is the condition in which others are deprived of access to you.* Under *access*, I include experience alongside information, since I think that privacy is about more than information. Your ability to take a shower unwatched is part of your privacy even though watchers may gain no information about you that they didn't already get in their high school biology course. Or, if you think that they might after all gain some information about your particular physiognomy, I would say that it is a matter of privacy that you are able to keep your body unobserved even by people who have already seen it and thus who already have that particular information. This said, I shall primarily speak of the value of privacy regarding information, since it is information about us that will be collected by IVHS.

Note that I have defined privacy in terms of the condition of others' lack of access to you. Some writers, for example Charles Fried, have claimed that it is *your control* over who has access to you that is essential to privacy. According to Fried, it would be ironic to say that a person alone on an island has privacy.[11] I don't find this ironic at all. But, more importantly, including control as part of privacy leads to anomalies. For example, Fried writes that "in our culture the excretory functions are shielded by more or less absolute privacy, so much so that situations in which this privacy is violated are experienced as extremely distressing."[12] But in our culture one does not have control over who gets to observe one's performance of the excretory functions, since it is generally prohibited to execute them in public.[13] Since prying on someone in the privy is surely a violation of privacy, privacy must be a condition independent of the issue of control.[14]

It's easy to get confused here, since there are some private matters in which control is of great importance. For example, we don't simply want to restrict access to our naked bodies; we want to be able to decide who gets to see or touch them. The privy should remind us, however, that cases like these do not exhaust our interest in privacy. To include control in the definition of privacy would restrict our understanding of the value of privacy to only that part of privacy in which control is important—which is precisely the result in Fried's case. He ends up taking privacy to be a value because it gives us a kind of scarce resource (access to ourselves) to distribute. And he claims that our ability to distribute this resource is the key to our ability to have intimate relations.[15] I think that Fried is wrong about intimate relations, since I think that intimate relations are a function of how much people care about each other, not how much they know about each other. One may have an intensely intimate relationship with someone without—or at least before—sharing a lot of private information with them, and one can share private information with one's shrink or priest or even with a stranger on an airplane without thereby having an intimate relationship with them.

If we include control in the definition of privacy we will find the value of the sort of privacy we want in the bedroom, but not of the sort we want in the bathroom. In our bedrooms, we want to have power over who has access to us; in our bathrooms, we just want others deprived of that access. But notice here that the sort of privacy we want in the bedroom presupposes the sort we want in the bathroom. We cannot have discretion over who has access to us in the bedroom unless others lack access at their discretion. In the bathroom, that is all we want. In the bedroom, we want additionally the power to decide at our discretion who does have access. What is common to both sorts of privacy interests, then, is that others not have access to us at their discretion. If we are to find the value of privacy generally, then it will have to be the value of this restriction on others. Sometimes its value will lie precisely in the fact that the restriction leaves room for our own control. But other times it will lie just in that others lack the access. This is important for our purposes, since the information that IVHS will gather is not the sort that it will be terribly important for us to be able to give out at our discretion. It will be information that we simply do not want others to have.

From the definition of privacy just given follows a specific conception of the *right to* privacy. The right to privacy is not my right to control access to me—it is my right that others be deprived of that access.[16] In some cases, though not all, having this right will protect my ability to control access to me.

Having privacy is not the same thing as having a right to privacy. I can have either without the other. I can have privacy without the right to privacy, say, when I successfully conceal my criminal activities. And I can have a right to privacy and not have privacy, say, when others successfully violate the right.

For there to be a right to privacy, there must be some valid norm that specifies that some personal information about, or experience of, individuals should be kept out of other people's reach. Such norms may be legal. I've already quoted some of the legal norms governing the right to privacy in the United States.[17] If, however, we think that individuals ought to have others deprived of access to some of their personal affairs whether or not a law says so, then we think that there is (something like) a moral right to privacy. And we will want our laws to protect this moral right by backing it up with an effective legal right. Since I think that IVHS threatens our privacy in ways that go beyond current legal rights, I am concerned to defend a moral right to privacy.

To say that someone has a moral right to privacy doesn't say much unless we know what the scope of that right is, what things or activities a person has a right to keep out of other people's view. For anyone who doesn't live in a cave or in a desert, a completely private life is impossible. Normally, we will think that some things are rightly within the scope of a person's privacy (say, their religious beliefs) and other things (say, the color of their eyes) are not. Often, as cases like *Roe v. Wade* and *Bowers v. Hardwick* show, precisely what should or should not come under the scope of the right to privacy is controversial.[18] As these cases testify, some will argue that citizens of a free society should have as extensive a right to privacy as is compatible with reasonably safe social coexistence, while others will argue that only certain specific areas of people's lives (for example, bodily processes, intimate relationships, activities relating to the formation of political opinions and plans) should be protected. As the tension between current law and fears about IVHS shows, there is disagreement over whether the accumulation of bits of public information should come under the scope of privacy.

To resolve such disagreements, we must get clear on the value of privacy. If we know why having privacy, or, equivalently, having an effective right to privacy, is an especially important and good thing for human beings, we will be able to determine what must come under the scope of privacy for that value to be realized.

To do this, I propose that we imagine together the world in which the full IVHS project is completed, and then see what losses we might suffer as a result of the information about us that would then be gathered. Here it is of great importance that a fully developed IVHS will not exist in an informational vacuum. IVHS's information will exist alongside that provided by other developments already in existence and likely to grow, such as computerization of census and IRS information; computer records of people's credit-card purchases, their bank transactions, their credit histories generally, their telephone calls, their medical conditions, and their education and employment histories; and, of course, the records of their brushes with the law, even of arrests that end in acquittal. Add to this the so-called information highway on which we will all soon be riding, with its automatic recording of all interactions, not to mention the FBI's desire to keep it eternally wiretappable.[19] It has been observed, by the way, that as people conduct the business of their daily lives more and more via digital communications, mere knowledge of whom people call—knowledge now readily available to police agencies—"would give law enforcers extensive access to people's habits and daily activities."[20]

It is this whole complex of information gathering that, I think, threatens us. It is this whole complex that, in its potential to make our lives as a whole visible from a single point, brings to mind the panopticon. Accordingly, it is as a factor in helping to bring about this whole complex that I shall consider the threat posed by IVHS.

It might seem unfair to IVHS to consider it in light of all this other accumulated information—but this is the only way to see the threat accurately. The reason is this: We have privacy when we can keep personal things out of the public view. Information gathering in any particular realm may not seem to pose a very grave threat precisely because it is generally possible to preserve one's privacy by escaping into other realms. Consequently, as we look at each kind of information gathering in isolation from the others, each may seem relatively benign.[21] However, as each is put into practice, its effect is to close off yet another escape route from public access, so that, when the whole complex is in place, its overall effect on privacy will be greater than the sum of the effects of the parts. What we need to know is IVHS's role in bringing about this overall effect, and it plays that role by contributing to the establishment of the whole complex of information-gathering modalities.

I call this whole complex, of which IVHS will be a part, the *informational panopticon*. It is the risks posed to privacy by the informational panopticon as a whole that I shall explore.

Ride with me, then, into the informational panopticon and consider what we stand to lose if our lives become generally visible. We can characterize the potential risks under four headings: (*a*) the risk of extrinsic loss of freedom; (*b*) the risk of intrinsic loss of freedom; (*c*) symbolic risks; and (*d*) the risk of psycho-political metamorphosis. All these strange headings will become clear in due course. I have given the last category a particularly unwieldy and ugly heading precisely because it is the one that I regard as least familiar, most speculative, and most ominous. The reference to Kafka is intentional. This said, I should add that these headings are not put forth as airtight metaphysical divisions. They are meant simply to get unruly ideas under control. Like many philosophical categories, they will crumble if pressed too hard. If, however, we see them for what they are, they will give us an orderly picture of the risks that IVHS and the rest of the informational panopticon pose to privacy. But, more, this picture will be just a negative image of the value of privacy.

The Risk of Extrinsic Loss of Freedom

By extrinsic loss of freedom, I mean all those ways in which lack of privacy makes people vulnerable to having their behavior controlled by others. Most obviously, this refers to the fact that people who want to do unpopular or unconventional actions may be subject to social pressure in the form of denial of certain benefits—jobs, promotions, or membership in formal or informal groups—or even blackmail, if their actions are known to others. Even if they have reason to believe that their actions *may* be known to others and that those others *may* penalize them, this is likely to have a chilling effect on them that will constrain the range of their freedom to act.[22] Remember, it is by inducing the consciousness of visibility that the panopticon, in Foucault's words, "assures the automatic functioning of power."

Ruth Gavison writes, "Privacy . . . prevents interference, pressures to conform, ridicule, punishment, unfavorable decisions, and other forms of hostile reaction. To the extent that privacy does this, it functions to promote liberty of action, removing the unpleasant consequences of certain actions and thus increasing the liberty to perform them."[23] This is not just a matter of the freedom to do immoral or illegal acts. It applies equally to unpopular political actions that have nothing immoral or illegal about them.

Moreover, in a free society, there are actions thought immoral by many or even a majority of citizens that a significant minority thinks are morally acceptable. The preservation of freedom requires that, wherever possible, the moral status of these actions be left to individuals to decide for themselves and thus that not everything that a majority of citizens thinks is immoral be made illegal. (Think here of pornography, gambling, drunkenness, homosexual or pre- or extra-marital heterosexual sex.) If it would be wrong to force people legally to conform to the majority's views on such issues, it would be equally wrong to use harsh social pressure to accomplish the same effect. For this reason, Mill argued in *On Liberty* against both legal enforcement of morality and its informal social enforcement by stigmatization or ostracism.[24]

Mill was not, by the way, against people trying to persuade one another about what is moral. Actually, he thought we should do more of that than we normally do. He distinguished, however, between appeals to reason and appeals to force or its equivalent, harsh informal social penalties. Trying to persuade the minority by making arguments and producing evidence can be done in public forums without pointing fingers, and thus without putting any particular person at risk. Most importantly, it leaves the members of the minority free to make up their own minds.[25] Threatening the minority with stigmatization or ostracism works like force because it changes people's actions by attaching painful consequences to them, without changing their minds at all. Privacy protects people from the operation of this force and thus preserves their freedom.

Some may wonder whether the idea that people need privacy to act freely is based on too dim a view of human character. Those who raise this doubt think that people with strong characters will be able to resist social pressure and thus only those with weak characters need dark private corners in order to act freely. In different ways, this objection can be raised against all the risks to privacy that I shall describe, and so I want to give a general answer to it. The answer has three parts:

First, laws and social practices generally have to be designed for the real people that they will govern, not for some ideal people that we would like to see or be. Just as Madison observed that if people were angels we wouldn't need government at all,[26] so we might add that if people were heroes we wouldn't need privacy at all. Since people are neither angels nor (except in a few instances) heroes, we need both government and privacy.

Second, just because people are not angels, some will be tempted to penalize those who act unconventionally. Even if people should ideally be able to withstand social pressure in the form of stigmatization or ostracism, it remains unjust that they should suffer these painful fates simply for acting in unpopular or unconventional ways. In any actual society, we will need privacy to prevent this injustice.

Third, suppose we wanted to make our citizens into the sorts of strong-willed people who can resist social pressures. We would still have to give them experience in formulating their own judgments and in acting upon those judgments. And this experience would have to be given to them before they have the strong characters we want them to attain. They would have to be sheltered from pressures toward social conformity while they are still vulnerable, in order to become the sorts of people who are not vulnerable. They would need privacy in order to become the sorts of people who don't need it.[27] Much as liberty is, as Mill felt, a school for character,[28] so too is privacy. And since this school must provide continuing education for adults as well teach children, we need privacy as an abiding feature of the society. In short, the vast majority of actual people need privacy for free action, and those who do not, needed privacy to become that way. With or without heroes, we need privacy.

The Risk of Intrinsic Loss of Freedom

By intrinsic loss of freedom, I point to ways in which denial of privacy limits people's freedom directly, independently of the ways in which it makes them susceptible to social pressure or penalties. Put differently, I want here to suggest that privacy is not just a means of protecting freedom; it is itself constitutive of freedom in a number of important ways.

To start, recall the discussion about the place of control in the definition of privacy.[29] I concluded there that control is not part of privacy but that in some cases it is part of what privacy makes possible. For me to be able to decide who touches my body, or who knows the details of my personal history, those things must not be generally accessible to others at their discretion. That means that if those things are not shielded by privacy, I am automatically denied certain important choices. This is what I mean by an intrinsic loss of freedom. I am not here denied the choices by fear of certain consequences; I am denied them directly because privacy is the condition of their being choices for me in the first place.

Another intrinsic loss of freedom is the following. A number of writers have emphasized the ways in which some actions have a different nature when they are observed than they do when they are not.[30] This is clearest in cases that are distant from IVHS: Criticizing an individual in front of others is a different act from uttering the same critical words to him in private. And, of course, making love before an audience is something quite different from the same act done in private. In the case of our informational panopticon, the alteration is more subtle. Every act, say, driving to destination X at time T, is now a more complex event. It now becomes driving to X at T *and creating a record of driving to X at T.* These differ from one another as leaving a message on someone's answering machine differs from rehearsing the same words in one's imagination. If my every driving act (not to mention all the other acts visible in the informational panopticon) is also the depositing of a record, not only are my acts changed, but my freedom is limited. I am no longer free to do the act of simply driving to X at T *without leaving a record.*

With this, I lose as well the freedom of acting spontaneously. In a society that collected data on all of an individual's transactions,

> one would be both buying a tank of gas and leaving a part of a systematic record of where one was on that particular date. One would not just be applying for life insurance; one would also be recording in a permanent way one's health on that date and a variety of other facts about oneself. No matter how innocent one's intentions and actions at any given moment . . . , persons would think more carefully before they did things that would become part of the record. Life would to this degree become less spontaneous and more measured."[31]

When you know you are being observed, you naturally identify with the outside observer's viewpoint and add that alongside your own viewpoint on your action. This double vision makes your act different, whether the act is making love or taking a drive. The targets of the panopticon know and feel the eye of the guard on them, making their actions different than if they were done in private. Their repertoire of possible actions diminishes as they lose those choices whose intrinsic nature depends on privacy.

Symbolic Risks

Elsewhere I have argued that privacy is a social ritual by which we show one another that we regard each person as the owner of herself, her body, and her thoughts.[32] It is for this reason that privacy is generally absent from organizations like monasteries, armies, communist cells, and madhouses, where individuals are thought to belong to some larger whole or greater purpose. This is also why invasions of privacy are wrong even when they don't pose any risk to reputation or freedom, even when the invader will not use what he observes in any harmful way, even when the individual is unaware that her privacy is being invaded. Aside from any harms that invasions of privacy threaten, such invasions are *insults*. They slight an individual's ownership of herself and thus insult her by denying her special dignity. The peeping tom treats his prey with unmerited, and thus unjust, contempt.

Privacy conveys to the individual his self-ownership precisely by letting him know of his ability and his authority to withdraw himself from the scrutiny of others. Those who lose this ability and authority are thereby told that they don't belong to themselves; they are specimens belonging to those who would investigate them.[33] They are someone else's data. It is no accident that the panopticon was a design for a prison, an institution that in effect suspends a person's ownership of himself because he committed a crime. Since our informational panopticon effectively suspends self-ownership though no crime has been committed, it conveys an unmerited, and thus unjust, insult.

I said earlier that I wanted to emphasize the way in which the panopticon makes our lives visible from a single point. Here it is worth noting that that point is outside of us, where the guardian stands. The panopticon symbolizes a kind of draining of our individual sovereignty away and outside of us into a single center. We become its data to observe at its will—our outsides belong to its inside rather than to our own.

I have called this a symbolic risk because it affects us as a kind of message, a message inscribed in an institutional structure. We are not deprived of our self-ownership in the way that slaves are deprived permanently or the way that prisoners are deprived temporarily. Rather, the arrangement of the institution broadcasts an image of us, to us, as beings lacking the authority to withdraw ourselves from view. It conveys the loss of self-ownership to us by announcing that our every move is a fitting datum for observation by others. As a symbolic message, it insults rather than injures.

But, of course, what is symbolic is almost never merely symbolic. By such symbols do we come to acquire our self-conceptions. They shape the way we identify ourselves to ourselves and to one another, and thus they shape our identities themselves. Growing up in the informational panopticon, people will be less likely to acquire selves that think of themselves as owning themselves. They will say *mine* with less authority, and *yours* with less respect. And I think that selves that think of themselves as owning themselves are precisely what we understand as "moral selves." They are selves that naturally accept ownership of their actions and thus responsibility for them. They naturally insist on ownership of their destinies and thus on the right to choose their own way. Here the loss of privacy threatens an incalculable loss. What will it be worth if a man should gain the world but lose his soul?

The Risk of Psycho-Political Metamorphosis

The risk just discussed is, not that we shall lose something we now enjoy, but that we shall become something different than we currently are, something less noble, less interesting, less worthy of respect. This is the fear expressed in the quote from Hubert Humphrey at the beginning of this chapter.[34] What I shall say now continues in this vein.

The popular science-fiction film *Demolition Man* portrays a future society characterized by widespread information gathering, including a full IVHS system. However, to me, the most interesting feature of the film is that the denizens of the society depicted there speak, and thus seem to think, in a way that can only be described as childish. They have an oversimplified way of labeling things and experiences and appear to have a repertoire of responses that is limited in number and nuance. Their emotional lives are, you might say, reduced to the primary colors, without shade or tone, disharmony or ambiguity. I want to suggest that this is a product of the informational panopticon in which they live. Total visibility infantilizes people. It impoverishes their inner life and makes them more vulnerable to oppression from without.

There is already a widely recognized correlation between privacy and adulthood. But it is normally understood in the reverse direction: The less mature a person is, the less privacy he gets, and, as he moves toward adulthood, he gets more privacy. I want to suggest that this is a two-way street. The deprivation of privacy stunts maturity and keeps people suspended in a childish state.

How does this happen? Consider the words of Edward Bloustein, president of Rutgers University:

> The man who is compelled to live every minute of his life among others and whose every need, thought, desire, fancy or gratification is subject to public scrutiny, has been deprived of his individuality and human dignity. Such an individual merges with the mass. His opinions, being public, tend always to be conventionally accepted ones; his feelings, being openly exhibited, tend to lose their quality of unique personal warmth and to become the feelings of every man. Such a being, although sentient, is fungible; he is not an individual.[35]

But this is only the beginning. Consider the process and where it leads: To the extent that a person experiences himself as subject to public observation, he naturally experiences himself as subject to public review. As a consequence, he will tend to act in ways that are publicly acceptable. People who are shaped to act in ways that are publicly acceptable will tend to act in safe ways, to hold, express, and manifest the most widely accepted views, indeed, the lowest common denominator of conventionality.[36] (Think of the pressure that television sponsors exercise against anything unconventional, in their fear of offending any segment of the purchasing population.) But thought and feeling follow behavior. (Pascal said: "Kneel down, move your lips in prayer, and you will believe.")[37] Trained by society to act conventionally at all times, people will come so to think and so to feel. Their inner lives will be impoverished to the extent that their outer lives are subject to observation. Infiltrated by social convention, their emotions and reactions will become simpler, safer, more predictable, less nuanced, more interchangeable. This much is noted by Bloustein, but I think the process goes further.

As the inner life that is subject to social convention grows, the still deeper inner life that is separate from social convention contracts and, given little opportunity to develop, remains primitive. Likewise, as more and more of your inner life is made sense of from without, the need to make your own sense out of your inner life shrinks. You lose both the practice of making your own sense out of your deepest and most puzzling longings and the potential for self-discovery and creativity that lurk within a rich inner life. Your inner emotional life is impoverished, and your capacity for evaluating and shaping it is stunted.

Thus will be lost—and this is the most ominous possibility of all—the inner personal core that is the source of criticism of convention, the source of creativity, rebellion, and renewal. To say that people who suffer this loss will be easy to oppress doesn't say enough. They won't have to be oppressed, since there won't be anything in them that is tempted to drift from the beaten path or able to see beyond it. They will be the "one-dimensional men" that Herbert Marcuse feared.[38] The art of such people will be insipid decoration, and their politics fascist.

Here, I think, we reach something deep and rarely noted about the liberal vision—something that shows the profound link between liberalism and privacy, and between those two and democracy. The liberal vision is guided by the ideal of the autonomous individual, the one who acts on principles that she has accepted after critical review, rather than simply absorbing them unquestioned from outside.[39] Moreover, the liberal stresses the importance of people making sense of their own lives, and of their having authority over the sense of those lives. All this requires a kind of space in which to reflect on and entertain beliefs, and to experiment with them—*a private space.*

Deeper still, however, the liberal vision has an implicit trust in the transformational and ameliorative possibilities of private inner life. Without this, neither democracy nor individual freedom has worth. Unless people can form their own views, democratic voting becomes mere ratification of conventionality, and individual freedom mere voluntary conformity.[40] And, unless, in forming their own views, people can find within themselves the resources for better views, neither democracy nor individualism can be expected to improve human life.

Protecting Privacy in the Panopticon

This concludes my catalogue of the risks posed by loss of privacy. As I suggested earlier, the risks give us a negative image of the value to us of maintaining privacy. I can sum up that value as the protection of freedom, of moral personality, and of a rich and critical inner life. If IVHS endangers this value, then we will have to bring the heretofore public information about travel on public streets under the scope of privacy.

But that is just the beginning of what is necessary. We should remember Bentham's and Foucault's recognition that the panopticon works even if no one is in the guardhouse. The risks that are posed by the informational panopticon come, not from being seen, but from the knowledge that one is visible. This means that protecting ourselves from the risks I have described will be harder than we might imagine.

Consider that privacy can be protected in two ways, which I shall call the formal conditions of privacy and the material conditions. By the *formal* conditions of privacy, I mean generally the rules that either specifically give one a right to privacy or have a similar effect (such as conventions of modesty or reserve or of appropriate levels of curiosity or prying). Such rules might be legal, customary, or moral or some combination of these. By the *material* conditions of privacy, I mean physical realities that hinder others in gathering information about, or experiences of, you: things like locks, fences, doors, curtains, isolation, and distance.

It should be clear that one might have formal conditions without the material and that the formal conditions might be effective without the material being in place. For example, people packed like sardines into a rush-hour subway train have a way of respecting each other's privacy even though they have, materially, extensive access to one another's bodies. On the other hand, one can have the material conditions of privacy without the formal, and the material conditions might be effective without the formal being in place. For example, after my students are duly shocked by Hobbes's defense of absolute political authority,[41] I remind them that, when Hobbes wrote, it took about a week to travel from the west coast of England to the east coast, and about two weeks from north coast to south.[42] An absolute sovereign in Hobbes's time, without any formal constraints, surely had less actual ability to invade his subjects' lives than, say, a contemporary U.S. president, even with all our constitutional safeguards.

That constitutional safeguards can be and have been ignored by the powerful bears a lesson for us: Material conditions of privacy more reliably prevent invasions of privacy than formal conditions can. Material conditions have a kind of toughness that the formal conditions never can match. Thus, formal conditions of privacy can never fully guarantee protection of privacy when the material conditions for protecting privacy are lacking or, equivalently, when the material conditions for invading privacy are at hand. The material conditions for invading privacy are a kind of power, and power is always tempting and often corrupting, and, to paraphrase Lord Acton, the more power there is, the more corrupting it is likely to be.

This is important because the accumulation of detailed information about people's goings and comings is a material condition for invading privacy. What is more, the continued and increasing amassing of this and all the other sorts of information that make up the informational panopticon seems to me to be inevitable. This is for the simple reason that, as with IVHS, all of the elements of the informational panopticon serve good purposes and can and will be put in place with the best of intentions. We should remember Louis Brandeis's warning, quoted at the outset of this chapter,[43] and watch out for threats of liberty dressed in beneficent intentions. The existence of all this collected information and of the technical ability to bring these different records together will add up to an enormous capacity to amass detailed portraits of people's lives—in short, material conditions for invasion of privacy on an unheard-of scale. One has to be very optimistic indeed about the power of rules, to think that formal guarantees of privacy will protect us. To the extent that we are not so optimistic, we will experience ourselves as visible even if we are not being observed, which will bring in its train all the risks earlier described.

To the extent that the material conditions for our virtually total visibility come ineluctably into place in the years ahead, we will need, not only to prevent the misuse of information, but *to prevent the fear that it is being misused.* That is the lesson of the panopticon. We will have to protect people, not only from being seen, but from feeling visible. Thus, we will need more than ever before to teach and explain the importance of privacy, so that respect for it becomes second nature, and violation of it repugnant. And, of course, we will need more than ever to make sure that our fellows are complying with the formal rules that protect privacy. If we are going to protect privacy in the informational panopticon, we're really going to have to keep an eye on one another!

Notes

This chapter is a revised version of a paper originally presented at the Symposium on Privacy and Intelligent Vehicle Highway Systems (sponsored by the Federal Highway Administration, U.S. Department of Transportation, and Santa Clara University School of Law), held in Santa Clara, California, on 29–30 July 1994. The paper was published in *Santa Clara Computer and High Technology Law Journal* 11, no. 1 (March 1995): 27–44. Reprinted with permission.

1. IVHS AMERICA Legal Issues Committee, " 'Strawman' Privacy Principles: Comment Form," p. 2.

2. Jeremy Bentham, "Panopticon, or, The Inspection-House," in *The Works of Jeremy Bentham*, ed. John Bowring (New York: Russell & Russell, 1964), vol. 4, pp. 40–41, inter alia.

3. Michel Foucault, *Discipline and Punish: The Birth of the Prison*, trans. Alan Sheridan (New York: Vintage Books, 1979), pp. 195–228. See p. 200 for a description of the architecture envisioned by Bentham.

4. Ibid., p. 228.

5. "[I]t is at once too much and too little that the prisoner should be constantly observed by an inspector: too little, for what matters is that he knows himself to be observed; too much, because he has no need in fact of being so." Ibid., p. 201.

6. Ibid., pp. 202–3.

7. "The panoptic schema . . . was destined to spread throughout the social body; its vocation was to become a generalized function." Ibid., p. 207, see also pp. 211–16.

8. *U.S. v. Knotts*, 460 U.S. 276, 281 (1983).

9. *U.S. v. Karo*, 468 U.S. 705, 714 (1984), see 468 U.S. at 720–21.

10. Richard Wasserstrom, "Privacy: Some Arguments and Assumptions," in *Philosophical Dimensions of Privacy*, ed. Ferdinand Schoeman (Cambridge: Cambridge University Press, 1984), pp. 325–26. (Schoeman, ed., *Philosophical Dimensions of Privacy* is cited hereafter as *PDOP*.) Originally published in *Philosophical Law*, ed. Richard Bronaugh (Westport, Conn.: Greenwood, 1978), pp. 148–66.

11. Charles Fried, "Privacy," *PDOP*, pp. 209–10.

12. Ibid., p. 214.

13. If it is said that such prohibition doesn't take away one's ability to display such functions but only ups the cost of doing so, then it will follow that no one has any privacy in his home, since crooks can break in even though it is prohibited. On the other hand, it might be objected that I can, after all, invite someone to watch me perform my excretory functions, and in this sense even the privacy that I have here includes my control over who gets access to me. But, to think that this shows that such privacy necessarily includes control, one would have to maintain that if I couldn't invite a witness in to watch (say, because of draconian laws or unfailing taboos against doing so), that would mean that those functions were no longer shielded by privacy—and that sounds quite implausible.

14. Ruth Gavison gives additional reasons for excluding control from the definition of privacy, in her "Privacy and the Limits of Law," *PDOP,* pp. 349–50.

15. "But intimacy is the sharing of information about one's actions, beliefs, or emotions which one does not share with all, and which one has the right not to share with anyone. By conferring this right, privacy creates the moral capital which we spend in friendship and love." Fried, "Privacy," p. 211. I criticize this view in chapter 6 of this volume, previously printed in *PDOP,* pp. 300–16.

16. It might be objected that, if I have a right that others be deprived of access to me, then I can waive that right, and thus effectively I would have the right to grant individuals access to me. This would bring control back in, not back into the definition of privacy, but into the definition of the right to privacy. But there are rights that people have but cannot waive in the sense here needed. For example, my right to life is not generally taken as one that I can waive and thereby have a right to stop living, and my right not to be enslaved is not generally taken as one that I can waive and thereby have a right to sell myself into slavery.

17. See notes 8 and 9 above and accompanying text.

18. *Roe v. Wade,* 410 U.S. 113 (1973); *Bowers v. Hardwick,* 478 U.S. 186 (1986).

19. Interestingly, the "information highway" is the inverted image of IVHS: here the intelligence comes first and then the roadways.

20. John Schwartz, "Industry Fights Wiretap Proposal: Group Says Clinton Plan Would Scare Consumers Off 'Data Highway,' " *Washington Post,* 12 March 1994, pp. C1, C7 (quote from p. C7).

21. Fried observes in a note that "so long as the mails are still private, wire tapping may not be so severe an imposition, particularly if people do not in any case consider telephone conversations as necessarily private." Fried, "Privacy," p. 221 n. 18.

22. "The usual arguments against wiretapping, bugging, a National Data Center, and private investigators rest heavily on the contingent possibility that a tyrannical government or unscrupulous individuals might misuse them for

blackmail or victimization. The more one knows about a person, the greater one's power to damage him." Stanley I. Benn, "Privacy, Freedom, and Respect for Persons," *PDOP*, p. 226.

23. Gavison, "Privacy and Limits of Law," *PDOP*, pp. 363–64.

24. John Stuart Mill, *On Liberty* (Harmondsworth, England: Penguin Books, 1974; originally published 1859), p. 141–46, inter alia.

25. It also forces the majority to test their own beliefs in the open court of public discussion.

26. *Federalist* No. 51, in Alexander Hamilton, James Madison, and John Jay, *The Federalist Papers*, ed. Clinton Rossiter (New York: New American Library, 1961), p. 322.

27. "[P]rivacy also contributes to learning, creativity and autonomy by insulating the individual against ridicule and censure at early stages of groping and experimentation." Gavison, "Privacy and Limits of Law," p. 364.

28. "He who lets the world, or his own portion of it, choose his plan of life for him has no need of any other faculty than the ape-like one of imitation. He who chooses his plan for himself employs all his faculties." Mill, *On Liberty*, p. 123.

29. See notes 11 through 16 above and accompanying text.

30. "The observer makes the act impossible . . . in the sense that the actor now sees it in a different light." Benn, "Privacy, Freedom, and Respect for Persons," p. 226. "Aware of the observer, I am engaged in part in viewing or imagining what is going on from his or her perspective. I thus cannot lose myself as completely in the activity." Wasserstrom, "Privacy: Some Arguments and Assumptions," p. 324; see also the sensitive discussion in Robert S. Gerstein, "Intimacy and Privacy," *PDOP*, pp. 265–71.

31. Wasserstrom, "Privacy: Some Arguments and Assumptions," p. 328.

32. See chapter 6 of this volume.

33. "A man whose home may be entered at the will of another, whose conversation may be overheard at the will of another, whose marital and familial intimacies may be overseen at the will of another, is less of a man, has less human dignity, on that account." Edward J. Bloustein, "Privacy as an Aspect of Human Dignity: An Answer to Dean Prosser," *PDOP*, p. 165.

34. Hubert H. Humphrey, foreword to *The Intruders*, by Edward V. Long (New York: Praeger, 1967), p. viii.

35. Bloustein, "Privacy as an Aspect of Human Dignity," p. 188.

36. "In the absence of privacy we would dare less, because all our failures would be on record." Gavison, "Privacy and Limits of Law," p. 364.

37. This is attributed to Pascal, without citation, by Louis Althusser, in his *Lenin and Philosophy*, trans. B. Brewster (London: New Left Books, 1971), p. 158.

38. Herbert Marcuse, *One-Dimensional Man* (Boston: Beacon, 1964).

39. See Benn, "Privacy, Freedom, and Respect for Persons," p. 241ff., for a statement of this ideal and a discussion of its relation to privacy.

40. "Part of the justification for majority rule and the right to vote is the assumption that individuals should participate in political decisions by forming judgments and expressing preferences. Thus, to the extent that privacy is important for autonomy, it is important for democracy as well." Gavison, "Privacy and the Limits of Law," pp. 369–70.

41. Thomas Hobbes, *Leviathan* (Amherst, N.Y.: Prometheus Books, 1988; originally published 1651).

42. J. Crofts, *Packhorse, Waggon and Post: Land Carriage and Communications under the Tudors and Stuarts* (London: Routledge & Kegan Paul, 1967), pp. 84–88, 122–24, 141–42; and Sidney Webb and Beatrice Webb, *The Story of the King's Highway*, vol. 5 of *English Local Government* (Hampden, Conn.: Archon Books, 1963; originally published 1913), pp. 62–84. I am indebted to my colleague Terence Murphy of the American University Department of History for these references.

43. *Olmstead v. U.S.*, 277 U.S. 438 (1928) (Brandeis, J., dissenting).

8

Abortion, Infanticide, and the Asymmetric Value of Human Life

Why . . . has it been imagined that to die is an evil—when it is clear that not to have been, before our birth, was no evil?

Voltaire

Love, Respect, and the Asymmetric Value of Human Life

The pro-life position on abortion is that abortion is morally wrong because a fetus is an innocent human being and killing it is, at least morally speaking, murder.[1] This claim does not challenge our normal way of evaluating something morally as murder. On the contrary, this claim appeals to that normal evaluation and insists that, according to it, killing fetuses counts as murder. Our normal evaluation of a killing as murder hinges on our normal valuation of the lives of those whom we think it uncontroversially wrong to kill, namely, children and adults. Rational assessment of the pro-life position, then, requires determining whether there is something about fetuses that provides a plausible basis for applying to them the value we normally apply to the lives of children and adults.[2] In conducting this assessment, we are aided by a clue that has been largely overlooked in the abortion debate, namely, that the way we normally value human life is quite unusual, quite unlike the normal way in which we value other things. This has the consequence that only a very specific kind of feature of humans at any stage can provide a plausible basis for the normal valuation. I shall follow out this clue and show that there is something about children and adults that provides a plausible basis for the way we value their lives but that there is nothing about fetuses that will do the job. The result is a refuta-

189

tion of the pro-life position, and a defense of the pro-choice position on abortion.

The question whether killing fetuses is wrong for the same reasons we think it wrong to kill children or adults is more general than whether a fetus has a right to life. To avoid the mistake of thinking that having a right to life is the only moral basis for the wrongness of destroying a human life,[3] we look for whatever might make it wrong to kill humans generally and see if this applies to fetuses. Of course, if it is not wrong to kill fetuses for the same reasons that it is wrong to kill humans generally, it might be wrong on other grounds.[4] I shall not pursue this, however, since it seems extremely unlikely that such grounds could be strong enough to justify requiring a woman to stay pregnant against her will (especially in these days of abundant reproduction). In any event, it is an implication of my argument here that there is nothing about fetuses that could provide a plausible basis for thinking that their lives should be protected in the way we protect the lives of children or adults.

There are some pro-choicers who think that the abortion dispute can be settled without addressing the moral status of the fetus. They think the fact (and I regard it as a fact) that a woman has a right to control her body is enough to justify her right to abortion. But this is not enough because a person's right to control her body ends if it comes up against a being with comparable moral status and thus comparable rights—"your right to swing your fist ends where my nose begins" and all that.[5] So we shall still have to figure out if the fetus has a moral status comparable to that of the woman carrying her. On the other hand, there are even some arguments in favor of a woman's right to abortion that accept per argumentum that killing a fetus is as seriously wrong as killing a human adult. But such arguments can, at best, give a woman a right to expel an unwelcome fetus from her body, and only to end its life if necessary for the expulsion.[6] As early as a living fetus can be safely and easily removed from a pregnant woman, her right to abortion might be transformed into a duty to provide extrauterine care for her expelled fetus. If (when!) medical technology pushes this point back toward the earliest moments of pregnancy, the right to abortion will disappear entirely. The surest way to secure a woman's right to abortion is to show that nothing about fetuses warrants including them under our normal way of valuing human life. For this, we get some help from Voltaire.

Voltaire's question, quoted at the outset of this chapter,[7] reminds us that we normally believe the moral wrongness of killing human beings to be something much worse than not creating them (if the latter is bad at all). This implies that the loss due to ending a human life under way is much worse than the loss that would have been the result of not starting that life. In short, we normally think that murder is much worse than failure to procreate via contraception or voluntary abstinence. But this means that the value of a human life is quite unusual: it is temporally *asymmetric*.

The standard kind of value is temporally *symmetric*. Normally, if something has x units of value, then destroying it (after it exists) and intentionally not producing it (before it exists) equally deprive the world of x units of value. Or, equivalently, that it has that value is equally a reason (before it exists) for a suitably situated moral agent to produce one and a reason (after it exists) for that agent to refrain from destroying it.

One way the value of something existing may seem not to be symmetric is that destroying the existent thing wastes the effort that already went into producing it, while not producing it does not. Likewise, trying to produce a new one courts a risk of failure, while an existing one is a sure thing. Thus, it would be more precise to say that the standard way in which something is thought to have value is symmetric except for considerations of wasted effort and uncertainty. However, these considerations are not large enough to account for the very large moral difference that people generally think exists between killing an existing human being and not bringing a new one into existence.[8] Consequently, I shall say that a value is symmetric if the only difference between the value of producing it and the value of not destroying it stems from considerations such as those of already invested effort and newly faced risk. Thus, I will continue to say the value of normally valued things is symmetric, while the value we place on human life is asymmetric.

The upshot is that, to determine whether killing a fetus is morally wrong for the same reasons that killing human beings generally is thought to be wrong, we need to figure out whether there is anything about the fetus that provides a plausible basis for thinking that to end its life is asymmetrically disvaluable—or, as I shall sometimes say, asymmetrically wrong. Is there anything about the fetus that makes killing it seriously worse than not having produced it, due to contraception or voluntary abstinence practiced by fertile couples? Though I don't argue for it here, I think that contraception and abstinence are not morally wrong at all. Nonetheless, my argument will work even if these are thought to be moderately wrong, since even people who think contraception is wrong think that abortion is much worse, and very few people who think that abortion is gravely evil think that abstinence is.

To help us think about the different ways in which things might have value, I want to distinguish roughly between the ways in which *love* and *respect* each value their objects. Love, though it may be triggered by the appeal of certain traits or properties of the beloved, comes to value the beloved as such—"unconditionally," we sometimes say—and thus values the sheer existence of the beloved. Respect, though it is aimed at individuals, is, in my view, a way of honoring some property possessed by the respected one, where "honoring" involves at least not interfering with the normal functioning of that property. Thus, for Kant, we are to respect human beings because they possess the trait of rational agency, and we do so by honoring that property, which is to say, not interfering with or undermining the normal functioning of their rational agency.[9] Further, love is *given* freely by the lover, while respect is *deserved* by the respected because of the property she possesses. Love expresses the will of the lover, while respect responds to the worth of the respected.

Now, I think that there are only two possible ways in which something can have asymmetric value: either its existence itself (somehow) gives it a value that is not temporally symmetric, or its value is the value it has to itself or someone else. Some important writers—for example, Ronald Dworkin[10]—adopt the first alternative, and I think that the assumption that existence does add asymmetric value is tacitly held by many people who think that abortion is morally questionable. Consequently, I shall consider this assumption in the next section, "The Priority of Morality over Metaphysics in the Abortion Question," and try to show that, to paraphrase Kant, existence is not a morally relevant property.[11] Since love cherishes the sheer existence of its object, while respect honors some property possessed by its object, I speculate that the widespread error of thinking that existence as such lends value is the result of confusing love with respect. Then, "the priority of morality over metaphysics in the abortion question" implies "the priority of respect over love in the abortion question."

The second way in which something might have asymmetric value is more promising. If the value of something lies in its value to itself or to someone else, then its value exists only for itself or someone else. With our focus on the normal valuation of human life, we can eliminate the "someone else" from this formulation, since a human life is thought to have its value even if no one else cares about the individual whose life it is. If, then, the value of life is its value to the one whose life it is and who cares about its continuation, then its value exists only for the one who cares about it, and only once it is cared about and not before. That gives us asymmetric value. Note that, here, respect has priority over love. It is not so much that we care about the one whose life it is, or care about what she cares about, as it is that we respect her because she possesses the property of caring about her life and that we respect her by honoring that property, which is to say, not interfering with or undermining her having what she cares about. I shall defend this account of the asymmetric value of human life in the section of this chapter on "Voltaire's Question." As confirmation, in the section on "Personhood Revisited," I shall show how the account supports the widely held (but vaguely formulated) view that it is only once humans are *persons* that it is seriously wrong to kill them.

One implication of my argument that may trouble some readers is that the life of newborn infants is not yet asymmetrically valuable. However, this doesn't imply that it is okay to kill infants; rather, it implies that, if infanticide is morally wrong, it is wrong on other grounds and in a different way than the killing of children and adults. I shall take this up in the final section of this chapter, "The Priority of Love over Respect in the Infanticide Question."

The Priority of Morality over Metaphysics in the Abortion Question

There are, broadly speaking, two ways to approach the question of abortion, which we can call the metaphysical way and the moral way. The metaphysical way is to start with a human being that it seems uncontroversially wrong to kill and work backwards to see if the fetus is, so to speak, a phase of this same individual entity. For example, up until the end of the first two weeks of pregnancy, a zygote or embryo may split into identical twins, who have the same genetic code and yet become two unique human beings. Noting this, Norman Ford maintains that, starting at two weeks, the fetus is the same individual entity that, in the normal course of events, will become a full-fledged person and thus it ought to have its life protected from then on.[12] One reason that this approach is bound to fail is that the assumption that being a human individual is enough to earn one moral protection of one's life smacks of *speciesism*—arbitrary or dogmatic preference for our own species.[13] Once we recognize that what makes the killing of human beings seriously wrong cannot be the sheer fact of their membership in the human species, the wrongness must be based on a property (it could be one or more features) that human beings normally have but that could, in principle, turn up in other species.

Accordingly, we are looking for a property, not a kind. Of course, the property might be just that by which we identify beings as of a certain kind, but even then—even if the property is strictly coterminous with the kind (for example, rationality in the case of humans)—it will be the property that does the moral work, not the kind.[14] On the other hand, once it is clear that it is a property we seek, it cannot be taken for granted that the property is coterminous with the kind. We look for a property (ever) possessed by human beings that explains the wrongness of killing them, all the while leaving open the question whether the property is possessed by all human beings or at all stages. We answer the abortion question by determining whether that property is possessed by fetuses. This is the moral approach to the question, which I shall follow.

There is yet a deeper way in which morality has priority over metaphysics in answering the abortion question. Imagine that we found the special property that is the basis of our objection to killing humans, and suppose that this property is something (for example, a functioning cerebral cortex)[15] that emerges in the seventh month of pregnancy. Someone following the metaphysical approach outlined in the previous paragraphs might be tempted to say that the fetus from two weeks on is the same continuous, self-identical individual as will have the special property at seven months and thus that it would be as wrong to kill it at two weeks as it is at seven months. If this were so, it would follow as well that the fetus is entitled to vote, since it is also the same continuous, self-identical individual as will have that right at age eighteen. What's wrong in this argument is not the assumption that the being that traverses the span from conception to death is a self-identical individual. That is a more or less natural extension of the common belief that a human being from birth to death is a self-identical individual—the one named by its proper name.

The argument goes wrong by confusing metaphysical identity with moral identity, or assuming that the former entails the latter. Metaphysical identity from conception on means that the being is the same individual in all its temporal phases. Moral identity would mean that it has the same moral status in all its temporal phases or, at least, that earlier phases have a moral claim on the properties (and thus the moral status) possessed at later phases. If we are to grant the metaphysical identity of the human from conception on and avoid the inference that the fetus currently has the right to vote, we must grant that metaphysical identity is not equivalent to, and does not imply, moral identity. Here morality is prior to metaphysics in the sense that metaphysical identity will not supply us with the moral status needed to answer the abortion question: rather than looking for the (metaphysical) beginning of the human individual that somewhere down the line has a life it is wrong to take, we must look for the (morally relevant) property that makes it wrong to take a human life, and see when the human individual starts to have that property.

The priority of morality over metaphysics has important implications for the significance of *existence* in the abortion debate. It may turn out that the fetus possesses, from the moment of conception, the property that makes killing it seriously wrong, and then its metaphysical and moral identity in this regard will coincide. However, given the possibility that this property is acquired later (either during pregnancy or later still), then the fetus may exist for some time without the property. Since the fetus's metaphysical identity with the human being that will have the property does not entail their moral identity, it follows that the pre-property fetus has no moral claim to the property. Moreover, since what the property gives is precisely the moral wrongness of stopping the fetus from continuing on to later phases, there is nothing morally wrong with ending the fetus's life before the property is there. The fetus's existence prior to its possession of the property gives it no moral claim to continue existing. And, if the pre-property fetus has no moral claim to get the property, then there is no moral difference between a fetus that stops existing before it gets the property and a fetus that never starts to exist.

If this seems counterintuitive, I think it is because we tend to read a kind of personal identity backwards into fetuses, and personal identity carries connotations of moral identity beyond mere metaphysical identity. If we think of the pre-property fetus as a kind of quasi-person "who" loses the chance to have the special property, then we will think of the pre-property fetus as a personlike victim—which is a moral status that a not-yet-existing fetus lacks. Just because it is so natural to us to think this way, I believe that this ("retroactive empersonment") is the single greatest source of confusion in the abortion debate. If we resist it, then that the fetus has already been existing has no bearing on the moral status of its loss of future existence. Consequently, that loss is morally equivalent to the simple failure of that future stretch of fetal life to begin. Then, it is no worse morally to end the life of a pre-property fetus than to refuse to produce a new one. Existence as such cannot provide asymmetrical value.

Mistakes about this are so common in the abortion dispute that I think that my argument will be strengthened by a plausible explanation of the appeal of the mistaken view. Recall the difference between the respect and (unconditional) love sketched earlier. Respect is something that we have toward some property that an individual has—reason, moral agency, what have you—and we respect that individual because of that property. Love, by contrast, is directed at individuals as such. Then, love naturally cherishes the sheer existence of its object. If this is so, then it is our natural love of our fellows (the sentiment that Hume called "humanity")[16] that leads us to cherish their sheer existence—before there is a moral warrant for this. And, cherishing their sheer existence, we are naturally led to cherish their existence for as long as they can be said to exist as the same individuals, metaphysically speaking. But that love is given freely by us, not deserved by the beloved. Thus, it does not imply anything about the beloved deserving to continue to exist. It tells us, rather, about our own sentiments. Consequently, the argument for the priority of morality over metaphysics is equally an argument for the priority of respect over love in the abortion question. This isn't to say that love counts for nothing in morality; it says only that love cannot justify the belief that its object possesses a moral standing of its own. Only possession of the appropriate property can do that.

Voltaire's Question

Voltaire's question reminds us that we view the ending of a human life underway as much worse than the failure of a life to start. This gives us a surprisingly exclusive requirement because it rules out any attempt to explain the wrongness of killing human beings by invoking their "objectively" good properties—by which I mean properties whose appeal (roughly speaking) is that their existence makes the world a better place than it would be without them. Such objectively good properties are symmetrically valuable. That human beings possess such objectively good properties as rationality, or capacity for joy and attachment, cannot explain the serious wrongness of killing humans because contraception and abstinence also cause the nonexistence of these good properties. Then, these properties cannot be the basis of the asymmetric wrongness of killing human beings.

It might be thought that destroying an existing being that has objectively good properties is inherently worse than not creating a being with those properties. But this runs afoul of the priority of morality over metaphysics because it counts existence itself as giving an existing being a moral claim to continue existing. Nor can the force of Voltaire's question be escaped by recourse to the so-called acts-omissions princi-ple, which holds that acting to produce a bad outcome is always much worse than simply failing to prevent that same outcome. This principle is far from universally accepted, so we cannot assume that it holds in the controversial cases we are here considering. Anyway, contraception and abstinence are acts, so they get no special dispensation from the principle.

The problem is to find a property whose nature involves existence in a way that makes the destruction of a being with that property signifi-cantly wrong while the noncreation of such a being is only mildly wrong, if wrong at all. That this is just what objectively good properties lack suggests that it is a *subjective* property we need. I will argue that this suggestion is correct but that not just any subjective property will do. For example, L. W. Sumner contends that sentience brings any crea-ture into the realm of moral consideration and therefore that we should protect the lives of fetuses from the point at which they become sen-tient.[17] Now, aside from the fact that consistency would require that we extend the same protection to most animals, the most important fact for our purposes is that there is nothing about sentience as such that ac-counts for the asymmetric values of beings that possess it. It may be good that a six-month-old sentient being continue on for another six months, but this is no better than ending its life painlessly and replacing it with another that will have six months of sentience. There is nothing about being sentient that makes it worse to end a sentient being's life than to fail to create another sentient being.

The failure of sentience points us to the kind of subjective property that can do the job: The *subjective* awareness that one is already alive and counting on staying alive fits the requirement suggested by Vol-taire's question. The loss to an aware individual of the life whose con-tinuation she is counting on, is a loss that can only exist once an aware individual exists. Moreover, it is a loss that remains a loss, a frustration of an individual's expectations, even if that individual is replaced by another equally aware one. Thus it is a loss that can explain why ending a human life is significantly worse than not creating one.

The point is precisely *not* to say that it is good that such awareness or such aware individuals exist. That would turn the property into one whose goodness is objective, and then we would lose the distinction needed to cope with Voltaire's question. It would then be just as good to create new aware individuals as to continue existing ones, and the harm of killing would be no worse than that of contraception or absti-nence.

We need a way to say how it is valuable that individuals who care about their lives going on get to live on, without entailing that it is good that such aware individuals exist. We can do this by adverting to the moral attitude of respect: The asymmetric value of human life is a function of our respecting human beings because they possess the property of caring about the continuation of their lives. We express that respect by honoring that property, which is to say, by not interfering with or undermining people's ability to have or get what they care about. If it be thought that care about one's life is too thin a reed upon which to rest respect, remember that that care is the affective response to awareness of oneself as a being living out a life, so to speak, a minute or a day at a time—and such awareness is available only to rational beings. Consequently, respecting beings because they possess the property of caring about the continuation of their lives is respecting them for caring as only a rational being can care. Thus such caring can account for the asymmetric value we place on human life.

Note that I am not arguing that ending the life of a human being who is aware of and caring about his life is wrong because it thwarts an occurrent desire to stay alive or a felt expectation that one will.[18] Rather, our inquiry has led us to a unique human vulnerability, and to a distinctive moral response to that vulnerability. Once a human being has begun to be aware of her life, that life unfolds before a kind of inner audience that has an expectation of its continuation, an affective stake in living on. This expectation persists until the audience shuts down for good—even if, before that, the audience dozes off from time to time. We defeat this expectation even if we kill a temporarily sleeping or comatose individual who has begun to be aware of her life. Because of this special awareness, humans are vulnerable to a special harm from the ending of a life already under way.[19] We protect people from this harm because we respect them, not because we love them—though, of course, we may also do that.

My argument here should not be confused with the "logic of rights" approach used by Michael Tooley and S. I. Benn, to which it bears a certain surface resemblance.[20] Tooley has argued that a necessary logical condition for having a right is having some interest that the right protects. Fetuses, he contends, cannot have an interest in staying alive. Consequently, fetuses are logically disqualified from possessing a right to life, and abortion is okay. As interesting as this strategy is, it relies too heavily on the logic of the concept of a right. Tooley's mistake is not just that his argument works only against a fetal right to life—but that he supposes us to be so much the prisoners of our existing moral concepts that we need only determine what their logic allows to answer our moral questions. The simple fact is that, if a moral concept logically excludes some case that there is good reason to include, we need only modify the concept or create a new one. Benn takes the logic of rights even further than Tooley. Benn thinks that the concept of a right is so exclusive that it applies only to agents. Then, since neither fetuses nor newborns are agents, they cannot have rights, and abortion and infanticide are okay. Benn's version seems to me extreme enough to qualify as a reductio ad absurdum of the "logic of rights" approach. Surely it cannot be that our concept of a right is so locked into its connection with agency that we cannot pry it loose and use it for other defensible purposes. Suppose we agreed that our concept of a right applied only to agents, and found that, say, people on respirators (or in comas), though unable to act, ought to be protected against certain forms of molestation. What would happen if we simply modified the concept of a right so that it could cover such cases? Or if we created a new concept with all the attributes of rights, except the restriction to agents? Would we slide into an abyss of incoherence? Would our lexicographers go on strike?

As I see it, the answer to the question of whether we should protect fetal life with a right to life or in some other way hinges on whether there are good reasons for doing so, not on the logical preconditions of applying the concepts of rights or protection. My argument is that the interest that conscious human beings have in the continuation of the lives of which they are already aware is a good reason for protecting their lives morally in the asymmetric way that we do and that no such good reason obtains in the case of fetuses. The loss suffered by the aborted fetus is precisely the same sort of loss caused by contraception or by abstinence and thus provides no better reason for protecting fetuses than for prohibiting contraception or abstinence. Then, abortion can be no worse morally than these.

This train of argument may seem counterintuitive. It looks like abortion is different because it has a victim while contraception and abstinence do not. But recall the priority of morality over metaphysics: Since a property is what makes it seriously wrong to kill something, the fetus that exists before the property is not a victim in the morally relevant sense. The fetus's existence as such does not make the harm of depriving it of its future life morally different from the harm of the failure to produce a new fetus with its own future life, in the way that existing consciousness and expectation do for the harm of ending an aware human being's life.[21] *The loss to the fetus of its future life is morally no worse a loss than the loss to the world of any future life.*

Personhood Revisited

In an important article, Mary Anne Warren argues that it is personhood that warrants the right to life. Appealing to common usage, she lists the traits of personhood as consciousness, reasoning, self-motivated activity, capacity to communicate, and the presence of self-concepts and self-awareness. Contending that the fetus lacks these elements, she concludes that the fetus doesn't have a right to life.[22] What we are not told is why any or all of these elements makes it appropriate to hold the killing of a being that possesses the elements seriously wrong. Warren's position, then, amounts to a report of our common practice of awarding rights to the beings we call persons.[23] This renders her conclusion problematic because the pro-lifer can simply assert that the common practice is mistaken, or that there are grounds other than being a person for protecting fetuses. The only way out of these interminable disputes is to show that there is something about the nature of persons that explains the serious wrongness of killing them and that there is no such thing about a fetus.

My argument up to this point provides a way of showing what it is about persons that makes it asymmetrically wrong to kill them. Guided by Voltaire, I urged that the only plausible basis for asymmetrically valuing human life is that humans are aware of, and counting on, continuing the particular lives they already have. This is possible only for a being who is aware of his or her self as the same self enduring over time. And a hallowed philosophical tradition defines personhood by this very awareness. Locke defined a "person" as "a thinking intelligent being, that . . . can consider itself as itself . . . in different times and places."[24] Kant wrote: "That which is conscious of the numerical identity of itself at different times is in so far a *person*."[25]

Not only does this argument rescue the idea that it is persons who are morally entitled to protection against killing; it also reinforces my claim that the asymmetric value of human life is based on our respect for our fellows as beings who care about their lives. Persons are commonly thought to be proper objects of respect.

The Priority of Love over Respect in the Infanticide Question

The newborn infant does not yet have awareness that it is alive, much less that it is the selfsame person enduring over time.[26] Its relationship to the future person that it is on the way to becoming is more like a fetus's than like an adult's or a child's relationship to the life of which she is already aware. If already being aware of one's life is the necessary condition of the objection to killing human beings, what follows about the moral status of infanticide? This question is important because some philosophers (and many nonphilosophers) take their intuition that infanticide is as wrong as killing adults or children so seriously as to rule out any account of the wrongness of killing that doesn't apply equally to infants.[27] What I shall say in response to this is not an attempt to settle the issue about the moral status of infanticide. I wish only to say enough to suggest how the wrongness of infanticide can be accounted for on terms that are compatible with what I have said about abortion and the wrongness of killing children and adults.

The attitude that we have when we think it wrong to kill a child or adult because they care about their lives going on is a form of respect. We respect the property of being aware of, and caring about, their lives (and all this brings in its wake), and we respect them for having this attribute. We show this respect by not undermining what they care about. We are not (necessarily) either caring about them independently of what they care about or directly caring about what they care about, either of which would characterize love, rather than respect.[28]

Now, I think that the normal reaction to infants is a loving one (though, of course, it is not the only reaction, or the only normal one). This has probably been built into us as a result of evolution. Human babies are born at a very early stage of their development and must therefore be tended to by their parents (primarily their mothers, at least until recently) for a long time before they can get along on their own, and surely a long time before they can begin to pay their own way.[29] There are numerous evolutionary advantages of the long extrauterine development of humans. Most importantly, this long development allows adult human beings to have larger brains than could pass through a human female's birth canal. It is inconceivable that parents would have provided the necessary care for their helpless offspring over the hundreds of thousands of years of human evolution, if they had not developed a strong tendency to love infants. This is love, rather than respect, precisely because it must happen automatically, before the infant can do anything to deserve or be worthy of it.

But there is more. The love that we naturally direct toward infants is arguably a necessary condition of the development of the infant into a being worthy of respect. This is so for at least two reasons, and probably more. First of all, by loving infants, we are moved to devote the energy and attention necessary to bring infants into the community of language users, which, in turn, brings infants to awareness of their lives, which is also a necessary condition of their caring about their lives and our respecting them for that.[30] (The *Oxford English Dictionary* gives the root of "infant" as *infans*, Latin for "unable to speak.") Second of all, by loving infants, we convey to them a positive valuation of their sheer existence, which, in turn, underlies their valuation of their own particular lives once they are capable of it. Indeed, since it is precisely people's own valuation of their lives that is the condition of our respect for them, we can say that our loving infants is part of the process by which infants develop into worthy objects of respect.

In short, we might say that we respect the lives of children and adults because they love their own lives and that loving infants prepares them for loving their own lives and thus for being worthy of respect. *Love is respect's pioneer.* It goes on ahead, clears the field, and prepares the soil where respect will take root. Respect is what infants will get once they qualify for full membership in the human moral community, but love is what reaches out and brings them into that community and necessarily does so before they qualify.

This gives us enough to characterize the special status that infants have as natural objects of adults' love. As I suggested earlier, love cherishes the sheer existence of its object. Thus, love makes us want very much to protect infants and make sure that they survive. On the other hand, since that love is unconditional—given rather than deserved—it is not based on anything that makes the infants worthy of it. Thus, we find ourselves strongly inclined to believe that it is wrong to kill infants, yet unable to point to some property of infants (not shared by human fetuses, or even animals that we think may be acceptably killed) that justifies this belief.

If this is correct, then we can say that the strong belief in the wrongness of killing infants is the product of our natural love for them, coupled with (or strengthened by) our respect for our fellows' love of them. And this love is worth supporting because it is respect's pioneer. That is, by loving infants, we treat them as asymmetrically valuable before they really deserve it, but as part of the process by which they come really to deserve it. Then, it will be wrong to kill infants because it will be wrong generally to block or frustrate this love, both because we and our fellows naturally feel this love and because it is good that we feel it inasmuch as it is essential to infants' development into children and adults worthy of respect.

Note that this won't apply to fetuses. They may be objects of love, but not of such love as can play a role in their psycho-moral development. That requires a real, interactive social relation such as can only occur after birth. That is not to say that the fact that many people love fetuses counts for nothing. Much as respect for our fellows' love for infants justifies protecting infants' lives, respect for those who love fetuses may, for example, justify treating aborted fetuses with special care. But, since this is a matter of other people's love rather than fetuses' own worthiness for respect, it surely won't be enough to justify requiring women to stay pregnant against their wills.

This account does not say that killing infants is wrong for the same reasons as killing children or adults. Quite the contrary. Killing children or adults is wrong because it violates the respect they are due as creatures aware of, and caring about, their lives. Killing infants is wrong because it violates the love we give them as a means to making them into creatures aware of, and caring about, their lives. The killing of children and adults is wrong because of properties *they* possess that make it wrong, while the killing of infants is wrong because of an emotion that *we* naturally and rightly have toward infants. Then, it will be harder to justify exceptions to the rule against killing adults and children than to the rule against killing infants, because adults and children possess in their own right a property that makes it wrong to kill them. Infants, for the moment, do not. Killing them collides with our love for them, not with their love for their lives. For this reason, there will be permissible exceptions to the rule against killing infants that will not apply to the rule against killing adults or children. In particular, I think (as do many philosophers, doctors, and parents) that ending the lives of severely handicapped newborns will be acceptable because it does not take from the newborns a life that they yet care about and because it is arguably compatible with, rather than violative of, our natural love for infants. But, of course, I have not proven this here.

Notes

This chapter is a revised version of an article originally published in *Journal of Social Philosophy* 27, no. 3 (Winter 1996). Reprinted with permission.

1. A few words about terminology are in order. "Pro-life" and "pro-choice" are political labels, not technically accurate philosophical terms. I use them because of their familiarity, not because I think that only pro-lifers are pro-life or that only pro-choicers are pro-choice. Further, I use the term "murder" in its moral sense, meaning any killing that is bad or wrong for the same reasons it is bad or wrong to kill children and adults. When I speak of it being bad or wrong to kill children or adults, I mean killing that takes place voluntar-

ily and in the absence of such conditions as mental illness or duress that would normally block the imputation of wrongdoing. For the purpose of simplicity, I normally omit these necessary qualifications and assume that the reader will fill them in where needed. Finally, I join in the widespread, though technically incorrect, practice of using the term "fetus" to refer to the being that develops in a pregnant woman from the moment of conception to the moment of birth. Speaking strictly, the single cell resulting from the fertilization of the egg is a *zygote*; shortly thereafter, when it becomes somewhat more complex, it is a *blastocyst*; when it implants in the uterine wall about six days after fertilization, it is a called an *embryo*. It is only technically a *fetus* at about sixty days after conception. See Harold J. Morowitz and James S. Trefil, *The Facts of Life* (New York: Oxford University Press, 1992), p. 46.

2. The pro-life claim is rightly understood and evaluated as a rational claim inasmuch as it is meant to persuade citizens of a modern secular state, since religious claims (such as that the fetus has an immortal soul from conception on) are neither testable nor provable, and thus not (or, anyway, no longer) a plausible basis for securing widespread conviction or requiring compliance of nonbelievers.

3. This mistake is all too prevalent in the literature on the abortion question, although, in a recent article, James Q. Wilson makes the mistake in reverse. He distinguishes the rights-based approach to abortion from the moral approach. Apparently, he has never heard of moral rights. I shall try to steer clear of both errors. See James Q. Wilson, "On Abortion," *Commentary* 27, no. 1 (January 1994): 21–29.

4. Arguments that focus on the fact that the fetus is a *potential* human being or person make such a claim, but they are widely thought to fail because having the potential to realize a status does not entail having the rights that come with the actual status. (That newborn babies are potentially eighteen-year-olds doesn't give them the right to vote now.) Perhaps those pro-lifers who exhibit pictures of fetuses to show that they look like babies are making an argument of this sort, since being a baby is a property that adult humans don't have. But being a baby is something that fetuses share with animals widely thought acceptable to kill. It is that fetuses look like baby humans that is thought to make them special, and their membership in the human species is something that fetuses share with adult humans. In any event, the positive emotional response that most people will have to pictures of babylike fetuses cannot decide their moral status, contrary to a claim recently made by James Q. Wilson. He proposes that we show people films of fetuses at different stages of gestation and that we outlaw abortion at the point at which the fetus looks like a baby to most people and, so to speak, engages their moral sentiments in its favor. If this really were a moral test, one wonders why Wilson doesn't also recommend that we show people films of women at different stages of legally enforced involuntary pregnancy and that we permit abortion from the point at which the woman looks like a human being to most people and engages their moral sentiments in

her favor. But, of course, it is not a moral test. Our emotional response to what things look like is, at best, a hint about what they really are and really are entitled to. To determine what things are and what they are entitled to, we must use our reason. Mere feelings will not do. See Wilson, "On Abortion"; and my "The Impotency of the Potentiality Argument for Fetal Rights: Reply to Wilkins," *Journal of Social Philosophy* 24, no. 3 (Winter 1993): 170–76.

5. Put more technically: A pregnant woman has a right to control her body because she is a human being with the full complement of rights that humans are normally thought to have. If the fetus turns out to be a human being with the full complement of rights also, consistency with the very grounds of the woman's right will require according the fetus the same right to control its body as the woman has over hers. Then, the woman's right will normally be thought to end at the point that it interferes with the fetus's control over its body. I am indebted to Karen Dolan for this clear statement of the principle.

6. For example, Judith Thomson argues that, even if the fetus is already a person with a right to life (like a normal human adult), at least in most pregnancies and at least prior to viability, a woman has a right to abortion because a (fetus's) right to life doesn't entail a right to use another's resources (such as her uterus). Consequently, a woman has the right to expel the unwanted fetus, but to kill it only if that is the only way to expel it. Thomson's view might be thought to vindicate the idea, which I rejected above, that a woman's right to control her body suffices to establish her right to an abortion. However, Thomson's argument works only against the idea that the fetus has a right to life. It won't work if the fetus has some other special moral status that requires us to save it, rather than merely not to kill it unjustly. (Suppose you found an abandoned baby on your doorstep and had no means of bringing it to other shelter. Would you have no duty to take it in, even if it had no right to use your resources?) It will still be necessary to determine the moral status of the fetus. See Judith Jarvis Thomson, "A Defense of Abortion," *Philosophy and Public Affairs* 1, no. 1 (1971): 47–66; cf. Nancy Davis, "Abortion and Self-Defense," *Philosophy and Public Affairs* 13, no. 3 (1984): 175–207. The question about the baby at the doorstep is raised by John Arthur, *The Unfinished Constitution: Philosophy and Constitutional Practice* (Belmont, Calif.: Wadsworth, 1989), pp. 198–200.

7. The question is from Voltaire's article "The Whys," in *A Philosophical Dictionary* (originally published 1764), vol. 10, in *The Works of Voltaire*, trans. W. F. Fleming (Paris: E. R. DuMont, 1901), vol. 14, p. 214. I make no claim about what Voltaire actually meant by this question.

8. If the moral difference between killing and not procreating were due to the loss of investment that results from killing, then this would surely not be a large enough difference to make abortions as bad as killing children or adults, since abortions come when there is much less investment than goes into raising babies to become children and children to become adults. Similar things can be said about risk. The risk of not producing a fetus that reaches the stage at which

most abortions occur is much less than the risk of not producing a being that survives until childhood or adulthood. In any event, until birth, both the investment and the risk are the pregnant woman's, and thus hers to waste or venture.

9. "When I observe the duty of respect, I . . . keep myself within my own bounds in order not to deprive another of any of the value which he as a human being is entitled to put upon himself." Immanuel Kant, "The Metaphysical Principles of Virtue," pt. 2 of *The Metaphysics of Morals*, in *Ethical Philosophy*, trans. James W. Ellington (Indianapolis, Ind.: Hackett, 1983; originally published 1797), p. 114; see also Kant's *Groundwork of the Metaphysics of Morals*, trans. James W. Ellington (Indianapolis, Ind.: Hackett, 1981; originally published 1785), pp. 35–37. While I think my account of respect is in line with Kant's, I do not put it forth as a gloss on Kant's.

10. In *Life's Dominion*, Ronald Dworkin maintains that we regard human life as sacred: "The hallmark of the sacred as distinct from the incrementally valuable is that the sacred is intrinsically *valuable because*—and therefore only once—*it exists*" (emphasis mine). Dworkin gives two examples of things we value as sacred: works of great art and distinct animal species. What our valuation of these shares, and which Dworkin calls "the nerve of the sacred," is that we value the process that has brought them into existence. Individual human life is, for Dworkin, all the more eligible for sacredness than works of art or nature because it is, so to speak, the product of both natural and human creative efforts. But our valuing of the natural processes and the human creative efforts that bring something into existence does not explain (much less justify) our asymmetric valuing of that thing. If it did, then we would value asymmetrically—find sacred—*every product* of human effort or natural process, which we obviously do not, and surely should not. See Ronald Dworkin, *Life's Dominion: An Argument about Abortion, Euthanasia, and Individual Freedom* (New York: Vintage Books, 1994), pp. 73–83.

11. " '*Being*' is obviously not a real predicate; that is, it is not a concept of something which could be added to the concept of a thing." Immanuel Kant, *Critique of Pure Reason*, trans. Norman Kemp Smith (London: Macmillan, 1963), p. 504 (emphasis in original).

12. Norman M. Ford, *When Did I Begin?* (Cambridge: Cambridge University Press, 1991), pp. xvi–xviii, inter alia. I suspect that Ford is a decent fellow trying to find a little space for a woman's autonomy within an otherwise strict rendition of the Roman Catholic condemnation of abortion. Nonetheless, it is difficult to understand why it would be okay to kill something while it still might become two things that it would be wrong to kill separately. Others who take some form of the metaphysical approach are Richard Werner, "Abortion: The Moral Status of the Unborn," *Social Theory and Practice* 3, no. 2 (Fall 1974): 201–22; Jean Beer Blumenfeld, "Abortion and the Human Brain," *Philosophical Studies* 32, no. 3 (October 1977): 251–68; Warren Quinn, "Abortion: Identity and Loss," *Philosophy and Public Affairs* 13, no. 1 (Winter 1984): 24–54; Michael Lockwood, "Warnock versus Powell (and Harradine): When

Does Potentiality Count?" *Bioethics* 2, no. 3 (1988): 187–213; John T. Noonan, "An Almost Absolute Value in History," in *The Problem of Abortion*, ed. Joel Feinberg, 2d ed. (Belmont, Calif.: Wadsworth, 1984), pp. 9–14; Philip E. Devine, "The Scope of the Prohibition against Killing," in *Problem of Abortion*, ed. Feinberg, pp. 21–42; Norman C. Gillespie, "Abortion and Human Rights," in *Problem of Abortion*, ed. Feinberg, pp. 94–101; and Joel Feinberg, "Potentiality, Development, and Rights," in *Problem of Abortion*, ed. Feinberg, pp. 145–50.

13. "That term, [*speciesism*,] coined by the Oxford psychologist Richard Ryder in 1970, has now entered the *Oxford English Dictionary*, where it is defined as 'discrimination against or exploitation of certain animal species by human beings, based on an assumption of mankind's superiority.' As the term suggests, there is a parallel between our attitudes to nonhuman animals, and the attitudes of racists to those they regard as belonging to an inferior race." Peter Singer, *Rethinking Life and Death* (New York: St. Martin's Press, 1995), p. 173.

14. I think this will hold even if, say, one thinks of morality as an agreement among human beings to protect their shared interests. Such an agreement will have to identify the stage of development at which humans have an interest in being protected that is strong enough to override women's interest in being protected against forced pregnancy. This stage will have to coincide with the possession of some property that accounts for how humans become vulnerable to the sort of injury it would be reasonable for all to protect against.

15. This is the defining property of our humanity according to Morowitz and Trefil, who recommend that abortion be restricted from seven months on. Since this view cannot explain why it is worse to kill fetuses with functioning cerebral cortexes than to refuse to produce new ones who will have functioning cerebral cortexes, it is refuted by considerations raised in this chapter. Morowitz and Trefil, *Facts of Life*, pp. 17, 119, inter alia.

16. David Hume, *An Enquiry Concerning the Principles of Morals* (Indianapolis, Ind.: Hackett, 1983; originally published 1751), p. 75.

17. Writes Sumner, "If the creatures we meet have interests and are capable of enjoyment and suffering, we must grant them some moral standing. We thereby constrain ourselves not to exploit them ruthlessly for our own advantage." On these grounds, he proposes that we treat the advent of fetal sentience (sometime in the second trimester of pregnancy) as bringing with it an entitlement to protection. L. W. Sumner, "A Third Way," in *Problem of Abortion*, ed. Feinberg, pp. 71–93, especially p. 84. Some scientists hold that fetal sentience is impossible before the beginning of the seventh month, that "before the wiring up of the cortex [around the twenty-fifth week], the fetus is simply incapable of feeling anything, including pain." See Morowitz and Trefil, *Facts of Life*, p. 158.

18. The wrong involved in being killed is the loss of the life of which we have begun to be aware; it is not the pain of being aware of losing one's life.

Causing the latter pain is a wrong to be sure, one that may make it worse to kill someone who is aware of what's happening than, say, to kill him in his sleep. But killing someone in his sleep is bad enough to count as murder, and that's what counts here.

19. It isn't easy to capture the way in which staying alive becomes specially important to us once we are aware of it, though I think everyone can recognize it in his or her own experience. One writer who has given expression to part of what is at stake here is Richard Wollheim. Arguing that death is a misfortune even when life is bad, Wollheim writes, "It is not that death deprives us of some particular pleasure, or even of pleasure. What it deprives us of is something more fundamental than pleasure: it deprives us of that thing which we gain access to when, as persisting creatures, we enter into our present mental states. . . . It deprives us of phenomenology, and, having once tasted phenomenology, we develop a longing for it which we cannot give up: not even when the desire for cessation of pain, for extinction, grows stronger." Richard Wollheim, *The Thread of Life* (Cambridge, Mass.: Harvard University Press, 1984), p. 269. I say that this captures part of what is at stake because I think that we long for more than phenomenology, understood simply as perceptual experience. We would not, I think, care so much about continuing if we were, and knew we were, just experiencing fictional appearances, if our experience were, say, a continuing series of movies. It is because we seem to experience a real world in which people (including ourselves) act and produce, or fail to produce, outcomes that matter, that we long for experience to go on. If philosophers' epistemological nightmare came true and we really were brains in vats, I think that our attachment to life would diminish.

20. See Michael Tooley, *Abortion and Infanticide* (Oxford: Clarendon Press, 1983); and S. I. Benn, "Abortion, Infanticide, and Respect for Persons," in *Problem of Abortion*, ed. Feinberg, pp. 135–44.

21. This is what Don Marquis overlooks in holding that "loss of a future life" is what makes killing human adults and human fetuses equally wrong: "Since the loss of the future to a standard fetus, if killed, is, however, at least as great a loss as the loss of the future to a standard adult human being who is killed, abortion . . . is presumptively very seriously wrong, where that presumption is very strong—as strong as the presumption that killing another adult human being is wrong." Don Marquis, "Why Abortion Is Immoral," *Journal of Philosophy* 86, no. 4 (April 1989): 183–202 (the quote is from p. 194). Responding to Marquis, Peter McInerney lists some of the many differences in the ways fetuses and adult humans are related to their futures. He concludes: "Although there is some biological continuity between them so that there is a sense in which the later person stages 'are the future' of the fetus, the fetus is so little connected to the later personal life that it can not be deprived of that personal life. At its time the fetus does not already 'possess' that future personal life in the way that a normal adult human already 'possesses' his future personal life." Peter K. McInerney, "Does a Fetus Already Have a Future-Like-Ours?"

Journal of Philosophy 87, no. 5 (May 1990): 266–67. While McInerney raises enough concerns about the difference between a fetus's relation to its future and an adult's to its to show that Marquis cannot simply assert that abortion does the same thing to a fetus that murder does to a normal adult, McInerney does not do enough to support his conclusion that a fetus cannot be deprived of its future personal life. Indeed, since he admits that there is at least biological continuity between the fetus and the future personal life it will have if not aborted, there remains at least some sense in which abortion does deprive the fetus of its future. The question whether the fetus's loss is enough to make killing it morally like killing an adult requires a moral comparison of the various losses, which McInerney doesn't undertake. Another case of failure to respect the priority of morality over metaphysics.

22. Mary Anne Warren, "On the Moral and Legal Status of Abortion," in *Problem of Abortion*, ed. Feinberg, pp. 110–14.

23. This fact enables Jane English to stymie Warren's attempt by claiming that, as the concept of a person functions in our actual practice of recognizing some creatures as persons, that concept is too indefinite to "be captured in a strait jacket of necessary and/or sufficient conditions." Jane English, "Abortion and the Concept of a Person," in *Problem of Abortion*, ed. Feinberg, p. 152.

24. John Locke, *An Essay concerning Human Understanding*, ed. and abridged John Yolton (London: Everyman, 1994; originally published 1690), bk. 2, chap. 27, sec. 9, p. 180.

25. Kant, *Critique of Pure Reason*, p. 341 (emphasis in original).

26. One expert on infant cognitive development writes: "it is a most un-Proustian life, not thought, only lived. Sensorimotor schemata . . . enable a child to walk a straight line but not to think about a line in its absence, to recognize his or her mother but not to think about her when she is gone. It is a world difficult for us to conceive, accustomed as we are to spend much of our time ruminating about the past and anticipating the future. Nevertheless, this is the state that Piaget posits for the child before one-and-a-half, that is, an ability to recognize objects and events but an inability to recall them in their absence. Because of this inability . . . the child cannot even remember what he or she did a few minutes ago. . . . These observations have been made by others as well, but more recently there have been occasional suggestions that recall may occur considerably earlier than Piaget believed, perhaps in the second 6 months of life." Jean M. Mandler, "Representation and Recall in Infancy," in *Infant Memory: Its Relation to Normal and Pathological Memory in Humans and Other Animals*, ed. Morris Moscovitch (New York: Plenum Press, 1984), pp. 75–76.

27. See, for example, Lockwood, "Warnock versus Powell (and Harradine)"; Werner, "Abortion: Moral Status of Unborn"; Noonan, "An Almost Absolute Value in History"; Devine, "Scope of Prohibition against Killing"; and Feinberg, "Potentiality, Development, and Rights"; see also Loren E. Lomasky, "Being a Person: Does It Matter?" in *Problem of Abortion*, ed. Feinberg, pp. 161–72.

28. Of course, we will normally be caring in these ways too. The point is that our doing so is not necessary to the way we value the lives of children or adults. For that, all that is necessary is that we respect their caring about their lives.

29. "Human babies are the most helpless in the animal kingdom; they require many years of care before they can survive on their own." Mary Batten, *Sexual Strategies: How Females Choose Their Mates* (New York: G.P. Putnam's Sons, 1992), p. 142.

30. "When infants become *attached* to their mothers many language-critical processes are encouraged: the desire to engage in playful vocalization, including vocal exploration, the emergence of turn taking and dialogue structure, and the desire to imitate vocal patterns. In turn, mothers who are attached to and feeling nurturant toward their infants provide them with a number of opportunities to learn. Among the other processes encouraged by attachment are the use of eye gaze and manual gestures to signal attentional focus and convey labels, and the use of voice to designate and convey." John L. Locke, *The Child's Path to Spoken Language* (Cambridge, Mass.: Harvard University Press, 1993), p. 107 (emphasis in original). Elsewhere Locke points out that infants who do not find this emotional responsiveness in their mothers seek it elsewhere. Ibid., pp. 109–10.

9

On Euthanasia and Health Care

Some people think that the discussion of health care and euthanasia, particularly euthanasia, is dangerous and would be better avoided. A striking example is provided by philosopher Peter Singer's account of his attempts to speak about euthanasia at several conferences organized by German universities during 1991.[1] Germans are understandably uncomfortable about the topic of euthanasia because of troubling memories of the Nazi era. Some among them think that the discussion of euthanasia legitimates asking which lives are more worth living than others, which, in turn, opens the door to the horrible practices of the Third Reich. Moved by thoughts of this sort, a number of German organizations mobilized to protest and disrupt any conference on this subject, and they succeeded in making it impossible for Singer and many others to speak.

One might be glad to see this sensitivity on the part of Germans, particularly at a moment when their government is once again doing ominous things like deporting Gypsies. However, I think that this is a short-sighted reaction, on two grounds. First, while murders committed in the name of euthanasia were among the great horrors of the Nazi period, so, too, was the silencing of free discussion. Ultimately, that silencing was worse than the murders done in the name of euthanasia, since it provided cover for those murders and for many others. It's worth noting here, as well, that the Nazis' euthanasia program existed only as a euphemism for some of their murderous policies. They didn't start off by compassionately ending the lives of suffering patients and slide from there into the involuntary extermination of people thought undesirable. They started squarely with involuntary extermination.[2]

Second, refusal to discuss euthanasia makes sense only if there is a simple, obvious, and undangerous position that one can take on the issue. The German protesters implicitly assumed that it is morally acceptable simply to avoid euthanasia and preserve all human life, whatever the cost in resources. If that were obviously the case, then, concern about freedom of speech aside, the protesters would have had at least a reasonable moral position. However, things are more complicated than that. The cost of preserving all human life is not just a cost in resources; it is a cost in suffering. Euthanasia is not proposed primarily as a means to cut medical costs. It is proposed as a means to reduce suffering: the suffering of patients in the final stages of painful diseases, the suffering of newborns with severe and painful birth defects, and, of somewhat lesser importance but by no means morally irrelevant, the suffering of family members who must witness the awful suffering of a loved one in hopeless pain.

It is important to add that the suffering that prompts patients in final stages of terminal diseases to ask for euthanasia is not only physical pain. The report of the Remmelink Commission on euthanasia in the Netherlands indicates that "loss of dignity" was given more frequently than pain as a reason for requesting the termination of life. Pain was the only reason given in less than six percent of the cases studied.[3] Loss of dignity is a kind of suffering to which only a rational being can be subject, a mental suffering that comes from fearing that one's dying will be a denial of the self-possession that one strove to maintain in living. This is a real form of suffering, and to refuse to relieve it, to force a person to stay alive against her will, is to make her very life itself her enemy—and this is surely a cruel torture to add at a time that is already hard and sad enough.

I am not saying that this suffering justifies euthanasia. It may or may not. My point is that what it definitely does do is make the question of euthanasia a real moral question, with no easy answer. There is no moral free ride here, no possibility that we can keep our hands clean by keeping them in our pockets. To reject euthanasia in all cases is to consign some of our fellow human beings to great and avoidable suffering. Consequently, no one should assume that refusing to consider euthanasia puts him on the side of the angels. Determining whether to preserve life at the cost of suffering or to relieve suffering at the cost of life is an issue that must be addressed in a spirit of open-minded inquiry.

I make this point because I have noticed, in discussions on this and related issues with my colleagues and students, a tendency to think that the evils of the past (such as the Nazi horrors) mean that we should leave these issues alone. One sees this, not just on the very difficult issue of infanticide for severely defective newborns, but on related issues such as whether we should alter the gene pool, say, to eliminate certain congenital diseases or disabilities like blindness. In all these cases, leaving the issue alone means allowing conditions to persist that will cause suffering, incapacitation, or both to some of our fellow human beings. Accordingly, it is false, irresponsible, even downright reckless to think that one can avoid evil simply by refusing to consider these hard issues.

Nor will it do to rest content with one's "gut reactions" as if they were a sure guide to what's right. Defenders of racial segregation once appealed to their gut reactions to support their views, and that should be enough to make any thoughtful person think twice about accepting his own gut reactions as guides to moral truth. In the present situation, there is even more cause for concern. We all have very strong feelings about life and death and very strong reactions to the newly born, the suffering, and the dying. These feelings, however, give us little clear guidance for or against euthanasia, since they are enlisted on both sides: both for life and against suffering. Moreover, these feelings cannot simply be accepted on their own terms, because they developed in us in the course of evolution, during most of which period our task and need was simply to keep as many of our species alive as we could. When the emotional life of our species was taking shape, we did not have the possibility of keeping people alive on mechanical heart machines. Nor did we have the possibility of keeping people alive against their will. Thus, we should expect our instincts and emotions to be simpler in their urgings than our current situation requires. I am not saying that we should ignore our emotions, only that there is reason to suspect them and that their proddings must be subjected to rational evaluation before we can safely act on them.

Clearly, therefore, we cannot avoid a serious philosophical evaluation of the issues of life, health, and death, if we are to be morally responsible to ourselves and our fellows. Before turning to my own proposal for how to go about this evaluation, I want to comment briefly on a strategy commonly employed in such evaluation, a strategy that is both powerful and potentially misleading, namely, the "slippery slope" argument. For example: Party A says that terminally ill and suffering patients should have the right to have their lives ended at their request, when their request is made with comprehension of the options and reflects a stable desire, rather than a moment of desperation. Party B replies that, if we allow this, then before long we will be allowing people to have their lives ended just because they have some disability that makes them think their lives aren't worth living, and next we'll have relatives, legal guardians, doctors, or—God forbid—the government, deciding that people with certain disabilities should be killed because their lives aren't worth living. Thus B concludes that we should reject A's proposal.

Suppose that B's predictions are correct and thus that we are rightly persuaded by her slippery slope argument not to implement A's proposal. If, however, we think that this argument has shown that A's proposal is morally wrong, then it is we who are slipping. B's argument is that adopting A's proposal as a policy may make it more likely that other policies will exist that will be bad. This is an objection to adopting A's proposal as a policy even if A's proposal itself is right. B's argument does not show that it is wrong for people to have the right to have their lives ended. It shows that, though A's proposal may be right, implementing it as a policy may lead to the implementation of other policies that are wrong.[4]

Slippery slope arguments slip over the issue of whether a proposal itself is right and tar it with the wrongness of subsequent policies it may make more likely. That leaves us unsure about the moral status of the original proposal. Thus, if someone makes a slippery slope argument, even a good one, against a proposal, we should not think that this shows the proposal itself to be wrong. That must still be addressed. If the proposal turns out to be right itself, then, a successful slippery slope argument is an occasion for sadness. After all, what it implies is that a proposal that is right cannot be implemented because, to put it crudely, the world isn't good enough for it. And that means that we must be satisfied with something less than what is right. The lesson here is that we should keep separate questions separate. First, we should get clear on the rightness or wrongness of a given proposal, and, then, as a separate matter, we should take up the advisability of implementing it in light of the likely consequences of doing so.

With this in mind, let us now examine what it is about life that gives it the special moral status we attribute at least to human life. Note, at the outset, that we use the term life in two senses, which I call "biological" and "biographical."[5] Biological life is the ongoing functioning of our organisms. Biographical life is the unfolding dramas of our lives as those dramas are registered internally in our experiences, thoughts, memories, anticipations, and so on.

Biological life is life we share with birds and mosquitoes. By contrast, biographical life is life we share with no other animals (with the possible exception of some higher primates or the cetaceans). It is more than merely a conscious inner life, which dogs or cows surely have. It is more because it is self-conscious life, the life of a person, a being who is aware of its life as the life of one enduring individual, and with an awareness that is more than mere observation. Biographical life is the life of a being who has desires about how he wants to live, beliefs about how he should live, a being who cares about how his life turns out. This is what gives it a natural dramatic structure.

Biological life is the precondition for biographical life. But it is biographical life that is truly the locus of value for us; biological life is of value to us only insofar as it makes biographical life possible. Is being dead any worse than being alive in a state of permanent unconsciousness with no possibility of regaining consciousness? I think there is no reason to prefer one to the other, because for us the permanent loss of consciousness is no different from death. This suggests that what we treasure about our lives is not the continuation of our metabolic processes but the continuation of our inner biographies.

At least in secular moral doctrines, that something is greatly valued by humans counts toward its having moral value. At least part of what makes it immoral to hurt people is the fact that they so deeply dislike pain and try so hard to avoid it. Analogously, that human beings primarily value biographical life and value biological life only secondarily as a means to biographical life counts in favor of holding that biographical life has primary or intrinsic moral value, while biological life has only derivative or instrumental value. This presumption in favor of biographical life is no small matter. To overcome it requires showing (not just asserting) that biological life (alone) has greater value than biographical life even though those who have experience with both opt for the latter. I don't think that this can be convincingly done. One may, of course, make a religious affirmation of the supreme value of biological life. But, since no evidence can be given for such an affirmation, it is little more than a statement of someone's unsupported opinion. Individuals may direct their own lives by unsupported opinions, but such opinions are not a suitable basis for public policy or for publicly shared moral principles.

If I am right about the overriding importance of biographical life, then it cannot be that euthanasia is automatically wrong because it ends biological life. The rightness or wrongness of euthanasia will have to be based on euthanasia's role in the biography of the patient, that is, what it means to that person and how it meshes, or fails to mesh, with his own conception of what has made his life worth living. This, in turn, creates a presumption in favor of letting people decide when it fits their biographical life to end their biological life. In short, once the preeminence of biographical life is granted, then there will be a strong presumption in favor of allowing people to decide for themselves how long they should go on living.

There is another striking implication of the moral preeminence of biographical life. These days most people, including doctors, find it acceptable to allow patients to decide that they want no extraordinary efforts made to prolong their lives. So there is general acceptance of what is called *passive* euthanasia. As to whether doctors, or even the patients themselves, should be allowed intentionally to intervene to end life, however, there is much debate and doubt.[6] But, once we separate ourselves from the idea that it is biological life that is the locus of moral value, then the difference between passive and active euthanasia largely evaporates. Whether we let the body die or we intervene to make it die pales in importance compared to honoring the wishes of the person in whose biography that body plays but a supporting role.

Rachels reaches a similar conclusion in *The End of Life*. Taking a utilitarian tack, he argues that we are responsible for all the foreseeable consequences of whatever we choose to do, including the choice not to act. Thus, for him, the distinction between active and passive euthanasia is a distinction without a difference.[7] I think that, if the distinction between what we cause by our action and what results from our inaction is not maintained, then we are morally hostage to all the suffering in the world that we could prevent; and, in fact, Rachels goes on to argue that allowing starvation to go around the world is tantamount to murder.[8] I find this counterintuitive, since it essentially makes us slaves of any and every needy person in the world. On this issue, my approach would be to keep the distinction and then say that, insofar as passive euthanasia is undertaken intentionally with the aim of letting death come as soon as possible, it is an action and thus is morally no different in status from active euthanasia.

These considerations lead me to believe that, in principle, people should have the right to have their lives ended when they wish and that no great weight should be placed on whether their lives are ended actively or passively. In fact, where a person is in great suffering and pleading to have his life ended, I think that refusing to answer that plea with positive intervention is simply cruel.

These conclusions follow from the primacy of biographical over biological life. That primacy does not, of course, refute the slippery slope arguments against these conclusions. What it does do, rather, is suggest that the only arguments that will be successful against these conclusions are slippery slope arguments, namely, that implementing a right to active euthanasia may lead to abuses or worse. The primacy of biographical over biological life does, at least, give us a tool that weakens the force of such arguments. The point is this. Allowing active euthanasia seems to start us on a slippery slope toward allowing forced euthanasia if we think that the important moral boundary regarding killing is between forbidding the active ending of biological life and allowing it. Then, active euthanasia is the first step down a slope at the end of which is state-sanctioned murder. However, the primacy of biographical life suggests that the important moral boundary should be between forbidding killing people against their will and allowing it. Allowing active euthanasia on patients who request it does not cross that boundary, and, perhaps, if we can make clear that that is the important boundary, we can make sure that allowing active euthanasia does not lead to policies that step over it.

Turning now to the problem of allocating health care, we might think, at first glance, that it raises moral issues quite similar to those surrounding the termination of life. Staying healthy prolongs life, and death would seem to be the zero point of health. There are important differences, however. Euthanasia is largely a question of individual self-determination: of what the one whose life it is may do, and what others may or may not do to serve or block his wishes. The question of health care is different in that it is, in addition, a question of social and economic justice. Health care is produced by the efforts of others. While a right to life is generally a right not to be killed, a right to health care is a much grander thing, being a right to the services of numerous others, from brain surgeons to bedpan emptiers. Unlike the issue of euthanasia, which can be resolved largely in terms of the wishes of the patient, questions of health care require, in addition, considerations of the division of social labor and the distribution of the products of that labor, as well as a whole series of complex determinations about the allocation of resources *between* health care and other needs, and the allocation of resources *within* health care between generations, among different diseases, among people who live more and less healthy lifestyles, and so on.

As it was with euthanasia, the way people value their own lives is crucial to moral decisions about health care. It is because life without health is so much inferior to healthy life that health care matters morally at all. And it is because of a tension in the way that people look at their lives and the role of health in them that there is a tension in our thought about the best way to allocate health care. Consider that there is a special sadness when death strikes the young. This implies that early death is worse than late death, which, in turn, suggests a view of life as a finite resource of which one can have more or less. On the other hand, the criminal law holds a murderer equally culpable for killing a young or an old victim, indeed, even for killing a dying victim. This suggests a view of life in which the length of time left is irrelevant. However much one has is all one has, and in that sense the lives of young and old are alike. Before my grandmother died in her nineties, I asked her if she wanted to live to be a hundred. She said that no one wants to live to be a hundred except someone who is ninety-nine. This suggests a view of life in which each has all, and only what, he or she has left, and that much is of ultimate value to the one whose life it is.

These different ways of thinking about life are reflected in two opposing ways of thinking about the allocation of scarce health care resources. On the one hand, we devote enormous resources to treating the diseases of the aged. One out of every six health dollars is spent on treating people during the last year of life. On the other hand, some people have begun to think that we should reduce our investment in the last years of life down to only what is needed to keep people comfortable and as free of pain as possible and, instead, devote more of our resources to treating the diseases of youth and middle age. I am inclined to favor this latter view, not only because its implementation would improve more years of life overall than our current emphasis on treatment of the diseases of the elderly, but also because it manifests a kind of egalitarianism. Inasmuch as everyone starts out young and only some grow old, focusing on the treatment of the diseases of younger folks tends to spread the benefits of modern medicine more equally among all people in the society. Nonetheless, I wouldn't apply this by a rigid formula. We shouldn't forget that ninety-nine-year old whose little remaining time is all the time in eternity that she has left.

Notes

This chapter is based on a talk originally presented at the McDowell Conference on Philosophy and Social Policy, held at American University in Washington, D.C., on 20 November 1992.

1. Peter Singer, "On Being Silenced in Germany," *New York Review of Books* 38, no. 14 (15 August 1991): 36–42.

2. "Contemporary proponents of euthanasia advocate mercy-killing in response to the patient's request. Among the Nazis, there was never any thought of killing as a compassionate act for the benefit of suffering terminal patients;

indeed, this was not even used as a false excuse when they would lie about what they were doing. Families were informed that their sick or mentally retarded kin had died from such maladies as pneumonia or appendicitis. Nor was there ever any thought of securing the permission of the victims. The . . . killings were completely involuntary." James Rachels, *The End of Life: Euthanasia and Morality* (New York: Oxford University Press, 1986), p. 178.

3. P. J. van der Maas, J. J. M. van Delden, L. Pijnenborg, C. W. N. Looman, "Euthanasia and Other Medical Decisions concerning the End of Life," *Lancet* 338 (14 September 1991): 672.

4. Experience in the Netherlands gives some evidence against the slippery slope argument applied to euthanasia: "Many physicians who had practiced euthanasia mentioned that they would be most reluctant to do so again, thus refuting the 'slippery slope' argument." Ibid., 673. I have already suggested why the Nazi experience cannot be taken as evidence for the slippery slope argument applied to euthanasia. See note 2 above and accompanying text.

5. Rachels makes good use of this distinction in his *The End of Life*; see especially pp. 24–27.

6. As this book goes to press, the state of Michigan has failed once again to persuade a jury to convict Dr. Jack Kevorkian for assisting suicide, held by the Michigan Supreme Court to be a common law felony. Edward Walsh, "Kevorkian Critics Left with Dilemma: Legal System Failing to Halt Assisted Suicides," *Washington Post*, 18 May 1996, p. A3.

7. Rachels, *End of Life*, pp. 106–14.

8. Ibid., p. 130.

10

Is Police Discretion Justified in a Free Society?

By "police discretion," I understand the freedom of police officers to decide whether or not to arrest an individual when the conditions that would legally justify that arrest are present and when the officer can make the arrest without sacrificing other equally or more pressing legal duties. So I do not count under police discretion the choice of which individual to arrest when arrests of several are equally legally justified but only one arrest is physically possible. And, of course, I exclude all the other important, and I think inescapable, acts of judgment that police officers must make (for example, the decision that the conditions legally justifying arrest are there). Our question, then, is this: *Is it justified in a free society to allow police officers freedom to determine whether or not to arrest someone when they legally and physically can make the arrest?* The short answer is no. The long answer will require a look at the nature of free societies and the sort of law enforcement they require.

Before proceeding to this, I want to qualify my thesis in one important way. Police are commonly charged with the dual task of enforcing law and maintaining order. In pursuit of the latter aim, they disperse unruly crowds, quiet noisy neighbors, break up fights before they begin, clear the streets of drunks or prostitutes, and so on. In the context of such order maintenance, the police power to arrest is not so much a power to limit citizens' freedom as it is a threat available to police to back up their attempts to get troublesome individuals to desist from offending behavior or to clear the area. As long as arrest is used only in this way, I think it is acceptable for police to refrain from actually arresting troublesome individuals, even when they legally might, if they judge that milder means will serve the goal of order maintenance. Thus, here, it seems to me that discretion has a place.[1] However, whenever arrest is used to set in motion a series of events aimed at seriously limiting citizens' freedom, or when the threat of arrest itself seriously limits citizens' freedom, I contend that police ought not to have discretion. A brief detour through the history of political philosophy will help explain why.

Plato is well known for the (hopefully!) unrealistic claim, argued at great length in *The Republic*, that a good state will be possible only when philosophers become kings or kings philosophers.[2] In this good state, there are to be few laws, since Plato thought of laws the way he thought of medication: more than just a minimum betokens and promotes a permanently sickly constitution. More particularly, the philosopher-king doesn't need laws, since he or she knows the good and thus can determine in each new case exactly what is right to do. (I'm not being politically correct here; Plato actually argued for equal opportunity for women to become philosopher-kings.) It would make no sense to tie the philosopher-king's hands with laws, since laws bring about only generally good outcomes and they might prevent the philosopher-king from doing exactly what is right in each new particular situation.

But *The Republic* is not Plato's last word. His last dialogue, and thus his last word at least on the topic of the good state, is *The Laws*. The title should make clear that here, near the close of his life, Plato took a far more positive view of the role of and need for laws than he did as an idealistic young man. Midway (in content and in time) between *The Republic* and *The Laws* stands Plato's dialogue *The Statesman*. In it, we see unfold before our eyes the shift from the rule of the philosopher-king to the rule of law. It will be instructive to see what reasons ground this shift in Plato's views.

The dialogue in *The Statesman* takes place between a character called "the Eleatic stranger" and another called "the younger Socrates" (not to be confused with the Socrates who leads the discussion in *The Republic*). The stranger starts by speaking of the true statesman, the one who possesses the "royal art" of ruling wisely and justly, and young Socrates balks when the stranger suggests that such a statesman may rule without laws. The stranger then explains that

> the best thing of all is not that the law should rule, but that a man should rule, supposing him to have wisdom and the royal power. . . . Because the law does not perfectly comprehend what is noblest and most just for all and therefore cannot enforce what is best. The differences of men and

actions, and the endless irregular movements of human things, do not admit of any universal and simple rule.[3]

The stranger likens the royal art to other arts, such as those practiced by physicians or physical trainers. If these individuals truly possess their arts, it would be absurd to bind them by preestablished rules. If a physician gave a prescription to a patient, only later to discover a better way of curing the ailment, we would hardly insist that the physician stick to the earlier treatment. We would allow, even want, him to do just what his art teaches him is best in this particular case. So, too, the practitioner of the ruling art. Says the stranger, "Then if the law is not the perfection of right, why are we compelled to make laws at all? The reason of this has next to be investigated."[4]

Turning to this, the stranger points out that, like other arts, the royal art can never be mastered by more than a few individuals. Thus, there may be rulers who falsely claim to have that art and who therefore say that it is for the best that they rule without laws. Such false rulers are called tyrants, and their lawless rule is as bad as the genuine ruler's rule is good. Moreover, the fact that few are likely to possess the royal art, combined with the possibility of tyrants pretending to have it, makes people suspicious of anyone who rules without law, even those who do have the art. People "can never be made to believe that any one can be worthy of such authority . . . ; they fancy that he will be a despot who will wrong and harm and slay whom he pleases." This suspicion creates instability, which itself invites tyranny as worried citizens flock to demagogues for protection. In short, because there is no clear identifying mark of the true philosopher-king, no one can be allowed to rule without laws. Says the stranger, "as the State is not like a beehive, and has no natural head who is at once recognized to be the superior both in body and in mind, mankind are obliged to meet and make laws."[5]

Rule by laws is, then, for Plato, "second best."[6] Such rule cannot do justice (full, complete, perfectly tailored justice) to the complexity and variability of human affairs in the way that a genuine philosopher-king unconstrained by laws could. But, given how few true philosopher-kings there are, how difficult it is to know when we have got one, and, above all, how dangerous it would be if a phony philosopher-king ruled without laws, we must settle for second best—meet and make laws and hold everyone strictly to them. Ironically, laws are good for the same reason that makes them only second best: they limit the power of the ruler. They protect the citizens from the rulers, and the citizens pay for this protection by giving up the possibility of perfectly good solutions to their complex and variable problems.

Plato teaches, then, three lessons about the rule of law. First, the function of the rule of law is, not only to render justice to the citizens, but also to protect them from their governors. Second, the justification for the rule of law cannot be that it produces the best results in every case; its justification is that it gives generally good, albeit imperfect, results while protecting against tyranny. Law represents, to use a term not found in the Platonic corpus, a "trade-off." The possibility of perfect outcomes is traded off for security against the worst outcomes. Third, this trade-off, and thus the rule of law itself, would not be necessary if states were like beehives, in which those who are truly fit to rule are naturally marked and easily recognized.

From these Platonic lessons about the rule of law, we can draw some morals about police discretion, since police discretion begins where the rule of law ends: police discretion is precisely the subjection of law to a human decision beyond the law. Like rule by philosopher-kings unfettered by law, police discretion makes possible a tailoring of justice to the complexity and variability of human affairs. Thus, one moral to draw is that, if we give up police discretion, we also give up the possibility of some results that are better than what we get by strict application of the law. The second moral is that if we allow police discretion, we give certain citizens a special discretionary power over others, which can be used in tyrannical ways. Consequently, if police discretion is to be justified, we must be confident that it is more likely to be used to arrive at benefits superior to those the rule of law provides than to be used tyrannically. This confidence will be rash to the degree that states are unlike beehives. The final moral, then, is that the harder it is to identify those who are truly fit to exercise authority, the less confident we should be about allowing discretionary law enforcement.

Though these Platonic morals regarding police discretion continue to have relevance today, for us they are only a starting point. They do not give us the whole moral truth about police discretion—at least, not in terms that are adequate to modern political theory, or in terms adequate to the project promised in my title. Plato's republic was not, and was not meant to be, a free society. To shift our perspective and look at the problem from the standpoint of the conditions and nature of a free society is to move a greater distance than might immediately be apparent. My purpose, then, in starting with Plato is, in addition to distilling some general truths about the rule of law and its opposite, to use Plato as a backdrop against which the features of modern political theorizing, with its emphasis on the value of freedom, can most clearly be seen. For this, we must shift to modern thinkers like Hobbes and Locke, and to contemporaries like Rawls. Though all of these are broadly in the "social contract" tradition, their contractarianism as such is of secondary importance for our concerns. Far more important for our purposes is the way in which they understand the nature of political authority and its relationship to citizens' freedom. Here we will see the distinctive features of the modern conception of political authority in a free society.

Interestingly, both Hobbes and Locke started where the last of the Platonic morals had left off. They echoed, and in fact extended, Plato's observation that the human society is unlike a beehive, that there are no naturally marked and (thus) easily identifiable natural rulers. The crucial chapter 13 of Hobbes's *Leviathan*, the chapter in which he introduced his grim account of the state of nature and the reasons for getting out of it by creating a political commonwealth, begins:

> Nature hath made men so equall, in the faculties of body, and mind; as that though there bee found one man sometimes manifestly stronger in body, or of quicker mind then another; yet when all is reckoned together, the difference between man, and man, is not so considerable, as that one man can thereupon claim to himselfe any benefit, to which another may not pretend, as well as he. For as to the strength of body, the weakest has strength enough to kill the strongest. . . .
> And as to the faculties of the mind . . . , I find yet a greater equality amongst men, than that of strength.[7]

And chapter 2 of Locke's *Second Treatise of Government*, the chapter in which he introduced his own not-so-grim view of the state of nature, begins by making the same point as Hobbes:

> To understand political power right, and derive it from its original, we must consider, what state all men are naturally in, and that is, a *state of perfect freedom* to order their actions . . . as they think fit . . . , without asking leave, or depending on the will of any other man.
> A *state* also *of equality*, wherein all the power and jurisdiction is reciprocal, no one having more than another; there being nothing more evident, than that creatures of the same species and rank, promiscuously born to all the same advantages of nature, should also be equal one amongst another.[8]

To these modern thinkers, human social life is less like a beehive than even Plato thought. For Plato, we are not like a beehive because natural rulers are not naturally marked and easily recognized. This led to suspicion and fear of a false ruler who might tyrannize people, and from there to preference, albeit reluctant, for the rule of law as second best. For Hobbes and Locke, and I daresay for us as well, we are not like a beehive because there are no natural rulers (period). No one has—by virtue of innate ability or some other trait—natural fitness to rule others. There are no natural rulers to recognize, no queen bees, no philosopher-kings. And this has new and profound implications for understanding the danger of tyranny and the attraction of the rule of law.

In the state of nature, each has authority over herself and none has authority over others. Let us call authority over oneself "personal authority" and authority over others "political authority." In the state of nature, then, there is no political authority, only everyone's full and equal personal authority. If there is no natural political authority, such political authority as exists is artificial—created by us. It should be clear that personal and political authority are mutually exclusive categories, for the creation and enlargement of political authority is necessarily at the expense of personal authority (and vice versa). Since any political authority that exists is humanly created, it is either taken by force from, or freely given by, those over whom it is exercised. Note that this is a claim in political theory, not in psychology. Neither the taking nor the giving of authority need be consciously or intentionally done.

Since political authority is at the expense of personal authority, it results from either a forced taking or a free giving up of some of people's personal authority. If political authority is taken by force, then it has no moral claim on those over whom it is exercised. Consequently, for political authority to be morally legitimate, for it to exercise a claim on citizens beyond the fear it evokes, it must be freely given. But the political authority essential to a state cannot be freely given in the form of an actual voluntary donation by citizens, since the benefits of a state depend on its already being in existence when people are born so that they can be protected and educated to the point at which they could make the donation. Thus, the test of whether political authority is legitimate becomes the theoretical one of whether it would be reasonable for citizens to make this donation. And that question is answered positively if what the citizens get from political authority amounts to the best possible bargain for what they give up for it.

Here lies the analytic power and normative force of the social contract: It embodies the terms on which it would be reasonable for humans equal and complete in their personal authority to grant to some individuals political authority over them. This is why it has never been important that the contract and the state of nature are historical fictions. The contract spells out conditions under which citizens' surrender of some of their equal personal authority is reasonable, and thus, though it is the purest fiction, the contract provides a standard for legitimate political authority over free people.

An important implication of this way of thinking is that legitimate political authority is literally concocted out of the parts of free people's personal authority that they surrender to the political commonwealth. The lawmaker's authority to make laws is made up out of the authority that free people have to make decisions about how they should live, and the law enforcer's authority to back laws up with force is derived from the authority that free people have to use force in defense of their authority to govern their own lives, and so on. Thus, Locke said of the extent of the political authority in a legitimate state,

> It is *not*, nor can possibly be absolutely *arbitrary* over the lives and fortunes of the people: for it being but the joint power of every member of society . . . ; it can be no more than those persons had in a state of nature before they entered into society, and gave up to the community.[9]

And Rawls can say of liberal democracies that "political power, which is always coercive power, is the power of the public, that is, of free and equal citizens as a collective body."[10]

A corollary of this point is that authority exercised by political officials beyond that which it would be reasonable for people to surrender in forming a state is illegitimate. Illegitimate here means morally indistinguishable from the sorts of invasions that characterized the state of nature and that, once a state exists, are called tyrannical or criminal. If political authority is understood to consist of the personal authority that free people reasonably deposit in a state, authority exercised by political officials beyond that amount is stolen, taken by force. The force may be that of habit, tradition, or ignorance, but forced taking, rather than free giving, it remains. Thus, authority exercised beyond what is rationally granted is morally indistinguishable from tyranny or crime—from the sorts of coercive invasions the avoidance of which makes the state reasonable in the first place. Rather than citizens having an obligation to respect such authority, they have the right to resist it. Said Locke,

> *Where-ever law ends, tyranny begins* . . . ; and whosoever in authority exceeds the power given him by the law, and makes use of the force he has under his command, to compass that upon the subject, which the law allows not, ceases in that to be a magistrate; and, acting without authority,

may be opposed, as any other man, who by force invades the right of another.[11]

It should be evident now that the political authority that governs a free society has a very different moral structure from that which governs Plato's republic. This will be clearest if we imagine, contrary to fact, that Plato's philosopher-king were dedicated, above all, to promoting the freedom of his or her subjects. Then, we could picture the philosopher-king's authority as a kind of unlimited all-purpose power to do whatever is needed to realize, or even maximize, people's freedom. This is not how political authority in a free society should be understood, however. The most important difference is that political authority that is created by free people is not authority to do whatever is necessary to realize any particular goal, even the maximization of freedom. It is rather a specific, limited grant of authority to do certain things, and only certain things.

Another way to put this difference is as follows. The Platonic ruler is authorized to accomplish a goal, and thus his authority is limited, not in its scope, but only in the purposes for which it can be exercised. By contrast, the modern ruler of a free society is authorized to perform certain actions, and thus her authority is limited in its scope. The political officials of a free society are not simply empowered to do whatever is necessary to bring about some overriding purpose, even the maximization of freedom itself. They have only the authority that they have been given, and they must keep within that even if going beyond would better achieve popular goals. In this respect, we can understand the efforts of the founders of the American republic, first, to list in the Constitution the specific powers granted to the central government and, then, when it became obvious that the central government could not realistically be limited that way, to list in the first ten amendments to the Constitution specific areas in which the government could not tread even in the service of desirable goals.

From this follows a very simple conclusion for police discretion: There are only two ways in which such discretion can be justified in a free society, either by explicit grant from the citizens or by showing that it would be reasonable for the citizens to make such a grant. I take it that there has been no such explicit grant to police. Judges, by contrast, are, or at least once were, explicitly given sentencing ranges within which they are to choose the most just outcome, all things considered. But the police are simply and explicitly authorized to enforce the laws that the people's representatives enact, and no more.

Would it, however, be reasonable for the people to grant the police some range of freedom of decision about whether or not to enforce laws that they legally and physically can? Here it seems to me that the answer is no. It would not be reasonable for four very important reasons. First, doing so renders the laws themselves vague and uncertain. Rather than stating forthrightly what will and what will not be permitted, laws subject to discretionary enforcement effectively contain the additional wild-card proviso "if a police officer judges it appropriate. . . ." Second, adding this proviso amounts to amending the laws as passed by the people's representatives. Third, police discretionary power is almost certain to be used frequently in ways that discriminate (in effect, if not in intent) against the poor, powerless, and unpopular in our society[12]— undermining the legitimacy of the law where it is most in need of legitimacy. Fourth, granting police discretion to decide whether or not to enforce the law gives police officers the ability to use that discretion as leverage over other citizens, say, by threatening arrest if a citizen won't reveal some desired information.

Notice that, with this fourth reason, the danger of tyranny lies not so much in police officers' power to arrest and thus limit citizens' liberty as in the new power police officers have when it is up to them whether or not to arrest. It might be thought that, as long as the police arrest only those who are legitimately subject to arrest, then the discretionary power not to arrest merely reduces state interference with the individual below what is legitimate—and thus cannot be tyrannical. But this overlooks the fact that discretion to arrest or not is itself a power over citizens, separate from the power to arrest as such. Over and above their power to enforce the laws, discretion gives the police a new power beyond what the law authorizes, the power to use their law enforcement authority as a threat. That such threats are the common fare of television police dramas, and sometimes the only means that real cops have to wring information out of small-time drug dealers, prostitutes, and the like, hardly shows that this is right or appropriate to the government of a free society. If we are not ready to endorse a law requiring all citizens to give the police whatever information they want, then such use of discretion as leverage to get information amounts to allowing police to exercise a power over some citizens that we would not allow them to exercise over all. Nor does public acceptance of this phenomenon amount to a public grant of the authority to do it. What it suggests, rather, is that most people don't mind if the police treat drug dealers and prostitutes in a tyrannical fashion.

Bear in mind, I do not doubt that treating drug dealers or prostitutes in a tyrannical fashion may be effective in achieving larger goals, such as catching more serious crooks. But political authority in a free society is not an unlimited grant to do whatever is needed to accomplish good goals (as Miranda warnings and search-and-seizure protections testify). If most people want the police to exercise discretion in enforcing drug or other vice laws, then the people must say so through their representatives, which, in turn, will require that this new authority be justified in open public discussion. In fact, I think the same about any area in which it might be thought good to grant the police discretion. Put the grant into the law, or forget about it.

Before concluding this chapter, I want to draw support for my argument from another modern political theorist who, while not a social contractarian, played an important role in the thinking of the founders of the American republic. I refer to "the celebrated Montesquieu" to whom Madison, writing in *Federalist* 47, attributed that "invaluable precept in the science of politics," the doctrine of the separation of powers.[13]

It is interesting that Montesquieu presented this precept in the context of his discussion of the conditions of political liberty. Interesting also is that Montesquieu understood this liberty as "a right of doing whatever the laws permit." He did not understand liberty, then, in the Millian sense, as a freedom from laws. Like Locke, Montesquieu spoke from an older, though still modern, tradition, in which freedom exists as long as all are governed by publicly promulgated laws and only by those laws.[14] He, too, then, accepted that the rule of law is the bulwark of liberty:

> The political liberty of the subject is a tranquility of mind arising from the opinion each person has of his safety. In order to have this liberty, it is requisite the government be so constituted as one man need not be afraid of another.
>
> When the legislative and executive powers are united in the same person . . . , there can be no liberty. . . .
>
> Again there can be no liberty, if the judiciary power be not separated from the legislative and executive. . . . Were it joined to the executive power, the judge might behave with violence and oppression.[15]

Police discretion is, in effect, a mixing of legislative and judiciary power with executive power and thus likewise a threat to political liberty. It mixes legislative power by deciding which laws really are to be enforced, and it mixes judiciary power by deciding who is to come under the laws that are enforced. Now, though neither Montesquieu nor Madison said so in so many words, I think the idea behind the separation of powers is simply that the more people there are who have to be in on an act of government, the less likely that the act will be evil or tyrannical. Thus, liberty will be protected if police do their thing, judges do theirs, and lawmakers theirs.

I conclude, then, that police discretion has no rightful place in a free society. Where such discretion appears appropriate, I believe it appears so because it compensates for flaws elsewhere in the system. For example, police sometimes hesitate to use their powers of arrest because they know that an arrestee may have to spend the night in a detention cell and will get a potentially damaging arrest record even if he is finally not charged or eventually acquitted.[16] But this could be dealt with by making sure that there is adequate prosecutorial and judicial staff to process arrestees quickly, and by providing for the expunging of arrest records that end in no charge or acquittal—something long overdue in a society that believes that people are innocent until proven guilty.

Where such institutional flaws are not the problem, then, I contend that seemingly appropriate exercises of police discretion reflect flaws in our laws. For any area in which it would be good to grant police discretion, it will be possible to spell out the rules governing that discretion and build them into the laws (thus eliminating it as discretion in the sense I have been using that notion here, that is, as freedom to decide whether to apply the law). It follows then, that, for any area in which it is contended that police should have discretion, such discretion will be either to compensate for institutional flaws or inadequate legal draftsmanship. At best, discretion solves a problem at the wrong place in the criminal justice system.[17]

Moreover, to the extent that sections of the public are content with police discretion and do not build this discretion into the laws, a dangerous duplicitousness is at play. The people, through their representatives, say one thing and, through their tacit acceptance, say another. They make categorical laws to vent publicly their moral outrage and then allow the police effectively to redraft the laws once the police are out of public sight.

Earlier, in passing, I suggested that there is a difference between Locke's and Montesquieu's view of the relation between law and liberty and Mill's view. Mill's view was that law limits liberty and thus that, to enlarge liberty, we should shrink the reach of the law. Locke's and Montesquieu's view was that law limits the arbitrary acts of others and thus that, to protect liberty, we should insist that officials act according to the laws and exercise no authority beyond them. Both views are correct: The simple fact is that a free society should have few and clear criminal laws that the police should be expected to enforce wherever they apply, whenever it is physically possible to do so, as long as doing so is not in conflict with enforcing even more important laws or with explicit legislative guidelines. The police already have enormous powers over citizens that other citizens lack. They should not be given the additional power of being able to use their authority to arrest at their own discretion.

Moreover, the laws should express, not society's moral aspirations, but its real will, the terms on which it is truly prepared to act. If the legislators make more laws than the police can enforce, they should reduce the number of laws or increase the number of police officers. The laws should express the actual treatment that the society wants, and police enforcement of those laws should be as automatic as possible. The reduction of discretion should be carried throughout the system. We should have sentencing guidelines for judges, though I would hope for something quite a bit less brutal than the current combination of guidelines plus mandatory minimum sentences. And we should correct the recent lamentable tendency of this combination to shift discretion from judges (who exercise discretion in open court and who are at least somewhat insulated from political pressures) to prosecutors (who exercise discretion out of public view and who are political through and through). Reasonable sentencing guidelines for judges should be matched with reasonable charging guidelines for prosecutors.[18] If these, as well as reasonable arrest guidelines for police, were built into the law, we would have moved a great distance toward realizing the requirements of a free society as understood by liberal political philosophers from Locke to Rawls.

Notes

This chapter is a revised version of an article originally published in *Handled with Discretion: Ethical Issues in Police Decision Making*, ed. John Kleinig (Lanham, Md.: Rowman & Littlefield, 1996), pp. 71–83. Reprinted with permission. I wish to express my appreciation to the participants in the Workshop on Ethical Issues in Police Discretion, held under the auspices of the Institute for Criminal Justice Ethics at the John Jay College of Criminal Justice of the City University of New York on 4–7 May 1995, for their many helpful comments, objections, and recommendations. In particular, I thank Professor William Heffernan of the John Jay College for his challenging and useful commentary on the original article.

1. I was convinced of the need to make this qualification on my thesis by Professor James Fyfe of Temple University.

2. Plato, *The Republic,* in *The Dialogues of Plato,* trans. B. Jowett (New York: Random House, 1937), vol. 1, p. 737.

3. Plato, *The Statesman,* in *The Dialogues of Plato,* trans. B. Jowett (New York: Random House, 1937), vol. 2, p. 322.

4. Ibid.

5. Ibid., p. 329.

6. Ibid., p. 325.

7. Thomas Hobbes, *Leviathan* (Amherst, N.Y.: Prometheus Books, 1988; originally published 1651), p. 63.

8. John Locke, *Second Treatise of Government* (Indianapolis, Ind.: Hackett, 1980; originally published 1690), p. 8 (emphasis in original).

9. Ibid., p. 70 (emphasis in original).

10. John Rawls, *Political Liberalism* (New York: Columbia University Press, 1993), p. 216.

11. Locke, *Second Treatise,* p. 103 (emphasis in original).

12. See, for example, Dennis D. Powell, "A Study of Police Discretion in Six Southern Cities," *Journal of Police Science and Administration* 17, no. 1 (1990): 1–7; as well as the studies reported in my *The Rich Get Richer and the Poor Get Prison: Ideology, Class and Criminal Justice,* 4th ed. (Needham, Mass.: Allyn & Bacon, 1995), pp. 105–8. For a general overview of the problem and recent attempts to solve it, see Samuel Walker, *Taming the System: The Control of Discretion in Criminal Justice, 1950–1990* (New York: Oxford University Press, 1993), especially chapter 2, "Police Discretion."

13. *Federalist* No. 47, in Alexander Hamilton, James Madison, and John Jay, *The Federalist Papers,* ed. Clinton Rossiter (New York: New American Library, 1961), p. 301.

14. Wrote Locke, "for *law,* in its true notion, is not so much the limitation as *the direction of a free and intelligent agent* to his proper interest, and . . . freedom is not, as we are told, *a liberty for every man to do what he lists:* (for who could be free, when every other man's humour might domineer over him?) but a *liberty* to dispose, and order as he lists, his person, actions, possessions, and his whole property, within the allowance of those laws under which he is, and therein not to be subject to the arbitrary will of another, but freely follow his own." Locke, *Second Treatise,* p. 32 (emphasis in original).

15. Charles Secondat, Baron de Montesquieu, *The Spirit of the Laws* (New York: Hafner, 1949; originally published 1748), pp. 151–52. Interestingly, Montesquieu recommends that judges, too, be deprived of discretion in applying the law: "judges are no more than the mouth that pronounces the words of the law, mere passive beings, incapable of moderating either its force or its rigor." Ibid., p. 159.

16. For a sensitive description of cases in which police hesitate to arrest individuals accused by a person of doubtful credibility, see H. Richard Uviller, "The Unworthy Victim: Police Discretion in the Credibility Call," *Law and Contemporary Problems* 47, no. 4 (1984): 15–33.

17. I think the same can be said to those who think that the police ought at least to have discretion not to enforce unjust laws. It is easy enough to point to some outrageously unjust law and say it would be better if police were free not to enforce that law. We, however, are concerned with general policies. And that implies that what must be argued for is a general right of police to decide which laws are unjust enough not to be enforced. For this to be justified, we would need (at the very least) evidence showing that in general the police will be better judges of the justice of the laws than the legislators who make them—whereas the evidence of discrimination by the police argues in the opposite direction. Moreover, it would most likely better serve the cause of justice if police were to enforce unjust laws so that the society would have to face the consequences of its unjust legislation, than if police corrected injustice through publicly invisible acts of nonenforcement. It is the legislature that should correct unjust legislation, not the police—another case in which police discretion corrects for a problem that should be corrected elsewhere. Beyond this, it is, I think, inappropriate to apply to the police the model of justifiable civil disobedience. When private citizens engage in civil disobedience, they characteristically submit to the judgment of the law, and thus they pose no threat to the rule of law itself (this is one reason that their disobedience is *civil*). When police or other public officials fail to enforce the law, then the rule of law itself is undermined. At a minimum, if the police refrain from enforcing a law because they believe it to be unjust, they should make their nonenforcement public, in the way that civil disobedients make their disobedience public. Then, we might hope that lawmakers will be pressured to respond by improving the law.

18. An interesting proposal to this effect is made in "Developments in the Law: Race and the Criminal Process," *Harvard Law Review* 101 (1988): 1550–51.

11

Justice, Civilization, and the Death Penalty

On the issue of capital punishment, there is as clear a clash of moral intuitions as we are likely to see. Some (now a majority of Americans) feel deeply that justice requires payment in kind and thus that murderers should die; others (once, but no longer, nearly a majority of Americans) feel deeply that the state ought not to be in the business of putting people to death.[1] Arguments for either side that do not do justice to the intuitions of the other are unlikely to persuade anyone not already convinced. Since, as I shall suggest, there is truth on both sides, such arguments are easily refutable, leaving us with nothing but conflicting intuitions and no guidance from reason in distinguishing the better from the worse. In this context, I shall try to make an argument for the abolition of the death penalty that does justice to the intuitions on both sides. I shall sketch out a conception of retributive justice that accounts for the justice of executing murderers, and then I shall argue that *though the death penalty is a just punishment for murder*, abolition of the death penalty is part of the civilizing mission of modern states. Before getting to this, let us briefly consider the challenges confronting those who would argue against the death penalty. In my view, these challenges have been most forcefully put by Ernest van den Haag.

The Challenge to the Abolitionist

The book *The Death Penalty: A Debate*, in which van den Haag argues for the death penalty and John P. Conrad argues against, proves how difficult it is to mount a telling argument against capital punishment.

235

Conrad contends, for example, that "to kill the offender [who has committed murder in the first degree] is to respond to his wrong by doing the same wrong to him."[2] But this popular argument is easily refuted.[3] Since we regard killing in self-defense or in war as morally permissible, it cannot be that we regard killing per se as wrong. It follows that the wrong in murder cannot be that it is killing per se, but that it is (among other things) the killing of an innocent person. Consequently, if the state kills a murderer, though it does the same physical act that he did, it does not do the wrong that he did, since the state is not killing an innocent person.[4] Moreover, unless this distinction is allowed, all punishments are wrong, since everything that the state does as punishment is an act that is physically the same as an act normally thought wrong. For example, if you lock an innocent person in a cage, that is kidnapping. If the state responds by locking you in prison, it can hardly be said to be responding to your wrong by doing you the same wrong in return. Indeed, it will be said that it is precisely because what you did was wrong that locking you up, which would otherwise be wrong, is right.[5]

Conrad also makes the familiar appeal to the possibility of executing an innocent person and the impossibility of correcting this tragic mistake. "An act by the state of such monstrous proportions as the execution of a man who is not guilty of the crime for which he was convicted should be avoided at all costs. . . . The abolition of capital punishment is the certain means of preventing the worst injustice."[6] This argument, while not so easily disposed of as the previous one, is, like all claims about what "should be avoided at all costs," not very persuasive. There is invariably some cost that is prohibitive such that if, for example, capital punishment were necessary to save the lives of potential murder victims, there must be a point at which the number of saved victims would be large enough to justify the risk of executing an innocent person—particularly where trial and appellate proceedings are designed to reduce this risk to a minimum by giving the accused every benefit of the doubt.[7] Since we tolerate the death of innocents, in mines or on highways, as a cost of progress and, in wars, as an inevitable accompaniment to aerial bombardment and the like, it cannot convincingly be contended that, kept to a minimum, the risk of executing an innocent is still so great an evil as to outweigh all other considerations.[8]

Nor will it do to suggest, as Conrad does, that execution implies that offenders are incapable of change and thus presumes the offenders' "total identification with evil," a presumption reserved only to God or, in any case, beyond the province of (mere) men.[9] This is not convincing, since no punishment, whether on retributive or deterrent grounds, need imply belief in the total evilness of the punishee—all that need be believed is (for retribution) that what the offender has done is as evil as the punishment is awful or (for deterrence) that what he has done is awful enough to warrant whatever punishment will discourage others from doing it. "Execution," writes van den Haag, "merely presumes an identification [with evil] sufficient to disregard what good qualities the convict has (he may be nice to animals and love his mother). . . . No total identification with evil—whatever that means—is required; only a sufficiently wicked crime." [10]

Thus far I have tried to indicate how difficult it is to make an argument for the abolition of the death penalty against which the death penalty advocate cannot successfully defend himself. But van den Haag's argument is not merely defensive—he poses a positive challenge to anyone who would take up the abolitionist cause. For van den Haag, in order to argue convincingly for abolition, one must prove either that "no [criminal] act, however horrible, justifies [that is, deserves] the death penalty" or that, if capital punishment were found to deter murder more effectively than life imprisonment, we should still "prefer to preserve the life of a convicted murderer rather than the lives of innocent victims, even if it were certain that these victims would be spared if the murderer were executed." [11]

If van den Haag is right and the abolitionist cause depends on proving either or both of these assertions, then it is a lost cause, since, I believe, they cannot be proven, for reasons of the following sort: If people ever deserve anything for their acts, then it seems that what they deserve is something commensurate in cost or in benefit to what they have done. However horrible executions are, there are surely some acts to which they are commensurate in cost. If, as Camus says, the condemned man dies two deaths, one on the scaffold and one anticipating it, then isn't execution justified for one who has murdered two people? If not two, then ten? [12] As for the second assertion, since we take as justified the killing of innocent people (say, homicidal maniacs) in self-defense (that is, when necessary to preserve the lives of their innocent victims), then it seems that we must take as justified the killing of guilty people if it is necessary to preserve the lives of innocent victims. Indeed, though punishment is not the same as self-defense, it is, when practiced to deter crimes, arguably a form of social defense—and parity of reason would seem to dictate that if killing is justified when necessary for self-defense, then it is justified when necessary for social defense.

It might be thought that injuring or killing others in self-defense is justifiable in that it aims to stop the threatening individual himself, but that punishing people (even guilty people) to deter others is a violation of the Kantian prohibition against using people merely as means to the well-being of others.[13] It seems to me that this objection is premised on the belief that what deters potential criminals are the individual acts of punishment. In that case, each person punished is truly being used for the benefit of others. If, however, what deters potential criminals is the existence of a functioning punishment system, then everyone is benefited by that system, including those who end up being punished by it, since they, too, have received the benefit of enhanced security due to the deterring of some potential criminals. Even criminals benefit from what deters other criminals from preying on them. Then, each act of punishment is done as a necessary condition of the existence of a system that benefits all, and no one is used or sacrificed *merely* for the benefit of others.

If I am correct in believing that the assertions that van den Haag challenges the abolitionist to prove cannot be proven, then the case for the abolition of the death penalty must be made while accepting that some crimes deserve capital punishment and that evidence that capital punishment is a substantially better deterrent to murder than life imprisonment would justify imposing it. This is what I shall attempt to do. Indeed, I shall begin the case for the abolition of the death penalty by defending the justice of the death penalty as a punishment for murder.

Just Deserts and Just Punishments

In my view, the death penalty is a just punishment for murder because the *lex talionis* (an eye for an eye, and so on) is just, although, as I shall suggest at the end of this section, it can be rightly applied only when its implied preconditions are satisfied. The *lex talionis* is a version of retributivism. Retributivism—as the word itself suggests—is the doctrine that the offender should be *paid back* with suffering he deserves because of the evil he has intentionally done (or attempted to do), and the *lex talionis* asserts that injury equivalent to what he intentionally imposed (or attempted to impose) is what the offender deserves. Note that the injury for which the offender is to be paid back is not necessarily limited to the harm done to his immediate victim. It may include as well the suffering of the victim's relatives, the fear produced in the general populace, and the like. For simplicity's sake, however, I shall continue to speak as if the injury for which retributivism would have us pay the offender back is the harm (intentionally attempted or done)[14] to his immediate victim.

The *lex talionis* is not the only version of retributivism. Another, which I shall call "proportional retributivism," holds that what retribution requires is, not equality of injury between crimes and punishments, but "fit" or proportionality, such that the worst crime is punished with the society's worst penalty, and so on, though the society's worst punishment need not duplicate the injury of the worst crime.[15] Later, I shall try to show how a form of proportional retributivism is compatible with acknowledging the justice of the *lex talionis*. Indeed, since I shall defend the justice of the *lex talionis,* I take such compatibility as a necessary condition of the validity of any form of retributivism.[16]

There is nothing self-evident about the justice of the *lex talionis* or, for that matter, of retributivism.[17] The standard problem confronting those who would justify retributivism is that of overcoming the suspicion that it does no more than sanctify the victim's desire to hurt the offender back. Since serving that desire amounts to hurting the offender simply for the satisfaction that the victim derives from seeing the offender suffer, and since deriving satisfaction from the suffering of others seems primitive, the policy of imposing suffering on the offender for no other purpose than giving satisfaction to his victim seems primitive as well. Consequently, defending retributivism requires showing that the suffering imposed on the wrongdoer has some worthy point beyond the satisfaction of victims. In what follows, I shall try to identify a proposition—which I call the *retributivist principle*—that I take to be the nerve of retributivism. I think this principle accounts for the justice of the *lex talionis* and indicates the point of the suffering demanded by retributivism. Not to do too much of the work of the death penalty advocate, I shall make no extended argument for this principle beyond suggesting the considerations that make it plausible. I shall identify these considerations by drawing, with considerable license, on Hegel and Kant.

I think that we can see the justice of the *lex talionis* by focusing on the striking affinity between it and the *golden rule*. The *golden rule* mandates "Do unto others as you would have others do unto you," while the *lex talionis* counsels "Do unto others as they have done unto you." It would not be too far-fetched to say that the *lex talionis* is the law enforcement arm of the golden rule, at least in the sense that if people were actually treated as they treated others, then everyone would necessarily follow the golden rule because then people could only willingly act toward others as they were willing to have others act toward them. This is not to suggest that the *lex talionis* follows from the golden rule, but rather to suggest that the two share a common moral inspiration: the equality of persons. Treating others as you would have them treat you means treating others as equal to you because it implies that you count their suffering to be as great a calamity as your own suffering, that you count your right to impose suffering on them as no greater than their right to impose suffering on you, and so on. The notion of the equality of persons leads to the *lex talionis* by two approaches that start from different points and converge.

I call the first approach "Hegelian" because Hegel held (roughly) that crime upsets the equality between persons and retributive punishment restores that equality by "annulling" the crime.[18] As we have seen, acting according to the golden rule implies treating others as your equals. Conversely, violating the golden rule implies the reverse: Doing to another what you would *not* have that other do to you violates the equality of persons by asserting a right toward the other that the other does not possess toward you. Doing back to you what you did "annuls" your violation by reasserting that the other has the same right toward you that you assert toward him. Punishment according to the *lex talionis* cannot heal the injury that the other has suffered at your hands; rather, it rectifies the indignity he has suffered, by restoring him to equality with you.

I think that this (roughly) Hegelian account of retributivism provides us with a conception of crime and punishment appropriate to a liberal moral theory. This is so because "equality of persons" here does not mean equality of concern for their happiness, as it might for a utilitarian. On a utilitarian understanding of equality, imposing suffering on the wrongdoer equivalent to the suffering he has imposed would have little point. Rather, equality of concern for people's happiness would lead us to impose as little suffering on the wrongdoer as is compatible with maintaining the happiness of others. In the Hegelian form of retributivism, by contrast, "equality of persons" is understood in distinctively liberal rather than utilitarian terms. Instead of seeing morality as administering doses of happiness to individual recipients, the Hegelian retributivist envisions morality as maintaining the relations appropriate to equally sovereign individuals. A crime, rather than representing a unit of suffering added to the already considerable suffering in the world, is an assault on the sovereignty of an individual that temporarily places one person (the criminal) in a position of illegitimate sovereignty over another (the victim). The victim (or his representative, the state) then has the right to rectify this loss of standing relative to the criminal by meting out a punishment that reduces the criminal's sovereignty in the degree to which he vaunted it above his victim's. It might be thought that this is a duty, not just a right, but that is surely too much. The victim has the right to forgive the violator without punishment, which suggests that it is by virtue of having the right to punish the violator— the authority over the violator's fate rather than the duty to punish him—that the victim's equality with the violator is restored.

I call the second approach "Kantian" because Kant held (roughly) that, since reason (like justice) is no respecter of the sheer difference between individuals, when a rational being decides to act in a certain way toward his fellows, he implicitly authorizes similar action by his fellows toward him.[19] A version of the golden rule, then, is a requirement of reason: acting rationally, one always acts as he would have others act toward him. Consequently, to act toward a person as he has acted toward others is to treat him as a rational being, that is, as if his act were the product of a rational decision. From this, it may be concluded that we have a duty to do to offenders what they have done, since this amounts to according them the respect due rational beings.[20] Here, too, however, the assertion of a duty to punish seems excessive, since, if this duty arose because doing to people what they have done to others is necessary to accord them the respect due rational beings, then we would have a duty to do to all rational persons *everything*— good, bad, or indifferent—that they do to others. The point, rather, is that, by his acts, a rational being *authorizes* others to do the same to him; he doesn't *compel* them to. Here, again, the argument leads to a right, rather than a duty, to exact the *lex talionis*. This is supported by the fact that we can conclude from Kant's argument that a rational being cannot validly complain of being treated in the way he has treated others, and where there is no valid complaint, there is no injustice, and where there is no injustice, others have acted within their rights.[21] It should be clear that the Kantian argument, like the Hegelian one, rests on the equality of persons, because a rational agent implicitly authorizes having done to him action similar to what he has done to another only if he and the other are similar in the relevant ways.

The "Hegelian" and "Kantian" approaches arrive at the same destination from opposite sides. The "Hegelian" approach starts explicitly from the victim's equality with the criminal and infers from it the victim's right to do to the criminal what the criminal has done to the victim. The "Kantian" approach starts explicitly from the criminal's rationality, and implicitly from his equality with his victim, and infers from these the criminal's authorization of the victim's right to do to the criminal what the criminal has done to the victim. Taken together, these approaches support the following proposition: The equality and rationality of persons imply that an offender deserves, and his victim has the right to impose on him, suffering equal to that which he imposed on the victim. This is the proposition I call the *retributivist principle*, and I shall assume henceforth that it is true. This principle provides that the *lex talionis* is the criminal's just desert and the victim's (or, as his representative, the state's) right. Moreover, this principle also indicates the point of retributive punishment, namely, to affirm the equality and rationality of persons, victims and offenders alike.[22] And the point of this affirmation is, like any moral affirmation, to make a statement. It impresses upon the criminal his equality with his victim (which earns him a like fate) and his rationality (by which his actions are held to authorize his fate), and it makes a statement to the society, so that recognition of the equality and rationality of persons becomes a visible part of our shared moral environment that none can ignore in justifying their actions to one another.

When I say that, with respect to the criminal, the point of retributive punishment is to impress upon him his equality with his victim, I mean to be understood quite literally. If the sentence is just and the criminal rational, then the punishment should normally *force* upon him recognition of his equality with his victim, recognition of their shared vulnerability to suffering and their shared desire to avoid it, as well as recognition of the fact that he counts for no more than his victim in the eyes of their fellows. For this reason, the retributivist requires that the offender be sane, not only at the moment of his crime, but also at the moment of his punishment—while this latter requirement would seem largely pointless (if not downright malevolent) to a utilitarian. Incidentally, it is, I believe, the desire that the offender be forced by suffering punishment to recognize his equality with his victim, rather than the desire for that suffering itself, that constitutes what is rational in the desire for revenge.

The retributivist principle represents a conception of moral desert whose complete elaboration would take us far beyond the scope of the present chapter. In its defense, however, it is worth noting that our common notion of moral desert seems to include (at least) two elements: (*a*) a conception of individual responsibility for actions that is "contagious," that is, one that confers moral justification on the punishing (or rewarding) reactions of others; and (*b*) a measure of the relevant worth of actions that determines the legitimate magnitude of justified reactions. Broadly speaking, the "Kantian" notion of authorization implicit in rational action supplies the first element, and the "Hegelian" notion of upsetting and restoring equality of standing supplies the second. It seems, then, reasonable to take the equality and rationality of persons as implying moral desert in the way asserted in the retributivist principle. I shall assume henceforth that the retributivist principle is true.

The truth of the retributivist principle establishes the justice of the *lex talionis*, but, since it establishes this as a right of the victim rather than a duty, it does not settle the question of whether or to what extent the victim or the state should exercise this right and exact the *lex talionis*. This is a separate moral question because strict adherence to the *lex talionis* amounts to allowing criminals, even the most barbaric of them, to dictate our punishing behavior. It seems certain that there are at least some crimes, such as rape or torture, that we ought not try to match. And this is not merely a matter of imposing an alternative punishment that produces an equivalent amount of suffering, as, say, some number of years in prison that might "add up" to the harm caused by a rapist or a torturer. Even if no amount of time in prison would add up to the harm caused by a torturer, it still seems that we ought not to torture him even if this were the only way of making him suffer as much as he has made his victim suffer. Or consider someone who has committed several murders in cold blood. On the *lex talionis*, it would seem that such a criminal might justly be brought to within an inch of death and then revived (or to within a moment of execution and then reprieved) as many times as he has killed (minus one), and then finally executed. But surely this is a degree of cruelty that would be monstrous.[23]

Since the retributivist principle establishes the *lex talionis* as the victim's right, it might seem that the question of how far this right should be exercised is "up to the victim." Indeed, this would be the case in the state of nature. But once, for all the good reasons familiar to readers of John Locke, the state comes into existence, public punishment replaces private, and the victim's right to punish reposes in the state. With this, the decision as to how far to exercise this right goes to the state as well. To be sure, since (at least with respect to retributive punishment) the victim's right is the source of the state's right to punish, the state must exercise its right in ways that are faithful to the victim's right. Later, when I try to spell out the upper and lower limits of just punishment, these limits may be taken as indicating the range within which the state can punish and remain faithful to the victim's right.

I suspect that it will be widely agreed that the state ought not to administer punishments of the sort described above even if required by the letter of the *lex talionis* and that thus, even granting the justice of *lex talionis,* there are occasions on which it is morally appropriate to diverge from its requirements. We must, of course, distinguish such morally based divergence from that based on practicality. Like any moral principle, the *lex talionis* is subject to "ought implies can." It will usually be impossible to do to an offender exactly what he has done—for example, his offense will normally have had an element of surprise that is not possible for a judicially imposed punishment, but this fact can hardly free him from having to bear the suffering he has imposed on another. Thus, for reasons of practicality, the *lex talionis* must necessarily be qualified to call for doing to the offender *as nearly as possible* what he has done to his victim. When, however, we refrain from raping rapists or torturing torturers, we do so for reasons of morality, not of practicality. And, given the justice of the *lex talionis,* these moral reasons cannot amount to claiming that it would be unjust to rape rapists or torture torturers. Rather, the claim must be that, even though it would be just to rape rapists and torture torturers, other moral considerations weigh against doing so.

On the other hand, when, for moral reasons, we refrain from exacting the *lex talionis* and impose a less harsh alterative punishment, it may be said that we are not doing full justice to the criminal, but it cannot automatically be the case that we are doing an injustice to his victim. Otherwise, we would have to say it was unjust to imprison our torturer rather than torturing him or to simply execute our multiple murderer rather than multiply "executing" him. Surely it is counterintuitive (and irrational to boot) to set the demands of justice so high that a society would have to choose between being barbaric and being unjust. This would effectively price justice out of the moral market.

The implication of the notion that justice permits us to avoid extremely cruel punishments is that there is a range of just punishments that includes some that are just though they exact less than the full measure of the *lex talionis.* What are the top and bottom ends of this range? I think that both are indicated by the *retributivist principle.* The principle identifies the *lex talionis* as the offender's desert and since, on retributive grounds, punishment beyond what one deserves is unjust for the same reasons that make punishment of the innocent unjust, the *lex talionis* is the upper limit of the range of just punishments.[24] On the other hand, if the retributivist principle is true, then denying that the offender deserves suffering equal to that which he imposed amounts to denying the equality and rationality of persons. From this it follows that we fall below the bottom end of the range of just punishments when we act in ways that are incompatible with the *lex talionis* at the top end.

That is, we fall below the bottom end and commit an injustice to the victim when we treat the offender in a way that is no longer compatible with sincerely believing that he deserves to have done to him what he has done to his victim. Thus, the upper limit of the range of just punishments is the point after which more punishment is unjust to the offender, and the lower limit is the point after which less punishment is unjust to the victim. In this way, the range of just punishments remains faithful to the victim's right that is their source.

This way of understanding just punishment enables us to formulate proportional retributivism so that it is compatible with acknowledging the justice of the *lex talionis*: If we take the *lex talionis* as spelling out the offender's just desert, and if other moral considerations require us to refrain from matching the injury caused by the offender while still allowing us to punish justly, then surely we impose just punishment if we impose the closest morally acceptable approximation to the *lex talionis*. Proportional retributivism, then, in requiring that the worst crime be punished by the society's worst punishment and so on, could be understood as translating the offender's just desert into its nearest equivalent in the society's table of morally acceptable punishments. Then, the two versions of retributivism (*lex talionis* and proportional) are related in that the first states what just punishment would be if nothing but the offender's just desert mattered and the second locates just punishment at the meeting point of the offender's just desert and the society's moral scruples.

Since this second version modifies the requirements of the *lex talionis* only in light of other moral considerations, it is compatible with believing that the *lex talionis* spells out the offender's just desert, much in the way that modifying the obligations of promisers in light of other moral considerations is compatible with believing in the binding nature of promises. As excusing a person from keeping a promised appointment because she acted to save a life is compatible with still believing that promises are binding, so doing less than *lex talionis* requires in order to avoid cruelty is compatible with believing that the offender still deserves what *lex talionis* would impose.

Proportional retributivism so formulated preserves the point of retributivism and remains faithful to the victim's right that is its source. Since it punishes with the closest morally acceptable approximation to the *lex talionis,* it effectively says to the offender, you deserve the equivalent of what you did to your victim and you are getting less only to the degree that our moral scruples limit us from duplicating what you have done. Such punishment, then, affirms the equality of persons by respecting, *as far as is morally permissible*, the victim's right to impose suffering on the offender equal to what he received, and it affirms the rationality of the offender by treating him as authorizing others to do to him what he has done, though they take him up on it only *as far as is morally permissible*. Needless to say, the alterative punishments must in some convincing way be comparable in gravity to the crimes that they punish, or else they will trivialize the harms those crimes caused and be no longer compatible with sincerely believing that the offender deserves to have done to him what he has done to his victim and no longer capable of impressing upon the criminal his equality with the victim. If we punish rapists with a small fine, we do an injustice to their victims because this trivializes the suffering rapists have caused and thus is incompatible with believing that they deserve to have done to them something comparable to what they have done to their victims. If, on the other hand, instead of raping rapists we impose on them some serious penalty, say a substantial term of imprisonment, then we do no injustice even though we refrain from exacting the *lex talionis*.

To sum up, I take the *lex talionis* to be the top end of the range of just punishments. When, because we are simply unable to duplicate the criminal's offense, we modify the *lex talionis* to call for imposing on the offender as nearly as possible what he has done, we are still at this top end, applying the *lex talionis* subject to "ought implies can." When we do less than this, we still act justly as long as we punish in a way that is compatible with sincerely believing that the offender deserves the full measure of the *lex talionis* but receives less for reasons that do not undermine this belief. If this is true, then it is not unjust to spare murderers as long as they can be punished in some other suitably grave way. I leave open the question of what such an alternative punishment might be, except to say that it need not be limited to such penalties as are currently imposed. For example, though rarely carried out in practice, a life sentence with no chance of parole might be a civilized equivalent of the death penalty—after all, people sentenced to life imprisonment have traditionally been regarded as "civilly dead."[25]

It might be objected that no punishment short of death will serve the point of retributivism with respect to murderers because no punishment short of death is commensurate with the crime of murder, since, while some number of years of imprisonment may add up to the amount of harm done by rapists or assaulters or torturers, no number of years will add up to the harm done to the victim of murder. But justified divergence from the *lex talionis* is not limited only to changing the form of punishment while maintaining equivalent severity. Otherwise, we would have to torture torturers, rather than imprison them, if they tortured more than could be made up for by years in prison (or by the years available to them to spend in prison, which might be few for elderly torturers), and we would have to subject multiple murderers to multiple "executions." If justice allows us to refrain from these penalties, then justice allows punishments that are not equal in suffering to their crimes. It seems to me that if the objector grants this much, then he must show that a punishment less than death is not merely incommensurate to the harm caused by murder but so far out of proportion to that harm that it trivializes the harm and thus effectively denies the equality and rationality of persons. Now, I am vulnerable to the claim that a sentence of life in prison that allows parole after eight or ten years does indeed trivialize the harm of (premeditated, cold-blooded) murder. But I cannot see how a sentence that would require a murderer to spend his full natural life in prison, or even the lion's share of his adult life (say, the thirty years between age twenty and age fifty), can be regarded as anything less than extremely severe and thus no trivialization of the harm he has caused.

I take it, then, that the justice of the *lex talionis* implies that it is just to execute murderers, but not that it is unjust to spare them as long as they are systematically punished in some other suitably grave way. Before developing the implications of this claim, a word about the implied preconditions of applying the *lex talionis* is in order.

Since the *lex talionis* calls for imposing on offenders the harms they are responsible for imposing on others, the implied preconditions of applying it to any particular harm include the requirement that the harm be one that the offender is fully responsible for, where responsibility is both psychological (the capacity to tell the difference between right and wrong and to control one's actions) and social. If people are subjected to remediable unjust social circumstances beyond their control, and if harmful actions are a predictable response to those conditions, then those who benefit from the unjust conditions and refuse to remedy them share responsibility for the harmful acts—and thus neither the doing nor the cost of those acts can be assigned fully to the offenders alone. For example, if a slave kills an innocent person while making his escape, at least part of the blame for the killing must fall on those who have enslaved him. And this is because slavery is unjust, not merely because the desire to escape from slavery is understandable. The desire to escape from prison is understandable as well, but if the imprisonment were a just sentence, then we would hold the prisoner, and not his keepers, responsible if he killed someone while escaping.

Since I believe that the vast majority of murders in America are a predictable response to the frustrations and disabilities of impoverished social circumstances,[26] and since I believe that impoverishment is a remediable injustice from which others in America benefit, I believe that we have no right to exact the full cost of murders from our murderers until we have done everything possible to rectify the conditions that produce their crimes.[27] But not many—who are not already susceptible—will be persuaded by this sort of argument.[28] This does not, in my view, shake its validity, but I want to make an argument whose appeal is not limited to those who think that crime is the result of social injustice.[29] I shall proceed then, granting, not only the justice of the death penalty, but also, at least temporarily, the assumption that our murderers are wholly deserving of dying for their crimes. If I can show that it would still be wrong to execute murderers, I believe I shall have made the strongest case for abolishing the death penalty.

Civilization, Pain, and Justice

As I have already suggested, from the fact that something is justly deserved, it does not automatically follow that the thing should be done, since there may be other moral reasons for not doing it such that, all told, the weight of moral reasons swings the balance against proceeding. The same argument that I have given for the justice of the death penalty for murderers proves the justice of beating assaulters, raping rapists, and torturing torturers. Nonetheless, I believe, and suspect that most would agree, that it would not be right for us to beat assaulters, rape rapists, or torture torturers, *even though it were their just deserts*— and even if this were the only way to make them suffer as much as they made their victims suffer. Calling for the abolition of the death penalty, though it be just, then, amounts to urging that as a society we place execution in the same category of sanction as beating, raping, and torturing and treat it as something it would also not be right for us to do to offenders, *even if it were their just deserts*.

To argue for placing execution in this category, I must show what would be gained therefrom. To show that, I shall indicate what we gain from placing torture in this category and argue that a similar gain is to be had from doing the same with execution. I select torture because I think the reasons for placing it in this category are, due to the extremity of torture, most easily seen—but what I say here applies with appropriate modification to other severe physical punishments, such as beating and raping. First, and most evidently, placing torture in this cate-gory broadcasts the message that we as a society judge torturing so horrible a thing to do to a person that we refuse to do it even when it is deserved. Note that such a judgment does not commit us to an absolute prohibition on torturing. No matter how horrible we judge something to be, we may still be justified in doing it if it is necessary to prevent something even worse. Leaving this aside for the moment, what is gained by broadcasting the public judgment that torture is too horrible to inflict even if deserved?

I think the answer to this lies in what we understand as civilization. In *The Genealogy of Morals*, Nietzsche says that in early times "pain did not hurt as much as it does today."[30] The truth in this puzzling remark is that progress in civilization is characterized by a lower toler-ance for one's own pain and that suffered by others. And this is appro-priate, since, via growth in knowledge, civilization brings increased power to prevent or reduce pain and, via growth in the ability to com-municate and interact with more and more people, civilization extends the circle of people with whom we empathize.[31] If civilization is charac-terized by lower tolerance for our own pain and that of others, then publicly refusing to do horrible things to our fellows both signals the level of our civilization *and, by our example, continues the work of civilizing.* This gesture is all the more powerful if we refuse to do horri-ble things to those who deserve them. I contend, then, that the more horrible things we are able to include in the category of what we will not do, the more civilized we are and the more civilizing. Thus we gain from including torture in this category, and if execution is especially horrible, we gain still more by including it.

Needless to say, the content, direction, and even the worth of civiliza-tion are hotly contested issues, and I shall not be able to win those contests in this brief space. At a minimum, however, I shall assume that civilization involves the taming of the natural environment and of the human animals in it, and that the overall trend in human history is toward increasing this taming, though the trend is by no means unbro-ken or without reverses. On these grounds, we can say that growth in civilization generally marks human history, that a reduction in the hor-rible things we tolerate doing to our fellows (even when they deserve them) is part of this growth, and that once the work of civilization is taken on consciously, it includes carrying forward and expanding this reduction.

This claim broadly corresponds to what Émile Durkheim identified, nearly a century ago, as "two laws which seem . . . to prevail in the evolution of the apparatus of punishment." The first, the law of quantitative change, Durkheim formulates thus:

The intensity of punishment is the greater the more closely societies approximate to a less developed type—and the more the central power assumes an absolute character.

And the second, which Durkheim refers to as the law of qualitative change, is this:

Deprivations of liberty, and of liberty alone, varying in time according to the seriousness of the crime, tend to become more and more the normal means of social control.[32]

Several things should be noted about these laws. First of all, they are not two separate laws. As Durkheim understands them, the second exemplifies the trend toward moderation of punishment referred to in the first.[33] Second, the first law really refers to two distinct trends, which usually coincide but do not always. That is, moderation of punishment accompanies both the movement from less to more advanced types of society and the movement from more to less absolute rule. Normally these go hand in hand, but where they do not, the effect of one trend may offset the effect of the other. Thus, a primitive society without absolute rule may have milder punishments than an equally primitive but more absolutist society.[34] This complication need not trouble us, since the claim I am making refers to the first trend, namely, that punishments tend to become milder as societies become more advanced; and that this is a trend in history is not refuted by the fact that it is accompanied by other trends and even occasionally offset by them. Moreover, I shall close this chapter with a suggestion about the relation between the intensity of punishment and the justice of society, which might broadly be thought of as corresponding to the second trend in Durkheim's first law, namely, that punishments become milder as political rule becomes less absolute. Finally, and most important for our purposes, is the fact that Durkheim's claim that punishment becomes less intense as societies become more advanced is a generalization that he supports with an impressive array of evidence from historical societies from pre-Christian times to the time in which he wrote—and this, in turn, supports my claim that the reduction in the horrible things we do to our fellows is in fact part of the advance of civilization.[35]

Against this it might be argued that there are many trends in history, some good, some bad, and some mixed, and thus that the mere existence of some historical trend is not a sufficient reason to continue it. Thus, for example, history brings growth in population, but we are not for that reason called upon to continue the work of civilization by continually increasing our population. What this suggests is that in order to identify something as part of the work of civilizing, we must show, not only that it generally advances over the course of history, but that its advance is, on some independent grounds, clearly an advance for the human species—that is, either an unmitigated gain or at least consistently a net gain. And this implies that even trends we might generally regard as advances may in some cases bring losses with them, such that when they did, it would not be appropriate for us to lend our efforts to continuing them. Of such trends, we can say that they are advances in civilization except when their gains are outweighed by the losses they bring—and that we are called upon to further these trends only when their gains are not outweighed in this way. It is clear, in this light, that increasing population is a mixed blessing at best, bringing both gains and losses. Consequently, population increase is not always an advance in civilization that we should further, though at times it may be.

What can be said of reducing the horrible things that we do to our fellows even when deserved? First of all, given our vulnerability to pain, it seems clearly a gain. Is it, however, an unmitigated gain? That is, would such a reduction ever amount to a loss? It seems to me that there are two conditions under which it would be a loss, namely, if the reduction made our lives more dangerous or if not doing what is justly deserved were a loss in itself. Let us leave aside the former, since, as I have already suggested and as I shall soon indicate in greater detail, I accept that if some horrible punishment is necessary to deter equally or more horrible acts, then we may have to impose the punishment. Thus my claim is that reduction in the horrible things we do to our fellows is an advance in civilization as *long as our lives are not thereby made more dangerous* and that it is only then that we are called upon to extend that reduction as part of the work of civilization. Assuming then, for the moment, that we suffer no increased danger by refraining from doing horrible things to our fellows when they justly deserve them, does such refraining to do what is justly deserved amount to a loss?

It seems to me that the answer to this must be that refraining to do what is justly deserved is a loss only where it amounts to doing an injustice. But such refraining to do what is just is not doing what is unjust, unless what we do instead falls below the bottom end of the range of just punishments. Otherwise, it would be unjust to refrain from torturing torturers, raping rapists, or beating assaulters. In short, I take it that if there is no injustice in refraining from torturing torturers, then there is no injustice in refraining from doing horrible things to our fellows generally, when they deserve them, as long as what we do instead is compatible with believing that they do nonetheless deserve those horrible things. Thus, if such refraining does not make our lives more dangerous, then it is no loss, and, given our vulnerability to pain, it is a gain. Consequently, reduction in the horrible things we do to our fellows, when those things are not necessary to our protection, is an advance in civilization that we are called upon to continue once we consciously take upon ourselves the work of civilization.

To complete the argument, however, I must show that execution is horrible enough to warrant its inclusion alongside torture. Against this it will be said that execution is not especially horrible, since it only hastens a fate that is inevitable for us.[36] I think that this view overlooks important differences in the manner in which people reach their inevitable ends. I contend that execution is especially horrible, and it is so in a way similar to (though not identical with) the way in which torture is especially horrible. I believe we view torture as especially awful because of two of its features, which also characterize execution: intense pain and the spectacle of one person being completely subject to the power of another. This latter is separate from the issue of pain, since it is something that offends us about unpainful things, such as slavery (even voluntarily entered) and prostitution (even voluntarily chosen as an occupation).[37] Execution shares this separate feature, since killing a bound and defenseless human being enacts the total subjugation of that person to his fellows. I think, incidentally, that this accounts for the general uneasiness with which execution by lethal injection has been greeted. Rather than humanizing the event, it seems only to have purchased a possible reduction in physical pain at the price of increasing the spectacle of subjugation, with no net gain in the attractiveness of the death penalty. Indeed, its net effect may have been the reverse.

Execution, even by physically painless means, is characterized, not only by the spectacle of subjugation, but also by a special and intense psychological pain that distinguishes it from the loss of life that awaits us all. Interesting in this regard is the fact that, although we are not terribly squeamish about the loss of life itself, allowing it in war, in self-defense, as a necessary cost of progress, and so on, we are, as the extraordinary hesitance of our courts testifies, quite reluctant to execute. I think this is because execution involves the most psychologically painful features of deaths. We normally regard death from human

Conc.

causes as worse than death from natural causes, since a humanly caused shortening of life lacks the consolation of unavoidability. And we normally regard death whose coming is foreseen by its victim as worse than sudden death because a foreseen death adds to the loss of life the terrible consciousness of that impending loss.[38] As a humanly caused death whose advent is foreseen by its victim, an execution combines the worst of both.

Thus far, by analogy with torture, I have argued that execution should be avoided because of how horrible it is to the one executed. But there are reasons of another sort that follow from the analogy with torture. Torture is to be avoided, not only because of what it says about what we are willing to do to our fellows, but also because of what it says about us who are willing to do it. To torture someone is an awful spectacle, not only because of the intensity of pain imposed, but because of what is required to be able to impose such pain on one's fellows. The tortured body cringes, using its full exertion to escape the pain imposed upon it—it literally begs for relief with its muscles as it does with its cries. To torture someone is to demonstrate a capacity to resist this begging, and that, in turn, demonstrates a kind of hard-heartedness that a society ought not to parade.

This is true, not only of torture, but of all severe corporal punishment. Indeed, I think this constitutes part of the answer to the puzzling question of why we refrain from punishments like whipping, even when the alternative (some months in jail versus some lashes) seems more costly to the offender. Imprisonment is painful to be sure, but it is a reflective pain, one that comes with comparing what is to what might have been and that can be temporarily ignored by thinking about other things. But physical pain has an urgency that holds body and mind in a fierce grip. Of physical pain, as Orwell's Winston Smith recognized, "you could only wish one thing: that it should stop."[39] By refraining from torture in particular and corporal punishment in general, we both refuse to put a fellow human being in this grip and refuse to show our ability to resist this wish. The death penalty is the last corporal punishment used officially in the Western world. It is corporal, not only because it is administered via the body, but also because the pain of foreseen, humanly administered death strikes us with the urgency that characterizes intense physical pain, causing grown men to cry, faint, and lose control of their bodily functions. There is something to be gained by refusing to endorse the hardness of heart necessary to impose such a fate.

By placing execution alongside torture in the category of things we will not do to our fellow human beings even when they deserve them, we broadcast the message that totally subjugating a person to the power of others and confronting him with the advent of his own humanly administered demise is too horrible to be done by civilized human beings to their fellows even when they have earned it: too horrible to do, and too horrible to be capable of doing. And I contend that broadcasting this message loud and clear would, in the long run, contribute to the general detestation of murder and be, to the extent to which it worked itself into the hearts and minds of the populace, a deterrent. In short, refusing to execute murderers though they deserve it both reflects and continues the taming of the human species that we call civilization. Thus, I take it that the abolition of the death penalty, though that penalty is a just punishment for murder, is part of the civilizing mission of modern states.

Civilization, Safety, and Deterrence

Earlier I said that judging a practice too horrible to do even to those who deserve it does not exclude the possibility that it could be justified if necessary to avoid even worse consequences. Thus, were the death penalty clearly proven a better deterrent to the murder of innocent people than life in prison, we might have to admit that we have not yet reached a level of civilization at which we can protect ourselves without imposing this horrible fate on murderers, and thus we might have to grant the necessity of instituting the death penalty.[40] But this is far from proven. The available research by no means clearly indicates that the death penalty reduces the incidence of homicide more than life imprisonment does. Even the econometric studies of Isaac Ehrlich, which purport to show that each execution saves seven or eight potential murder victims, have not changed this fact, as is testified to by the controversy and objections that Ehrlich's work has provoked from equally respected statisticians.[41]

Conceding that it has not been proven that the death penalty deters more murders than life imprisonment, van den Haag has argued that neither has it been proven that the death penalty does not deter more murders.[42] Thus, his argument goes, we must follow common sense, which teaches that the higher the cost of something, the fewer the people who will choose it. Therefore, at least some potential murderers who would not be deterred by life imprisonment will be deterred by the death penalty. Van den Haag continues:

Our experience shows that the greater the threatened penalty, the more it deters.

. . . Life in prison is still life, however unpleasant. In contrast, the death penalty does not just threaten to make life unpleasant—it threatens to take life altogether. This difference is perceived by those affected. We find that when they have the choice between life in prison and execution, 99% of all prisoners under sentence of death prefer life in prison. . . .

From this unquestioned fact a reasonable conclusion can be drawn in favor of the superior deterrent effect of the death penalty. Those who have the choice in practice . . . fear death more than they fear life in prison. . . . If they do, it follows that the threat of the death penalty, all other things equal, is likely to deter more than the threat of life in prison. One is most deterred by what one fears most. From which it follows that whatever statistics fail, or do not fail, to show, the death penalty is likely to be more deterrent than any other.[43]

Those of us who recognize how commonsensical it was, and still is, to believe that the sun moves around the earth will be less willing than Professor van den Haag to follow common sense here, especially when it comes to doing something awful to our fellows. Moreover, there are good reasons for doubting common sense on this matter. Here are four.

First, from the fact that one penalty is more feared than another, it does not follow that the more feared penalty will deter more than the less feared, unless we know that the less feared penalty is not fearful enough to deter everyone who can be deterred—and this is just what we don't know with regard to the death penalty. Though I fear the death penalty more than life in prison, I can't think of any act that the death penalty would deter me from that an equal likelihood of spending my life in prison wouldn't deter me from as well.[44] Since it seems to me that whoever would be deterred by a given likelihood of death would be deterred by an *equal* likelihood of life behind bars, I suspect that the commonsense argument only seems plausible because we evaluate it unconsciously assuming that potential criminals will face larger likelihoods of death sentences than of life sentences. If the likelihoods were equal, it seems to me that where life imprisonment were improbable enough to make it too distant a possibility to worry much about, a similar low probability of death would have the same effect. After all, we are undeterred by small likelihoods of death every time we walk the streets. And if life imprisonment were sufficiently probable to pose a real deterrent threat, it would pose as much of a deterrent threat as death. And this is just what most of the research we have on the comparative deterrent impact of execution versus life imprisonment suggests.[45]

Second, in light of the fact that roughly five hundred to seven hundred suspected felons are killed by the police in the line of duty every year, and the fact that the number of privately owned guns in America is substantially larger than the number of households in America, it must be granted that anyone contemplating committing a crime already faces a substantial risk of ending up dead as a result.[46] It's hard to see why anyone *who is not already deterred by this* would be deterred by the addition of the more distant risk of death after apprehension, conviction, and appeal. Indeed, this suggests that people consider risks in a much cruder way than van den Haag's appeal to common sense suggests—which should be evident to anyone who contemplates how few people use seatbelts (14 percent of drivers, on some estimates), when it is widely known that wearing them can spell the difference between life (outside prison) and death.[47]

Third, van den Haag has maintained that deterrence works, not only by means of cost-benefit calculations made by potential criminals, but also by the lesson about the wrongfulness of murder that is slowly learned in a society that subjects murderers to the ultimate punishment.[48] If, however, I am correct in claiming that the refusal to execute even those who deserve it has a civilizing effect, then the refusal to execute also teaches a lesson about the wrongfulness of murder. My claim here is admittedly speculative, but no more so than van den Haag's to the contrary. And my view has the added virtue of accounting for the failure of research to show an increased deterrent effect from executions, *without having to deny the plausibility of van den Haag's commonsense argument that at least some additional potential murderers will be deterred by the prospect of the death penalty.* If there is a deterrent effect from *not executing,* then it is understandable that while executions will deter some murderers, this effect will be balanced out by the weakening of the deterrent effect of not executing, such that no net reduction in murders will result.[49] This, by the way, also disposes of van den Haag's argument that, in the absence of knowledge one way or the other on the deterrent effect of executions, we should execute murderers rather than risk the lives of innocent people whose murders might have been deterred if we had executed. If there is a deterrent effect of not executing, it follows that we risk innocent lives either way. And if this is so, it seems that the only reasonable course of action is to refrain from imposing what we know is a horrible fate.[50]

Fourth, those who think that van den Haag's commonsense argument for executing murderers is valid will find that the argument proves more than they bargained for. Van den Haag maintains that, in the absence of conclusive evidence on the relative deterrent impact of the death penalty versus life imprisonment, we must follow common sense and assume that if one punishment is more fearful than another, it will deter some potential criminals not deterred by the less fearful punishment. Since people sentenced to death will almost universally try to get their sentences changed to life in prison, it follows that death is more fearful than life imprisonment and thus that it will deter some additional murderers. Consequently, we should institute the death penalty to save the lives these additional murderers would have taken. But, since people sentenced to be tortured to death would surely try to get their sentences changed to simple execution, the same argument proves that death-by-torture will deter still more potential murderers. Consequently, we should institute death-by-torture to save the lives these additional murderers would have taken. Anyone who accepts van den Haag's argument is then confronted with a dilemma: until we have conclusive evidence that capital punishment is a greater deterrent to murder than life imprisonment, he must grant *either* that we should not follow common sense and we should not impose the death penalty *or* that we should follow common sense and torture murderers to death. This is the reductio ad absurdum of van den Haag's commonsense argument.

History, Force, and Justice

I believe that, taken together, these arguments prove that we should abolish the death penalty though it is a just punishment for murder. Let me close with an argument of a different sort. When you visualize the lash falling upon the backs of Roman slaves, or the hideous tortures meted out in the period of the absolute monarchs, you see more than mere cruelty at work. Surely you suspect that there is something about the injustice of imperial slavery and royal tyranny that requires the use of extreme force to keep these institutions in place. That is, for reasons undoubtedly related to those that support the second part of Durkheim's first law of penal evolution, we take the amount of force a society uses against its own people as an inverse measure of its justness. Though no more than a rough measure, it is a revealing one nonetheless, because when a society is limited in the degree of force it can use against its subjects, it is likely to have to be a juster society, since it will have to gain its subjects' cooperation by offering them fairer terms than it would have to if it could use more force. From this, we cannot simply conclude that reducing the force used by our society will automatically make our society more just—but, I think, we can conclude that it will have this tendency, since it will require us to find means other than force for encouraging compliance with our institutions, and this is likely to require us to make those institutions as fair to all as possible.

Notes

This chapter is a revised version of an article that was originally published in *Philosophy and Public Affairs* 14, no. 2 (Spring 1985): 115–48. Copyright 1985 by Princeton University Press. Reprinted with permission. That article was based on my opening statement in a debate with Ernest van den Haag on the death penalty at an Amnesty International conference on capital punishment, held at John Jay College in New York City on 17 October 1983. I am grateful to the editors of *Philosophy and Public Affairs* for very thought-provoking comments, to Hugo Bedau and Robert Johnson for many helpful suggestions, and to Ernest van den Haag for his encouragement.

1. Asked, in a 1995 Gallup Poll, "Are you in favor of the death penalty for persons convicted of murder?" 77 percent were in favor, 13 percent were opposed, and 10 percent had no opinion. Asked the same question in 1966, 47 percent were opposed, 42 percent were in favor, and 11 percent had no opinion. Kathleen Maguire and Ann L. Pastore, eds., *Sourcebook of Criminal Justice Statistics 1994*. U.S. Department of Justice, Bureau of Justice Statistics (Washington, D.C.: U.S. Government Printing Office, 1995), p. 181.

2. Ernest van den Haag and John P. Conrad, *The Death Penalty: A Debate* (New York: Plenum, 1983) (cited hereafter as *DPAD*), p. 60.

3. Some days after the first attempt to execute J. D. Autry by lethal injection was aborted, an editorial in the *Washington Post* asked: "If the taking of a human life is the most unacceptable of crimes, can it ever be an acceptable penalty? Does an act committed by an individual lose its essential character when it is imposed by society?" 14 October 1983, p. A26.

4. See *DPAD*, p. 62.

5. "Does fining a criminal show want of respect for property, or imprisoning him, for personal freedom? Just as unreasonable is it to think that to take the life of a man who has taken that of another is to show want of regard for human life. We show, on the contrary, most emphatically our regard for it, by the adoption of a rule that he who violates that right in another forfeits it for himself." John Stuart Mill, "Parliamentary Debate on Capital Punishment within Prisons Bill," in *Philosophical Perspectives on Punishment*, ed. Gertrude Ezorsky (Albany, N.Y.: State University of New York Press, 1972), p. 276. Mill made the speech in 1868.

6. *DPAD*, p. 60.

7. Mill argues that the possibility of executing an innocent person would be an "invincible" objection "where the mode of criminal procedure is dangerous

to the innocent," such as it is "in some parts of the Continent of Europe. . . . But we all know that the defects of our [English] procedure are the very opposite. Our rules of evidence are even too favorable to the prisoner." Mill, "Parliamentary Debate," pp. 276–77.

8. See *DPAD*, pp. 230–31.

9. Ibid., p. 27, see also pp. 42–43.

10. Ibid., p. 35.

11. Ibid., p. 275.

12. "As a general rule, a man is undone by waiting for capital punishment well before he dies. Two deaths are inflicted on him, the first being worse than the second, whereas he killed but once." Albert Camus, "Reflections on the Guillotine," in *Resistance, Rebellion, and Death* (New York: Alfred A. Knopf, 1969), p. 205. Based on interviews with the condemned men on Alabama's death row, Robert Johnson presents convincing empirical support for Camus's observation, in *Condemned to Die: Life under Sentence of Death* (New York: Elsevier, 1981).

13. Jeffrie G. Murphy, "Marxism and Retribution," *Philosophy and Public Affairs* 2, no. 3 (Spring 1973): 219.

14. I shall not always repeat this qualification, but it should be taken as implied throughout; likewise, when I speak of the death penalty as punishment for murder, I have in mind premeditated, first-degree murder (completed or attempted). Also, retribution is not to be confused with *restitution*. Restitution involves restoring the *status quo ante,* the condition prior to the offense. Since it was in this condition that the criminal's offense was committed, it is this condition that constitutes the baseline against which retribution is exacted. Thus retribution involves imposing a loss on the offender measured from the status quo ante. For example, returning a thief's loot to his victim so that thief and victim now own what they did before the offense is *restitution*. Taking enough from the thief so that what he is left with is less than what he had before the offense is *retribution*, since this is just what he did to his victim.

15. "The most extreme form of retributivism is the law of retaliation: 'an eye for an eye.' " Stanley I. Benn, "Punishment," *The Encyclopedia of Philosophy*, ed. Paul Edwards (New York: Macmillan, 1967), 7:32. Hugo Bedau writes: "retributive justice need not be thought to consist of *lex talionis*. One may reject that principle as too crude and still embrace the retributive principle that the severity of punishments should be graded according to the gravity of the offense." Hugo Bedau, "Capital Punishment," in *Matters of Life and Death,* ed. Tom Regan (New York: Random House, 1980), p. 177. See also Andrew von Hirsch, "Doing Justice: The Principle of Commensurate Deserts," and Hyman Gross, "Proportional Punishment and Justifiable Sentences," both in *Sentencing*, ed. H. Gross and A. von Hirsch (New York: Oxford University Press, 1981), pp. 243–56 and 272–83, respectively.

16. In an article aimed at defending a retributivist theory of punishment, Michael Davis claims that the relevant measure of punishment is, not the cost

to the offender's victim ("property taken, bones broken, or lives lost"), but the "value of the unfair advantage [the offender] takes of those who obey the law (even though they are tempted to do otherwise)." Michael Davis, "How to Make the Punishment Fit the Crime," *Ethics* 93 (July 1983): 744. Though there is much to be said for this view, standing alone it seems quite questionable. For example, it would seem that the value of the unfair advantage taken of law-obeyers by one who robs a great deal of money is greater than the value of the unfair advantage taken by a murderer, since the latter gets only the advantage of ridding his world of a nuisance while the former will be able to make a new life without the nuisance and have money left over for other things. This leads to the counterintuitive conclusion that such robbers should be punished more severely (and regarded as more wicked) than murderers. One might try to get around this by treating the value of the unfair advantage as a function of the cost imposed by the crime. And Davis does this after a fashion. He takes the value of such advantages to be equivalent to the prices that licenses to commit crimes would bring if sold on the market, and he claims that these prices would be at least as much as what non-license-holders would (for their own protection) pay licensees not to use their licenses. Now, this obviously brings the cost of crime to victims back into the measure of punishment, though only half-heartedly, since this cost must be added to the value to the licensee of being able to use his license. And this still leaves open the distinct possibility that licenses for very lucrative theft opportunities would fetch higher prices on the market than licenses to kill, with the same counterintuitive result mentioned earlier.

17. "[T]o say 'it is fitting' or 'justice demands' that the guilty should suffer is only to affirm that punishment is right, not to give grounds for thinking so." Benn, "Punishment," p. 30.

18. "The sole positive existence which the injury [i.e., the crime] possesses is that it is the particular will of the criminal [i.e., it is the criminal's intention that distinguishes criminal injury from, say, injury due to an accident]. Hence to injure (or penalize) this particular will as a will determinately existent is to annul the crime, which otherwise would have been held valid, and to restore the right." G. W. F. Hegel, *The Philosophy of Right,* trans. T. M. Knox (Oxford: Clarendon, 1962; originally published 1821), p. 69, see also p. 331 n. I take this to mean that the right is a certain equality of sovereignty between the wills of individuals, that crime disrupts that equality by placing one will above others, and that punishment restores the equality by annulling the illegitimate ascendance. On these grounds, as I shall suggest below, the desire for revenge (strictly limited to the desire "to even the score") is more respectable than philosophers have generally allowed. And so Hegel wrote: "The annulling of crime in this sphere where right is immediate [i.e., the condition prior to conscious morality] is principally revenge, which is just in its content in so far as it is retributive." Ibid., p. 73.

19. According to Kant, "any undeserved evil that you inflict on someone

else among the people is one that you do to yourself. If you vilify him, you vilify yourself; if you steal from him, you steal from yourself; if you kill him, you kill yourself." Since Kant held that "[i]f what happens to someone is also willed by him, it cannot be a punishment," he took pains to distance himself from the view that the offender *wills* his punishment. "The chief error contained in this sophistry," Kant wrote, "consists in the confusion of the criminal's [i.e., the murderer's] own judgment (which one must necessarily attribute to his reason) that he must forfeit his life with a resolution of the will to take his own life." Immanuel Kant, "The Metaphysical Elements of Justice," pt. 1 of *The Metaphysics of Morals*, trans. J. Ladd (Indianapolis, Ind.: Bobbs-Merrill, 1965; originally published 1797), pp. 101, 105–106. I have tried to capture this notion of attributing a judgment to the offender rather than a resolution of his will, with the term "authorizes."

20. "Even if a civil society were to dissolve itself by common agreement of all its members . . . , the last murderer remaining in prison must first be executed, so that everyone will duly receive what his actions are worth." Ibid., p. 102. Interestingly, Conrad calls himself a retributivist but doesn't accept the strict Kantian version of retributivism. In fact, he claims that Kant "did not bother with justifications for his categorical imperative . . . , [but just] insisted that the Roman *jus talionis* was the reference point at which to begin." *DPAD*, p. 22. Van den Haag, by contrast, states specifically that he is "not a retributionist." Ibid., p. 32. In fact, he claims that "retributionism" is not really a *theory* of punishment at all but only "a feeling articulated through a metaphor presented as though a theory." Ibid., p. 28. This is so, he maintains, because a theory "must tell us what the world, or some part thereof, is like or has been or will be like." Ibid. "In contrast," he goes on, "deterrence theory is, whether right or wrong, a theory: It asks what the effects are of punishment (does it reduce the crime rate?) and makes testable predictions (punishment reduces the crime rate compared to what it would be without the credible threat of punishment)." Ibid., p. 29. Now, it should be obvious that van den Haag has narrowed his conception of "theory" so that it covers only the kind of things one finds in the empirical sciences. With so narrow a conception, there is no such thing as a theory about what justifies some action or policy and no such thing as a Kantian theory of punishment or, for that matter, a Rawlsian theory of justice—that is to say, no such thing as a *moral* theory. Van den Haag, of course, could use the term "theory" as he wished, were it not for the fact that he appeals to deterrence theory, not merely for predictions about crime rates, but also (indeed, in the current context, primarily) as a theory about what justifies punishment—that is, as a moral theory. And he must, since the fact that punishment reduces crime does not imply that we should institute punishment unless we *should* do whatever reduces crime. In short, van den Haag is about moral theories the way I am about airplanes: he doesn't quite understand how they work, but he knows how to use them to get where he wants to go.

21. "It may also be pointed out that no one has ever heard of anyone con-

demned to death on account of murder who complained that he was getting too much [punishment] and therefore was being treated unjustly; everyone would laugh in his face if he were to make such a statement." Kant, "Metaphysical Elements of Justice," p. 104, see also p. 133.

22. Herbert Morris defends retributivism on parallel grounds. See his "Persons and Punishment," *Monist* 52, no. 4 (October 1968): 475–501. Isn't what Morris calls "the right to be treated as a person" essentially the right of a rational being to be treated only as he has authorized, implicitly or explicitly, by his own free choices?

23. "Where criminals set the limits of just methods of punishment, as they will do if we attempt to give exact and literal implementation to *lex talionis,* society will find itself descending to the cruelties and savagery that criminals employ. But society would be deliberately authorizing such acts, in the cool light of reason, and not (as is often true of vicious criminals) impulsively or in hatred and anger or with an insane or unbalanced mind. Moral restraints, in short, prohibit us from trying to make executions perfectly retributive." Bedau, "Capital Punishment," p. 176.

24. I think that justice allows us to defend ourselves against injury, and thus that, if a punishment matching the suffering produced by a given offense were not generally sufficient to deter people from committing that offense, justice would permit inflicting the minimum amount of suffering necessary to deter reasonable people from committing that offense, even if this were more than the *lex talionis* would provide. However, given that the harm deserved by the offender according to *lex talionis* rightly includes—as I noted earlier—the harm he has imposed on others beyond his immediate victim, I think that it is extremely unlikely that deterrence will require more than the *lex talionis.* Consequently, with this unlikely exception noted, I shall continue to say that *lex talionis* supplies the upper limit of just punishment. I introduce this qualification of the principle of just punishment in response to an objection raised by Ernest van den Haag. See my *Justice and Modern Moral Philosophy* (New Haven, Conn.: Yale University Press, 1990), pp. 197–98, and Ernest van den Haag, "Refuting Reiman and Nathanson," *Philosophy and Public Affairs* 14, no. 2 (Spring 1985): 166–67.

25. I am indebted to my colleague Robert Johnson for this suggestion. Prisoners condemned to spend their entire lives in prison, he writes, "experience a permanent civil death, the death of freedom. The prison is their cemetery, a 6' by 9' cell their tomb. Interred in the name of justice, they are consigned to mark the passage of their lives in the prison's peculiar dead time, which serves no larger human purpose and yields few rewards. In effect, they give their civil lives in return for the natural lives they have taken." Robert Johnson, *Death Work: A Study of the Modern Execution Process* (Belmont, Cal.: Wadsworth, 1990), p. 158.

26. "In the case of homicide, the empirical evidence indicates that poverty and poor economic conditions are systematically related to higher levels of

homicide." Richard M. McGahey, "Dr. Ehrlich's Magic Bullet: Economic Theory, Econometrics, and the Death Penalty," *Crime and Delinquency* 26, no. 4 (October 1980): 502. Some of that evidence can be found in Peter Passell, "The Deterrent Effect of the Death Penalty: A Statistical Test," *Stanford Law Review* (November 1975): 61–80.

27. A similar, though not identical, point has been made by Jeffrie G. Murphy: "I believe that retributivism can be formulated in such a way that it is the only morally defensible theory of punishment. I also believe that arguments, which may be regarded as Marxist at least in spirit, can be formulated which show that social conditions as they obtain in most societies make this form of retributivism largely inapplicable within those societies." Murphy, "Marxism and Retribution," p. 221. Though my claim here is similar to Murphy's, the route by which I arrive at it differs from his in several ways. Most important, a key point of Murphy's argument is that retributivism assumes that the criminal freely chooses his crime, while, according to Murphy, criminals act on the basis of psychological traits that the society has conditioned them to have: "Is it just to punish people who act out of those very motives that society encourages and reinforces? If [Willem] Bonger [a Dutch Marxist criminologist] is correct, much criminality is motivated by greed, selfishness, and indifference to one's fellows; but does not the whole society encourage motives of greed and selfishness ('making it,' 'getting ahead'), and does not the competitive nature of the society alienate men from each other and thereby encourage indifference— even, perhaps, what psychiatrists call psychopathy?" Ibid, p. 239. This argument assumes that the criminal is in some sense unable to conform to legal and moral prohibitions against violence and thus, like the insane, cannot be thought responsible for his actions. This claim is rather extreme, and dubious as a result. My argument does not claim that criminals, murderers in particular, cannot control their actions. I claim, rather, that, though criminals can control their actions, when crimes are predictable responses to unjust circumstances, then those who benefit from, and do not remedy, those conditions bear some responsibility for the crimes. Thus the criminals cannot be held wholly responsible in the sense of being legitimately required to pay the full cost of their crimes. It should be noted that Murphy's thesis (quoted at the beginning of this note) is stated in a somewhat confused way. Social conditions that mitigate or eliminate the guilt of offenders do not make retributivism inapplicable. Retributivism is applied both when those who are guilty (because they freely chose their crimes) are punished and when it is held wrong to punish those who are not guilty (because they did not freely choose their crimes). It is precisely by the application of retributivism that the social conditions referred to by Murphy make the punishment of criminals unjustifiable.

28. Van den Haag notes the connection between crime and poverty and explains it and its implications as follows: "Poverty does not compel crime; it only makes it more tempting." *DPAD*, p. 207. And it is not absolute poverty that makes crime more tempting, only relative deprivation, the fact that some

have less than others. Ibid., p. 115. In support of this, van den Haag marshals data showing that, over the years, crime has risen along with the standard of living at the bottom of society. Since, unlike absolute deprivation, relative deprivation will be with us no matter how rich we all become as long as some have more than others, he concludes that this condition that increases the temptation to crime is just an ineradicable fact of social life, best dealt with by giving people strong incentives to resist the temptation. This argument is flawed in several ways. First, the claim that crime is connected with poverty ought not to be simplistically interpreted to mean that a low absolute standard of living itself causes crime. Rather, what seems to be linked to crime is the general breakdown of stable communities, institutions, and families, such as has occurred in our cities in recent decades as a result of economic and demographic trends largely out of individuals' control. Of this breakdown, poverty is today a sign and a cause, at least in the sense that poverty leaves people with few defenses against the breakdown and few avenues of escape from it. This claim is quite compatible with finding that people who have lower absolute standards of living, but who dwell in more stable social surroundings with traditional institutions still intact, have lower crime rates than contemporary poor people who have higher absolute standards of living. Second, the implication of this is not simply that it is relative deprivation that tempts to crime, since if that were the case, the middle class would be stealing as much from the rich as the poor do from the middle class. That this is not the case suggests that there is some threshold after which crime is no longer so tempting, and while this threshold changes historically, it is in principle one all could reach. Thus, it is not merely the (supposedly ineradicable) fact of having less than others that tempts to crime. Finally, everything is altered if the temptation to crime is the result, not of an ineradicable social fact, but of an injustice that can be remedied or relieved. Obviously, this would require considerable argument, but it seems to me that the current distribution of wealth in America is unjust whether one takes utilitarianism as one's theory of justice (given the relative numbers of rich and poor in America, as well as the principle of declining marginal returns, redistribution could make the poor happier without an offsetting loss in happiness among the rich) or Rawls's theory (the worst-off shares in our society could still be increased, so the difference principle is not yet satisfied) or Nozick's theory (the original acquisition of property in America was marked by the use of force against Indians and blacks, from which both groups still suffer).

29. In arguing that social injustice disqualifies us from applying the death penalty, I am arguing that unjust discrimination in the recruitment of murderers undermines the justice of applying the penalty under foreseeable conditions in the United States. This is distinct from the argument that points to the discriminatory way in which the death penalty has been applied to murderers (generally against blacks, particularly when their victims are white). This latter argument is by no means unimportant, nor do I believe that it has been rendered obsolete by the Supreme Court's 1972 decision in *Furman v. Georgia*, 408 U.S. 238

(1972), that struck down then-existing death penalty statutes because they allowed discriminatory application, or the Court's 1976 decision in *Gregg v. Georgia*, 428 U.S. 153 (1976), which approved several new statutes because they supposedly remedied this problem. There is considerable empirical evidence that much the same pattern of discrimination that led to *Furman* continues after *Gregg*. See, for example, William J. Bowers and Glenn L. Pierce, "Arbitrariness and Discrimination in Post-*Furman* Capital Statutes," *Crime and Delinquency* 26, no. 4 (October 1980): 563–635. Moreover, I believe that continued evidence of such discrimination would constitute a separate and powerful argument for abolition. Faced with such evidence, van den Haag's strategy is to grant that discrimination is wrong but claim that it is not "inherent in the death penalty"; it is a characteristic of the "distribution" of the death penalty. *DPAD*, p. 206. Thus, van den Haag maintains, discrimination is not an objection to the death penalty itself. This rejoinder is unsatisfactory for several reasons. First of all, even if discrimination is not an objection to the death penalty *per se,* its foreseeable persistence is—as the Court recognized in *Furman*—an objection to instituting the death penalty *as a policy*. Moral assessment of the way in which a penalty will be carried out may be distinct from moral assessment of the penalty itself, but, since the way in which the penalty will be carried out is part of what we will be bringing about if we institute the penalty, it is a necessary consideration in any assessment of the morality of instituting the penalty. In short, van den Haag's strategy saves the death penalty in principle, but fails to save it in practice. Second, it may well be that discrimination is (as a matter of social and psychological fact in America) inherent in the penalty of death itself. The evidence of its persistence after *Furman* lends substance to the suspicion that something about the death penalty—perhaps the very terribleness of it that recommends it to van den Haag—strikes at deep-seated racial prejudices in a way that milder penalties do not. In any event, this is an empirical matter, not resolved by analytic distinctions between what is distributed and how it is distributed. Finally, after he mounts his argument against the discrimination objection, van den Haag usually adds that those who oppose capital punishment "because of discriminatory application are not quite serious . . . , [since] they usually will confess, if pressed, that they would continue their opposition even if there were no discrimination whatsoever in the administration of the death penalty." Ibid., p. 225. This is preposterous. It assumes that a person can have only one serious objection to any policy. If he has several, then he would naturally continue to oppose the policy *quite seriously* even though all of his objections but one were eliminated. In addition to discrimination in the *recruitment* of murderers and in the *application* of the death penalty among murderers, there is a third sort that affects the justice of instituting the penalty, namely, discrimination in the *legal definition* of murder. I take this and related issues up in my *The Rich Get Richer and the Poor Get Prison: Ideology, Class, and Criminal Justice*, 4th ed. (Needham, Mass.: Allyn & Bacon, 1995).

   30. Friedrich Nietzsche, *The Genealogy of Morals*, in *The Birth of Tragedy*

and the Genealogy of Morals, trans. Francis Golffing (New York: Doubleday, 1956; originally published 1887), pp. 199–200.

31. Van den Haag writes that our ancestors "were not as repulsed by physical pain as we are. The change has to do not with our greater smartness or moral superiority but with a new outlook pioneered by the French and American revolutions [namely, the assertion of human equality and with it 'universal identification'], and by such mundane things as the invention of anesthetics, which make pain much less of an everyday experience." *DPAD*, p. 215; cf. van den Haag's *Punishing Criminals* (New York: Basic Books, 1975), pp. 196–206.

32. Émile Durkheim, "Two Laws of Penal Evolution," *Economy and Society* 2 (1973): 285, 294 (emphasis in original). This essay was originally published in French in *Année Sociologique* 4 (1899–1900). Conrad, incidentally, quotes Durkheim's two laws, but does not develop their implications for his side in the debate. *DPAD*, p. 39.

33. Durkheim writes that "of the two laws which we have established, the first contributes to an explanation of the second." Durkheim, "Two Laws of Penal Evolution," p. 299.

34. The "two causes of the evolution of punishment—the nature of the social type and of the governmental organ—must be carefully distinguished." Ibid., p. 288. Durkheim cites the ancient Hebrews as an example of a society of the less developed type that had milder punishments than societies of the same social type, due to the relative absence of absolutist government among the Hebrews. Ibid., p. 290.

35. Durkheim's own explanation of the progressive moderation of punishments is somewhat unclear. He rejects the notion that it is due to the growth in sympathy for one's fellows, since this, he maintains, would make us more sympathetic with victims and thus harsher in punishments. He argues instead that the trend is due to the shift from understanding crimes as offenses against God (and thus warranting the most terrible of punishments) to understanding them as offenses against men (thus warranting milder punishments). He then seems to come round nearly full circle by maintaining that this shift works to moderate punishments by weakening the religious sentiments that overwhelmed sympathy for the condemned: "The true reason is that the compassion of which the condemned man is the object is no longer overwhelmed by the contrary sentiments which would not let it make itself felt." Ibid., p. 303.

36. Van den Haag seems to waffle on the question of the unique awfulness of execution. For instance, he takes it not to be revolting in the way that ear cropping is, because "We all must die. But we must not have our ears cropped." *DPAD*, p. 190. Here he cites John Stuart Mill's parliamentary defense of the death penalty in which Mill maintained that execution only *hastens* death. Mill's point was to defend the claim that "[t]here is not . . . any human infliction which makes an impression on the imagination so entirely out of proportion to its real severity as the punishment of death." Mill, "Parliamentary Debate," p. 273. Van den Haag seems to agree, since he maintains that, since "we cannot

imagine our own nonexistence . . . [t]he fear of the death penalty is in part the fear of the unknown. It . . . rests on a confusion." *DPAD*, pp. 258–59. On the other hand, he writes: "Execution sharpens our separation anxiety because death becomes clearly foreseen. . . . Further, and perhaps most important, when one is executed he does not just die, he is put to death, forcibly expelled from life. He is told that he is too depraved, unworthy of living with other humans." Ibid., p. 258. I think, incidentally, that it is an overstatement to say that we cannot imagine our own nonexistence. If we can imagine any counterfactual experience (for example, how we might feel if we didn't know something that we do in fact know), then it doesn't seem impossible that we can imagine what it would "feel like" not to live. I think I can arrive at a pretty good approximation of this by trying to imagine how things "felt" to me in the eighteenth century. In fact, the sense of the awful difference between being alive and not that enters my experience when I do this, makes the fear of death—not as a state, but as the absence of life—seem hardly to rest on a confusion.

37. I am not here endorsing this view of voluntarily entered slavery or prostitution. I mean only to suggest that it is *the belief* that these relations involve the extreme subjugation of one person to the power of another that is at the basis of their offensiveness. What I am saying is quite compatible with finding that this belief is false with respect to voluntarily entered slavery or prostitution.

38. This is no doubt partly due to modern skepticism about an afterlife. Earlier peoples regarded a foreseen death as a blessing allowing time to make one's peace with God. Writing of the early Middle Ages, Phillippe Aries says, "In this world that was so familiar with death, sudden death was a vile and ugly death; it was frightening; it seemed a strange and monstrous thing that nobody dared talk about." Phillippe Aries, *The Hour of Our Death* (New York: Vintage, 1982), p. 11.

39. George Orwell, *1984* (New York: New American Library, 1983; originally published 1949), p. 197.

40. I say "might" here to avoid the sticky question of just how effective a deterrent the death penalty would have to be to justify overcoming our scruples about executing. It is here that the other considerations often urged against capital punishment—discrimination, irrevocability, the possibility of mistake, and so on—would play a role.

41. Isaac Ehrlich, "The Deterrent Effect of Capital Punishment: A Question of Life or Death," *American Economic Review* 65 (June 1975): 397–417. For reactions to Ehrlich's work, see Alfred Blumstein, Jacqueline Cohen, and Daniel Nagin, eds., *Deterrence and Incapacitation: Estimating the Effects of Criminal Sanctions on Crime Rates* (Washington, D.C.: National Academy of Sciences, 1978), especially pp. 59–63 and 336–60; Brian E. Forst, "The Deterrent Effect of Capital Punishment: A Cross-State Analysis," *Minnesota Law Review* 61 (May 1977): 743–67; Deryck Beyleveld, "Ehrlich's Analysis of Deterrence," *British Journal of Criminology* 22 (April 1982): 101–23; and Isaac Ehrlich, "On Positive Methodology, Ethics, and Polemics in Deterrence Re-

search," *British Journal of Criminology* 22 (April 1982): 124–39. Much of the criticism of Ehrlich's work focuses on the fact that he found a deterrence impact of executions in the period from 1933 to 1969, which includes the period of 1963 to 1969, a time when hardly any executions were carried out and crime rates rose for reasons that are arguably independent of the existence or nonexistence of capital punishment. When the 1963–1969 period is excluded, no significant deterrent effect shows. Prior to Ehrlich's work, research on the comparative deterrent impact of the death penalty versus life imprisonment indicated no increase in the incidence of homicide in states that abolished the death penalty and no greater incidence of homicide in states without the death penalty compared to similar states with the death penalty. See Thorsten Sellin, *The Death Penalty* (Philadelphia: American Law Institute, 1959).

42. "Other studies published since Ehrlich's contend that his results are due to the techniques and periods he selected, and that different techniques and periods yield different results. Despite a great deal of research on all sides, one cannot say that the statistical evidence is conclusive. Nobody has claimed to have disproved that the death penalty may deter more than life imprisonment. But one cannot claim, either, that it has been proved statistically in a conclusive manner that the death penalty does deter more than alterative penalties. This lack of proof does not amount to disproof." *DPAD*, p. 65.

43. Ibid., pp. 68–69. An alterative formulation of this "commonsense argument" is put forth and defended by Michael Davis in "Death, Deterrence, and the Method of Common Sense," *Social Theory and Practice* 7, no. 2 (Summer 1981): 145–77. Davis's argument is like van den Haag's except that, where van den Haag claims that people *do* fear the death penalty more than lesser penalties and *are* deterred by what they fear most, Davis claims that it is *rational* to fear the death penalty more than lesser penalties and thus *rational* to be more deterred by it. Thus, he concludes that the death penalty is the most effective deterrent *for rational people*. He admits that this argument is "about rational agents, not actual people." Ibid., p. 157. To bring it back to the actual criminal justice system that deals with actual people, Davis claims that the criminal law makes no sense unless we suppose the potential criminal to be (more or less) "rational." Ibid., p. 153. In short, the death penalty is the most effective deterrent because it would be rational to be most effectively deterred by it and we are committed by belief in the criminal law to supposing that people will do what is rational. The problem with this strategy is that a deterrence justification of a punishment is valid only if it proves that the punishment actually deters actual people from committing crimes. If it doesn't prove that, it misses its mark, no matter what we are committed to supposing. Unless Davis's argument is a way of proving that the actual people governed by the criminal law will be more effectively deterred by the death penalty than by lesser penalties, it is irrelevant to the task at hand. And if it is a way of proving that actual people will be better deterred, then it is indistinguishable from van den Haag's version of the argument and vulnerable to the criticisms of it that follow.

44. "[G]iven the choice, I would strongly prefer one thousand years in hell to eternity there. Nonetheless, if one thousand years in hell were the penalty for some action, it would be quite sufficient to deter me from performing that action. The additional years would do nothing to discourage me further. Similarly, the prospect of the death penalty, while worse, may not have any greater deterrent effect than does that of life imprisonment." David A. Conway, "Capital Punishment and Deterrence: Some Considerations in Dialogue Form," *Philosophy and Public Affairs* 3, no. 4 (Summer 1974): 433.

45. See note 41 above.

46. On the number of people killed by the police, see Lawrence W. Sherman and Robert H. Langworthy, "Measuring Homicide by Police Officers," *Journal of Criminal Law and Criminology* 70, no. 4 (Winter 1979): 546–60; on the number of privately owned guns, see Franklin Zimring, *Firearms and Violence in American Life* (Washington, D.C.: U.S. Government Printing Office, 1968), pp. 6–7.

47. *AAA World* (Potomac ed.) 4, no. 3 (May–June 1984): 18c, 18i.

48. *DPAD*, p. 63.

49. A related claim has been made by those who defend the so-called brutalization hypothesis by presenting evidence to show that murders increase following an execution. See, for example, William J. Bowers and Glenn L. Pierce, "Deterrence or Brutalization: What Is the Effect of Executions?" *Crime and Delinquency* 26, no. 4 (October 1980): 453–84. Bowers and Pierce conclude that each execution gives rise to two additional homicides in the month following and that these are real additions, not just a change in timing of the homicides. Ibid., p. 481. My claim, it should be noted, is not identical to this, since, as I indicate in the text, what I call "the deterrence effect of not executing" is, not something whose impact is to be seen immediately following executions, but an effect that occurs over the long haul and, further, my claim is compatible with finding no net increase in murders due to executions. Nonetheless, should the brutalization hypothesis be borne out by further studies, it would certainly lend support to the notion that there is a deterrent effect of not executing.

50. Van den Haag writes: "If we were quite ignorant about the marginal deterrent effects of execution, we would have to choose—like it or not—between the certainty of the convicted murderer's death by execution and the likelihood of the survival of future victims of other murderers on the one hand, and on the other his certain survival and the likelihood of the death of new victims. I'd rather execute a man convicted of having murdered others than put the lives of innocents at risk. I find it hard to understand the opposite choice." *DPAD*, p. 69. Conway was able to counter this argument earlier by pointing out that the research on the marginal deterrent effects of execution was *inconclusive*, not in the sense of *tending to point both* ways, but rather in the sense of *giving us no reason to believe that capital punishment saves more lives than life imprisonment*. He could then answer van den Haag by saying that the choice is, not between risking the lives of murderers and risking the lives of innocents,

but between killing a murderer with no reason to believe lives will be saved and sparing a murderer with no reason to believe lives will be lost. Conway, "Capital Punishment and Deterrence," pp. 442–43. This, of course, makes the choice to spare the murderer more understandable than van den Haag allows. Events, however, have overtaken Conway's argument. The advent of Ehrlich's research, contested though it may be, leaves us in fact with research that does tend to point both ways.

Index

abortion, moral problem of: love vs. respect and, 196, 198–200; moral significance of existence, 192, 195; moral vs. metaphysical approach, 193–96; need to determine moral status of fetus, 189–90; and U.S. Supreme Court, 123–24

ad hominem arguments, 55–56; and law of noncontradiction, 70n8

addiction, 75–76, 92n12; as vice, 83–85

antisubjugation argument for moral liberalism, 14–16

appropriateness, as relationship between facts and judgments about action, 10–11, 63–64, 71n10

Aquinas, St. Thomas, 45

Aristotle: on *eudaimonia*, 81; on the law of noncontradiction, 70n8; on the mean, 81–82; preference for aristocracy, 40; on reason being man himself, 60; on responsibility for virtue and vice, 85–88; on social nature of human beings, 45; on virtue, 81–82, 85–88

Asante, Molefi Kete, 43, 50

authority, claimed by rational subject, 9–11, 41–42, 57–64

Batten, Mary, on long extrauterine development of infants, 210n29

Bauman, Zygmunt, 54–55, 71n18

Bedau, Hugo: on death penalty, 262n23; on retributivism, 259n15

Benn, Stanley I.: on abortion, 198–99; on privacy, 159–60, 186n22, 187n30, 187n39

Bentham, Jeremy, 4; on panopticon, 170

Bergson, Henri, 16

Bloom, Allan, 35

Bloustein, Edward, on privacy, 181, 187n33

body: liberal right to control, 74; ownership of conferred by privacy, 161–65, 179–80; woman's right to control not sufficient for right to abortion, 190, 205n5

Boethius, 58–59

boxing, moral status of, 92n16

Brandeis, Louis, 169, 184

brutalization hypothesis, and death penalty, 269n49

Camus, Albert, on the death penalty, 237, 259n12

capitalism: and difference principle, 112–13; Marxian critique of, 19–23, 121n29, 122n30

cardinal virtues. *See* virtue, moral

care approach in ethics compared to justice approach, 45–48

About the Author

Jeffrey Reiman is William Fraser McDowell Professor of Philosophy at American University in Washington, D.C. Born in Brooklyn, New York, in 1942, Reiman received his B.A. in philosophy from Queens College in 1963 and his Ph.D. in philosophy from Pennsylvania State University in 1968. He was a Fulbright Scholar in India during 1966–67.

Reiman joined the American University faculty in 1970 in the Center for the Administration of Justice (now called the Department of Justice, Law and Society of the School of Public Affairs). After several years of holding a joint appointment in the Justice program and the Department of Philosophy and Religion, he joined the Department of Philosophy and Religion full-time in 1988, becoming director of the Master's Program in Philosophy and Social Policy. He was named William Fraser McDowell Professor of Philosophy in 1990.

Reiman is a member of the Phi Beta Kappa and Phi Kappa Phi honor societies and president of the American University Phi Beta Kappa chapter. He is the author of *In Defense of Political Philosophy* (Harper & Row, 1972), *Justice and Modern Moral Philosophy* (Yale University Press, 1990), and *The Rich Get Richer and the Poor Get Prison: Ideology, Class, and Criminal Justice* (4th edition, Allyn & Bacon, 1995), and more than fifty articles in philosophy and criminal justice journals and anthologies.